The Reagan Presidency

S0-AXP-179

A Garfield Foundation Public Affairs Study

R The
Reagan
Presidency
AN EARLY ASSESSMENT

Edited by Fred I. Greenstein
With Contributions by I.M. Destler,
Hugh Heclo, Samuel P. Huntington,
Richard P. Nathan, & Rudolph G. Penner

The Johns Hopkins University Press
Baltimore and London

© 1983 by The Johns Hopkins University Press
All rights reserved
Printed in the United States of America

The Johns Hopkins University Press, Baltimore, Maryland 21218
The Johns Hopkins Press Ltd., London

Library of Congress Cataloging in Publication Data
Main entry under title:

The Reagan presidency.

Includes index.
1. Presidents—United States—Addresses, essays,
lectures. 2. United States—Politics and government—
1981–   —Addresses, essays, lectures. I. Greenstein,
Fred I.
JK518.R42   1983   353.03′1′0924   83–48056
ISBN 0–8018–3056–7
ISBN 0–8018–3057–5 (pbk.)

Contents

Acknowledgments

The contributors to this Garfield Foundation Study are indebted to the Woodrow Wilson School of Public and International Affairs, Princeton University, for providing the forum at which a preliminary draft of this book was discussed—a November 19–20, 1982, conference on the Reagan presidency. In particular we thank Dean Donald E. Stokes and Assistant Dean Ingrid Reed. We also would like to express appreciation to the members of the Reagan administration, representatives of previous administrations, and scholars who served as conference discussants. They are: Larry Berman, Barry P. Bosworth, William P. Bundy, Congressman Dick Cheney, George C. Edwards III, Betty Glad, Patricia Roberts Harris, Stephen Hess, Alan F. Holmer, Dorothy B. James, John H. Kessel, Harvey C. Mansfield, Sr., Richard E. Neustadt, Joseph Pika, Nelson W. Polsby, Roger B. Porter, Lester G. Seligman, Norman C. Thomas, Jeffrey K. Tullis, Paul C. Warnke, Stephen J. Wayne, and Michael O. Wheeler.

Needless to say, it is the authors, not the commentators, who are responsible for this book, but it was invaluable to have such expert guidance.

The Reagan Presidency

1 The Need for an Early Appraisal of the Reagan Presidency

Fred I. Greenstein

Although several of the authors of this early appraisal of the Reagan presidency have been employed in the Executive Office of the President, we write as academics and not as political practitioners, spokesmen for the present or past administrations, or enunciators of our own political philosophies. We seek to arrive at a dispassionately analytic appraisal of the Reagan presidency, with attention both to the principal policies it has advanced and to how it has advanced them.

In our capacities as scholars, we might well have considered an incumbent administration to be a poor target of intellectual opportunity. Scholars normally cannot compete with journalists for direct exposure to members of the administration. Rather, while administrations are in progress, most scholars rely heavily on media coverage for information about the presidency. This coverage blurs their vision not only by its sheer volume and repetitiveness in making certain general points but also by its inconsistency on specific matters. The evidence derived from media reports is further complicated by the media's reliance on off-the-record sources of information. Many of these are private assertions by public figures who systematically leak news and release unattributed inside stories to advance their own or the president's purposes. As a consequence, evidence about presidential politics is confounded with exercises in presidential politics.

When appraising presidencies that are under way, scholars and journalists alike must strain to maintain professional, objective standards of analysis because both groups are bombarded by the polemical exchanges that are the grist of presidential politics, and, as citizens, may even be taking part in them. Moreover, when scholars and journalists write during a presidency, they address a phenomenon they know is in flux. I. M. Destler delineates the extraordinary shift from chaos to teamwork that occurred during the first two years of the Reagan administration's management of foreign policy. Richard Nathan documents the sharp decline in the administration's ability to dictate the budget, a decline that began even before the midterm election losses. Hugh Heclo and Rudolph Penner stress the administration's "midcourse correction" in year two, foreshadowing Reagan's need beginning in 1983 further to adjust his policy goals and strategies on encountering the more strongly Democratic and independent Ninety-eighth Congress. Samuel Huntington argues that even early in the second session of the Ninety-seventh Congress, legislators had begun contributing to the "downside" phase of the defense budget cycle.

In some cases what history "remembers" about a presidency is not even evident in its initial years. Obvious examples are the Fair Deal, which was not framed until the electoral politics of 1948 made it propitious for Truman to advance a liberal domestic program; Johnson's Vietnam debacle, which until 1967 was not widely perceived as such and in any event was overshadowed in 1965 and 1966 news accounts by the Great Society enactments; and Watergate, which unraveled soon after the date in January 1973 when "Vietnamization" was consummated and Nixon received the highest Gallup poll approval rating of his five-and-a-half years in office.

By the twenty-first century, scholars of the Reagan presidency will have clear advantages over journalists. Scholars will have at their disposal the unpublicized, and in many cases classified, presidential documents that began accumulating on January 20, 1981. They will gain major resources for analysis unavailable to those in the 1980s who while covering the presidency were in daily contact with Reagan administration representatives. There are, nevertheless, good reasons to begin scholarly analyses of modern presidencies while they proceed. And the reasons are compelling in the case of a presidency like Reagan's, which is distinctive in certain significant respects.

One reason for early appraisal arises from the recent transformation of the presidency into its modern incarnation. The post-1932 modern presidency differs qualitatively from the traditional presi-

→

dency in four ways: the president has vastly expanded autonomous policy-making powers; the president's role in shaping the annual legislative agenda and influencing Congress has been institutionalized; there has been a major expansion of official presidential staff, including the establishment of the Executive Office of the President; and the chief executive himself has come to be perceived by both the public and the principal governmental actors as the central figure in the federal government.[1]

The transformation of the office has been so profound that the modern presidencies have more in common with one another in the opportunities they provide and the demands they place on their incumbents than they have with the entire sweep of traditional presidencies from Washington's to Hoover's. The demands are the obverse of the strengths implicit in the changes: autonomous policy-making and legislative leadership expose presidents to blame for failed policies and for inability to achieve policies; presidential staffs encumber the president with the need to manage his own bureaucracy as well as to head the executive branch and deal with other national and international leaders; and personal visibility engenders vulnerability to blame for all that may go wrong in the body politic.

That the new demands are not trivial is evident from the fate of the eight modern presidents who preceded Reagan. Apart from Roosevelt and Kennedy, both of whom died in office, only Eisenhower did not end his incumbency short of its official limit as a result of insufficient political support. Truman and Johnson chose not to seek a further term, knowing that they were exceedingly unpopular and might well be defeated. Nixon was forced to resign. Ford and Carter were defeated.

In short, much remains to be learned about effective modern presidential leadership. But the data base is still small. With so few modern presidencies for the student of the institution to analyze—nine including Reagan's—scholars simply cannot afford to wait before taking stock of innovations and continuities each new administration appears to be exhibiting. Moreover, the breed of scholar represented in this volume specializes in contributing to contemporary discourse as well as to long-run accumulation of knowledge. The contemporary contribution comes in part from firsthand contact with public actors and scrutiny of the available contemporary resources, but most fundamentally from their ability to draw on historical and disciplinary perspectives to distinguish what is new in a presidency from recurring trends.

Scholars also need to produce "instant history" of each modern presidency because many questions central to analysis of the presidency and of public policy are not addressed in normal media coverage. By asking questions that are not raised in the media, and not answerable from the information that will find its way into archives, students of the presidency have—beginning at least as long ago as the early 1950s—generated original data about the dynamics of presidential politics that would never otherwise become available.[2] A striking example is the extensive examination by Richard Nathan and his research group of the effects of Reagan administration spending cuts.[3]

The Distinctiveness of the Reagan Presidency

The Reagan presidency needs to be tracked while under way because it is in some ways unique and in others extraordinary, even in the limited universe of nine modern presidencies. As a rare specimen it provides special perspective on what is and is not possible in public policy and presidential leadership. The Reagan presidency stands out by virtue of the chief executive's ideological closure, his propensity to act on his principles, his success in doing so, and the consequences of his success in transforming ideology into policy.

1. Extent and extremity of Reagan's ideological closure. As Heclo and Penner note, no other president has come to office after a remotely comparable prior career of making public an ideologically consistent (if very general) commitment to a political philosophy. Not only has Reagan been more devoted to and more uncompromising in his political principles than have previous presidents, but he has also departed from convention in the kinds of stands he takes. His abstract positions on issues are not centrist, even though at strategic times he has taken pains to avoid divisiveness by practicing the art of the possible and by dealing with his adversaries in a conciliatory manner. Anticipating the sketch of Reagan-the-man and of the political context of his accession to the presidency that concludes this chapter, we may simply note that his long-articulated, noncentrist views took shape during the mid-1950s and early 1960s phase of his post-Hollywood career. During this period, which coincided with the culmination of his transformation from youthful New Deal enthusiast to middle-aged conservative, he crystallized his new views while working

$\longrightarrow$

as a circuit-riding speaker to the many units of the vast General Electric company (GE) and to innumerable civic groups.

As a conservative orator, Reagan honed to perfection a talk couched in uncomplicated *Reader's Digest* prose that came to be known as "The Speech." A primer of conservative doctrine, it set forth a consistent, strongly stated series of admonitions: eliminate government restraint on the free market, devolve power from federal to lower jurisdictions, decrease taxes, and maintain a tough stance toward the Soviet Union. Delivered in the 1964 campaign, "The Speech" earned the erstwhile sports announcer, film actor, union leader, and public speaker a dominant position among conservatives who remained true to Goldwater's cause but sought a candidate with broad appeal.

Ideologues have regularly had their supporters in American politics, but to most observers of American politics, the 1964 defeat of an outspoken conservative vindicated the proposition that realistic American politicians would not choose true believers (much less noncentrist ones) as presidential nominees, a perception that was further reinforced by the overwhelming defeat of an outspoken liberal candidate, George McGovern, in 1972. But both Goldwater and McGovern lost support for reasons connected with such factors as their personalities, campaign styles, and strategies, as well as because citizens viewed them as too extreme. Reagan's attractive personality and style as political performer commended him as a candidate who might present an ideologically clear, strongly conservative choice rather than a centrist echo, but nevertheless be electable.

2. Reagan's proclivity once in office to transform faith into works. If on taking office Reagan had revealed himself to be only a campaign ideologue and had shifted to the middle-of-the-road policy proposals of Ford or Nixon, his distinctiveness as a position-taker while out of office would be of modest significance. Candidates with strong positions sometimes abandon them in office.

Reagan, however, sought to be true not only to the more orthodox conservative principles he had been propounding for years but also to a later appendage to his ideology—the beguiling supply-side doctrine that tax reductions would provide a painless remedy for the nation's economic woes. Especially in 1981, Reagan acted decisively to put his principles into practice in the spending and tax-cutting legislation discussed in the Nathan and the Heclo and Penner chapters, and to implement his campaign demands for drastic deregulation of the private sector, as described in Nathan's account of Reagan's extensive use of administrative policy-making. And he has been broadly consistent with his principles in his foreign as well as domestic policy practices, although (as Destler notes) with tactical exceptions and (as Huntington argues) by building incrementally on a commitment Carter had already made to increase military expenditures.

3. Reagan's initial success in putting his programs into practice. Though not unique among modern presidencies, the Reagan administration's early success in achieving its policy goals, notably in the case of economic and domestic programs and defense appropriations, was impressively distinctive. Modern presidents consistently propose policies, but usually Congress blocks or substantially alters their efforts. Truman's 1948 campaign was run on a platform calling for major domestic policy changes. None of consequence was enacted. Those portions of Kennedy's campaign promises to move the nation "forward" which called for congressional action were largely unachieved by the time of his death. Indeed, of the nine modern presidents only Roosevelt and Johnson had striking legislative success—until 1981.

When Reagan took office, it had become truistic among students of the presidency that while two of the previous four presidents (Johnson and Nixon) may have striven, to their ultimate regret, for "imperial" hegemony in the political system, the post-Watergate presidency was a distinctly nonimperial, "imperiled" institution. By 1980 presidency-curbing statutes and extralegal changes in institutions and practices appeared to have significantly sapped the president's ability to exercise influence.

Reagan and company reversed the notion that presidents were becoming increasingly powerless. By the summer of 1981, in a striking display of political skill that took advantage of such circumstances as a Republican-controlled Senate and a Democratic party in disarray, Reagan forces had achieved dramatic results on Capitol Hill above and beyond the administratively induced changes introduced by presidential appointees. And, while Reagan's results have been less dramatic since then, he has resisted welfare program restorations and sharp cuts in his defense spending requests. He and his aides have also been ingenious in maintaining his "success" record by advance negotiations that lead to legislative outcomes Reagan is prepared to accept and claim as accomplishments, even if they are not as striking as his 1981 achievements.

Of Reagan's first-year victories, the most significant were two enactments he signed on the same day in August—a major reduction in domestic expenditures and the Economic Recovery Tax Act of 1981. The massive tax cut—designed to reduce federal revenues by $737 billion over a five-year period—is of special interest to policy

$\rightarrow$

analysts because, to a degree extraordinary in American politics, it constitutes a massive policy change based on ideological premises.

To say that the tax cut has been consequential, however, is not to say it has been successful or even that there was prior evidence that it would succeed. As Heclo and Penner note, the rationale behind the tax cut was based on empirically untested political theory. The very groups the cut was designed to galvanize—investors and businesses—were from the start skeptical about the supply-side assumptions that underpinned such a drastic reduction in federal revenues. The assumptions of supply-side economics, which George Bush had most conspicuously criticized during the 1980 nomination campaign, were that funds made available to prosperous Americans by tax cuts would then be invested and that these investments would set off a chain reaction of increased productivity, higher employment, less need for public assistance subsidies, and a higher individual and corporate income base on which to collect taxes. The result would be a balanced federal budget. The failure of this scenario to take place is the single most conspicuous cause of the fourth way in which the Reagan presidency stands out.

4. The tension between principles and practice in Reagan's leadership. The Reagan presidency provides political analysts with a historically unique opportunity to examine the practicality of ideologically informed policy-making in the American context. American politicians have been both belabored and praised for their opportunism—for their disposition to advocate equivocal positions of the sort A. Lawrence Lowell epitomized in his sardonic 1897 reference to "a tariff for revenue only, so adjusted as to protect American industries."[6]

Heretofore, American politics has yielded little evidence of the consequences of ideologically informed policy-making. None of the modern presidents, nor for that matter their precursors, entered office with Reagan's degree of commitment to political abstractions. The Great Society was an extension of the New Deal. The New Deal was, as Heclo and Penner put it, an ideological hodgepodge.

By putting abstractly conceived policies into practice, the Reagan presidency constitutes a case study for the continuing controversy between planners and incrementalists about the desirability of basing policy on comprehensive political theories. In this debate the word "planner" includes not only visionaries of the Left who want to construct new institutions on the basis of their principles, but also policy advocates like President Reagan who propose radically conservative departures.

Defenders of incrementalism such as Dahl and Lindblom in *Politics, Economics and Welfare*,[7] and Braybrooke and Lindblom in *A Strategy of Decision*[8] argue that policy innovation should be incremental because cognitive limitations on comprehensive plans make ambitious policy ventures the likely victims of unanticipated consequences. Planning advocates such as Dror,[9] on the other hand, stress the need for major policy changes, even when the policies have had no previous use, especially when there are self-reinforcing obstacles to correcting complexly rooted evils. Racial discrimination is Dror's example. Reagan similarly applied the notion that major diseases sometimes must be treated with untested medicines to the economic stagflation that he inherited in 1981. Since American leaders rarely propose comprehensive changes and, when they do, usually fail to achieve them, Reagan's nonincremental economic policy departures of 1981—assessed by Heclo and Penner—are of profound interest. So are the domestic funding cuts and other changes that Nathan and his associates have been studying and on which Nathan presents his initial findings. For example an act of faith by the administration, rather than prior experience, led to the assumption that in 1981 when the working poor were deprived of income supplements, including Medicaid, they would not lose the incentive to work and fall back on unemployment compensation and other forms of public assistance.

Nathan's early findings suggest that the administration's inference was correct. But these findings relate only to initial effects. In many other matters connected with the administration's foreign and domestic policies, the consequences of ideology as an engine of policy-making are still being tested.

The Background of the Reagan Presidency

By way of transition to our discussions of policy and policy-making in the areas of domestic affairs, economic policy, defense, and foreign affairs, and of the lessons the Reagan experience provides for presidential leadership, it will be instructive to review the personal political development of the man himself, to note major way stations on his road to the White House, and to summarize the opportunities, restraints, and positioning for leadership that characterized the presidency that began on Inauguration Day 1981.

Reagan: Political Man—Late Entry Political Career

In contrasting the long governmental careers of European parliamentary leaders with the American candidate selection process in which a political novice can achieve high office, Anthony King has characterized Ronald Reagan as just such a political *arriviste*: "a retired film actor and professional after-dinner speaker" who "fought his first election in 1966 when he was already 55 years old."[10]

Yes, but. . . . If King's observations were all one knew about Reagan, it would be difficult to imagine that, once in office, he could have achieved a reputation among other political leaders as an impressively effective political operator. King's characterization, written before Reagan took office, appears in a discussion of why the presidential nominating system Americans developed in the 1970s permits the emergence of presidents who, once in Washington, perform with predictable ineptness. The then-incumbent Jimmy Carter, King noted, had previously been a "small-town businessman and former naval officer," whose governmental experience had consisted of two terms as state senator and one as governor of a state much less analogous to the nation than is California in size, complexity, and politics. It was not surprising that as national chief executive Carter had been spectacularly unsuccessful in enunciating and winning support for a political program.

Reagan has been far from apolitical, as Lou Cannon, the best-informed observer of his career, has made clear. In government, as a union leader, and even as an undergraduate campus leader, Reagan has been politically active, politically involved, and consistently drawn to partake of the generic enterprise of politics, in the sense of "who gets what, when, and how." He has been an enthusiastic political partisan for the entire period of the modern presidency, casting his first ballot in 1932 for Franklin Roosevelt, his idol of the Depression years and the model for his political style of reaching out rhetorically to the American people through the electronic media.

From the 1930s through the early postwar period, he held the view common among liberal Democrats that "Red-baiting" attacks on communism were covert attempts to smear liberals and trade unions. By 1948, however, he had shifted to the then equally common stance of cold war anti-Communist liberalism and made election speeches in support of Truman. His political views had evolved from non-Communist to anti-Communist liberalism.

Reagan's political activism was spurred by his trade union activism.

Shortly after arriving in Hollywood in the 1930s, he became an official of the Screen Actors' Guild and began to participate in its political position-taking and jurisdictional politics, as well as in its negotiations with the film studios. Reagan plunged into union activities with the cheerful affinity for politicking he had earlier displayed as campus politician. As a man whose profession called for persuasive public performances, who took politics seriously, and who (at some cost to his movie career) was deep in union activity, it was quite natural for him to become a political campaigner. In 1950, the last year he campaigned for Democrats, Reagan spoke for the entire California Democratic slate, in effect rejecting Richard Nixon's "pink lady" campaign efforts to brand his senatorial opponent, Helen Gahagan Douglas, as "soft on communism." His transition to conservatism was not yet consummated, but his principal avocational interests were following public affairs and engaging in grass-roots and union politicking.

The relative importance to Reagan of film acting and politicking even in his Hollywood years is suggested by the tone and distribution of chapters in his 1965 autobiographical memoir, *Where's the Rest of Me?*[11] The first nine chapters are a breezy, fast-paced account of his youth in Illinois, college antics, radio sportscasting, and life as an actor.

The final nine chapters shift pace. Several are almost pedantically devoted to the pull and haul of interests and personalities in the Screen Actors' Guild and the labor movement generally. All of the final chapters intertwine career narrative with references to union politics and national political issues. Appended to the book is the text of "The Speech," documenting the transformation Reagan made during the Eisenhower years to conservatism and to devoting his time to public exposition of conservative doctrine.

Reagan's GE experience as a business spokesman crystallized his conservatism. During this period he also became outstandingly successful as a political communicator, learning to convey his views equally persuasively in face-to-face conversation and in smooth, but not slick, speeches to large audiences. Rather than being a mere "after-dinner speaker," moreover, Reagan took on a virtually 'round-the-clock regimen of public appearances that were an outstanding preparation for political campaigning. He sometimes appeared before as many as a dozen forums in a day, repeating his basic message, but modifying it extemporaneously.

His GE years led in 1960 to his official transfer of loyalties to the Republican party. After the GE connection ended, he became generally available as a speaker to conservative audiences. This extended to his impressive 1964 campaign performance, which in turn persuaded a group of conservative California businessmen to back his successful 1966 campaign for governor.

Reagan's Prepresidential Career as Politician

In short, although Reagan first ran for elective office at age fifty-five, his affinity for politics was long-standing. Moreover, he had already built and sharpened skills that were highly appropriate for winning office and for use in political persuasion once in office. His skills, it must be stressed, were not well-attuned to the detailed side of policy-making and analysis. As a rhetorician who preferred anecdote to analysis he could be sold on policies or even political strategies without exploring their implications. Moreover, his stock-in-trade was general issues, not specific policy proposals. A generic politician may be gifted but may nevertheless invent square wheels out of inexperience with the problems of public policy.

Reagan spent eight years as governor of a state which, if it were a country, would have the seventh-largest gross national product in the world. Close accounts by Lou Cannon and others of the Reagan governorship illustrate that although Reagan's political enzymes and experience on the mashed-potato lecture circuit helped him politically, they did not make him into an instant gubernatorial success. His first term, in particular, was replete with episodes revealing a facet of his political style—the extensive use of delegation—that has been at once a strength and a source of one of the most persistent criticisms of his leadership, whether in the State House or the White House.

Because as governor-elect Reagan knew little about details of government and initially chose poor advisers, he assumed office with a flawed understanding of such fundamentals as the status of the state's finances, the requirements of preparing a budget, and even of what positions he should take on legislative proposals that directly impinged on his core ideological values. Moreover, at first he worked poorly with the legislature. The reader should turn to Lou Cannon's *Reagan* and to the many sources he cites for an account of the evolution of Reagan's state leadership. Suffice it to say that at age fifty-five he was capable of learning to operate as an effective political professional. In doing so, he developed a style of operation that closely presaged his White House procedures.

This style included regular use of advanced polling technology geared to media presentations that were timed to serve his purposes, a readiness to communicate with adversaries and to keep ideological cleavage from extending to the personal level, but an overall tendency to act on his ideological principles when possible. He also acquired governmental savvy and, perhaps more important, learned how to identify loyal aides who could handle the aspects of leadership that either did not interest him or were not his strength. A number of the devoted, technically able veterans of his California staff—Edwin Meese III, Michael Deaver, and William Clark, for example—were to follow him to Washington.

During the early seventies, when the impediments to presidential leadership were again the standard theme in writings about the presidency and proposals to reform it,[12] one common assertion was that modern presidential recruitment too rarely produced chief executives with previous comparable executive experience. The argument was that former legislators and vice-presidents (and presumably also one-term governors such as Jimmy Carter of states such as Georgia having archaic institutions and practices) were not as well suited for presidential leadership as the former New York governor (and assistant secretary of the Navy), Franklin Roosevelt, had been.

The ex-actor, ex–banquet speaker elected in 1980 had been governor for eight years. The duration and scope of his prepresidential experience as a state-level chief executive exceeded that of any other president. Still, he lacked exposure to federal-level issues and foreign policy. Moreover, neither he nor his aides had Washington experience. In this connection, it will be remembered that Richard Nixon's difficulties were in part a result of too much reliance on a "California mafia."

Nomination, Election, and Transition to Office

By the 1970s the American way of nominating presidents had evolved into an inordinately demanding and erratic enterprise. That decade saw a proliferation of state presidential primary elections and party caucuses running from the winter through the spring of the election year and making candidate selection a frenetic sequence of choices shaped by publicity, advertising, and campaigning in many highly diverse jurisdictions. What was always a decentralized nominating system became virtually atomized.[13]

The system, as often is said, is best suited for the sort of would-be nominee who fits Reagan's status in 1976—that of an unemployed millionaire. After completing his second term as governor in 1974, Reagan returned to public speaking, supplementing his current rendition of "The Speech" with accounts of how he had successfully employed conservative leadership practices in his two terms as California governor. Meanwhile, Richard Nixon's unelected successor was struggling to "put Watergate behind," working with deliberate speed to create his own administration. Ford was also seeking to rally from the plunge in public support that followed his pardon of Nixon and, saddled with a poorly performing economy, was preparing for the marathon nominating process that would consume the first half of 1976.

Ford's experience in 1976 was worlds apart from that of Harry Truman, the previous modern president to seek nomination despite low Gallup ratings. Indeed, Truman had far less backing among his party colleagues than Ford had with his. In 1948, Truman was quite easily nominated at the Democratic party convention. By 1976, however, conventions were little more than sites for ratifying the outcome of the previous half-year's gauntlet of state primaries and caucuses.

It was not difficult for Reagan the lecturer to begin seeking to become Reagan the presidential candidate, traversing the country to challenge his party's incumbent. Running against a conservative president, Reagan had to be a superconservative in 1976. He castigated the détente elements in the Ford-Kissinger foreign policy and opposed the Panama Canal sovereignty treaty on nationalistic grounds ("We bought it, we paid for it, it's ours, and we're going to keep it"). In addition, he raised the social issues dear to the fundamentalist right-wing movements that were gaining strength in the 1970s.

After a lackluster start, in which he was defeated by Ford in the initial New England primaries, Reagan carried North Carolina and a sufficient number of other conservative states, plus his own California, to remain in the race until the convention. Much like Reagan's first term as governor, his 1976 nominating campaign gave him on-the-job training. Moreover, it made him the most visible Republican after Ford and the discredited Nixon.

By 1978 Reagan was campaigning for the 1980 nomination. In the foundering Jimmy Carter he had a readier target than he had had in Ford. Prenomination surveys showed that Reagan was well ahead of the field in Republican party supporters' preferences for the 1980 Republican nomination, a field that included Ford. There was, however, a harbinger of the difficulties he would face during his presidency as the myth that the outcome of the 1980 election had been a mandate for his specific economic policies began to dissolve. Polls of the general electorate, however, found slightly more support for Ford than for Reagan against Carter. In short, Reagan was a party favorite, but his strong conservatism diminished his ability to appeal to the entire public.

In 1980, Reagan sought to temper his image as another Goldwater. Moreover, since he was running as the principal conservative in a field of less well known Republican moderates, he had the luxury of being able to moderate his conservative rhetoric, conducting what Charles Jones[14] has called a trifocal campaign—one designed first to win the nomination, then to unify the party, and finally to put the party in a favorable position to win the general election.

After an initial gaffe in Iowa, where he refused to participate in a debate with the other candidates and seemed about to lose his lead to George Bush, Reagan's race was nearly flawless. In the early sequence of primaries he won decisively in New Hampshire; ran better than expected in Massachusetts; was an upset winner in Vermont; overwhelmingly carried the four southern states of South Carolina, Georgia, Florida, and Alabama; and, after decisively beating Anderson in the Illinois congressman's home state on March 18, was widely conceded to be the certain nominee, despite the twenty-five remaining primaries. By the time of the convention he was to win twenty-nine primaries, losing only six—all of them to Bush. Bush was his leading moderate contender, apart from Ford, who had run in no primaries but had made it known that he was available for a draft if the convention became deadlocked.

Professor Charles Jones aptly contrasts Reagan's conciliatory rhetoric on accepting the Republican nomination in 1980 ("this convention has shown a party united, with positive programs for solving the nation's problems") with Goldwater's divisive acceptance speech of 1964 ("those who do not care for our cause, we don't expect to enter our ranks. . . ."). In contrast to other ideologues, Left as well as Right, Reagan, when pressed, has consistently put results over ideological purity. While he has used divisive rhetoric, he has shown a remarkable ability—aided by his winning personal style and a seeming lack of the burning anger that normally accompanies intense commitment to issues—to put conflicts behind him. A case in point: His abortive effort at the 1980 convention to arrange a Ford vice-presidency, followed by his offer of that position to Bush, suggested that he harbored no resentment of the latter's talk of "voodoo economics." As he had in Sacramento, Reagan acted on the old saw that in politics there come times when it is necessary to rise above principle and do what is right.

The 1980 Campaign and Election

No president has ever had lower Gallup Poll ratings than did Jimmy Carter. He was widely viewed as a good man who had no sense of direction and who consequently was responsible for what, by Election Day 1980, was the least satisfactorily performing national economy since the Great Depression. If the Iranian hostage crisis had not produced a temporary surge of patriotic support for Carter and given him an excuse not to debate Edward Kennedy, he might readily have been the first twentieth-century incumbent to be denied renomination.[15]

With a unified Republican party behind him and Anderson's third-party candidacy threatening Carter's support, Reagan might well have expected a landslide victory. Carter's weak appeal and the foundering economy put him in a league with Herbert Hoover as a highly vulnerable incumbent. Reagan had softened, if not obliterated, the divisively conservative themes in his appeal; he had gone to great lengths to reach ethnic and blue-collar members of the Democratic constituency; and all indicators suggested that as a television debater he had been more persuasive than Carter.

Nevertheless, the election was widely viewed as a toss-up.[16] Carter's unpopularity was clear, as was the powerful sense that the economy demanded new guidance. Yet, even watered down, Reagan's rhetoric and the baggage of his past commitments aroused fears that he might precipitate World War III or eliminate basic welfare benefits such as social security. Some voters were also skeptical of electing a septuagenarian president, and others presumably took into account Reagan's penchant for factual gaffes. In no other election on which survey data are available have more Americans indicated that they were unenthusiastic about both major party candidates.

In the event, a Reagan victory that encompassed more than 90 percent of the electoral vote and carried with it the first Republican control of the Senate since 1954 and a thirty-three-seat Republican surge in the House *looked* like a landslide. Reagan's aides inevitably treated the outcome as a mandate for his specific policy proposals, and, with far less justification, much of the press and many members of Congress accepted this reading of the election results. In fact, conservatism was at best a minor determinant of Reagan's election. The 1980 outcome was more a rejection of Carter than a demonstration of popular enthusiasm for Reagan or his policies. (In saying this I give less weight than Heclo and Penner do to grass-roots support for Reagan's antitax, antigovernment positions.)

Reagan's 51 percent of the three-way vote in 1980 represented a mere 2 percent increase over Ford's 1976 Republican tally. It is true that when Anderson, who clearly denied Carter victory in states such as Massachusetts and thus contributed to the landslide impression of the electoral college outcome, is excluded, Reagan did receive 55 percent of the two-party vote, but he won against a president whose stewardship of the economy had been discredited. The increases in Republican congressional strength that proved an absolute necessity in carrying through the 1981 legislative strategies were far from evidence of a conservative surge. Surveys generally showed little change between 1980 and earlier years in public approval of existing government spending levels and other issues that were part of the Reagan platform and taken by him to be elements of his mandate. The increase of 8 percent in House seats resulted from an increase of only 3 percent (from 50.6 percent to 53.5 percent) in votes for Republican House candidates, scarcely a Republican surge. Although the Republicans gained twelve seats in the Senate, they did so well in large part because more Democrats than Republicans were up for reelection: in twenty-four of the thirty-four Senate elections, Democratic incumbents were running. Overall, fewer votes were cast for Republican than Democratic senators.[17]

From Election to Inauguration: Strategic Consolidation

Reagan not only seized the nomination, unified the party, and won the election, but he also, in the common parlance, landed on his feet. In offering the vice-presidency first to Ford and then to Bush, he demonstrated his ecumenical commitment to include Republican moderates in his administration. Then, with remarkable speed, he and his chief aides began putting together the strategy for carrying out what Evans and Novak have only slightly hyperbolically called *The Reagan Revolution.*[18] Between the election and Inauguration Day, Reagan's forces prepared a package of domestic and economic policy proposals, and a strategy for rapidly enacting them, with a degree of technical skill that was to make the president's first year in office seem like a deliberate inversion of the standard catalogue of explanations of stalemated presidential leadership. That is, he was effective in legislative liaison, shaping the political agenda, and many of the other aspects of presidential politics that his immediate predecessors had not handled with favorable results. In effect, he set the stage for what two former Carter administration officials have concluded was needed for the presidency in the 1980s and what they realized their former boss had lacked—"a strategic approach to domestic affairs."[19]

Reagan promptly assembled a staff that was both congenial to him and Washington-wise. At its core, taking a central part in shaping the substance of and enactment strategy for the 1981 budget and tax cuts was the famous triumvirate of Meese, Deaver, and Baker. Edwin Meese and Michael Deaver, both Californians, know intimately the Reagan operating style. Meese is the man Reagan's conservative backers believe to be most ideologically "pure." Within the White House, he is the specialist in staff organization and in reducing issues to options for presidential choice. Deaver is nominally the scheduling aide, but more fundamentally serves as the personal friend and confidant of the president and the first lady. Reagan, however, did not content himself with employing Californians at the nerve center of his presidency. He appointed a skilled, effective Washington operator, George Bush's former chief of staff, James Baker III, to head the strategic effort of moving Reagan's principles through the Washington policy-making labyrinth.

In a similar matching of a long-time, California-based Reagan loyalist with an experienced Washington aide, the president appointed Lynn Nofziger, a veteran of all of his electoral campaigns, to the White House office specializing in grass-roots politicking. Nofziger's job was to influence legislators via their constituents, coordinating his efforts with direct appeals to the Hill by experienced Ford White House lobbyist Max Friedersdorf. The Nofziger-Friedersdorf combination was ideally suited for simultaneous persuasion of legislators in Washington and through their districts.

Reagan's appointment of Congressman David Stockman to head the Office of Management and Budget was critical for both the detailed domestic and economic policies and the operations of the new administration. A virtual Talmudic scholar of the federal budget, Stockman was relentless in identifying targets for cutting expenditures. His knowledge of budget minutiae and his ability to synthesize diverse economic projections of the consequences of cuts in spending and taxes was equaled by his appreciation for the possibilities of using congressional rules innovatively in the enactment of policy. Only a shrewd strategist of the current Congress could have conceived the plan to achieve expenditure cuts by employing the reconciliation provisions of the congressional budgeting procedures instituted in the wake of Watergate, thus permitting a single vote on an omnibus bill that had the effect of reducing or eliminating programs that inevitably would have survived had members of congress been forced to vote on them singly.[20]

In the transition period, Reagan assiduously built cordial relations with congressional leaders. The cooperation of Howard Baker, the first Republican Senate majority leader since William Knowland, in

1954, was vital to the strategy of initiating legislation in the Republican-controlled Senate and then winning its passage by forming a coalition of Republicans and southern Democrats in the House. But Reagan was broadly conciliatory to both parties and all factions in Congress, perhaps signaling his awareness that he would eventually have to play conventional, bipartisan, coalition politics to get legislative results.

We now know that Reagan's aides served him less well on substance than on procedure.[21] It may be that the president entertained fewer doubts than did his advisers about the feasibility, and even the technical adequacy, of the analyses used to justify the first year's economic and social programs. In foreign policy, Reagan's appointments were fated to produce the extraordinarily fractious first-year intramural conflicts that Destler carefully recounts later in this volume. Nevertheless, except for the foreign policy shambles, the administration took office displaying skill and team work that exceeded anything Washington had experienced in the previous decade. Moreover, just as there was seeming consensus among the President's policy advisers, there was a widespread sense of acceptance by other public figures of Reagan's claims that his election had been the result of strong public support for the specific details of his program.

Far more than most political observers would have imagined just after Reagan's election, or even at the time of his inauguration, the president and his associates entered office prepared to cut through the thicket that normally prevents the president from exercising substantial influence on Capitol Hill. The organizational and conceptual preparation of the Reagan forces for conducting foreign policy was not at all promising, however. And even in the case of the domestic and economic programs, which were based more on doctrinal reasoning than on experience, there was danger of the kind of boomeranging policy against which the incrementalists warn. By the same token, daring policy departures might just prove to be the necessary medicine for a profoundly ailing economy. In short, the Reagan administration took office with the potential, for better or worse, of making a unique contribution to American politics and policy. What ensued from this potential and from these hazards is the concern of the chapters that follow.

Notes

1. Fred I. Greenstein, "Change and Continuity in the Modern Presidency," in Anthony King, ed., *The New American Political System* (Washington, D.C.: American Enterprise Institute, 1978), pp. 45–87.

2. For a fascinating illustration of how scholarship conducted during a presidency can yield evidence complementing findings that will later become available when archives are opened, see Gary Reichard's impressive analysis of the Eighty-third Congress. Much of his data in *The Reaffirmation of Republicanism: Eisenhower and the Eighty-third Congress* (Knoxville: University of Tennessee Press, 1975) draws on Eisenhower's library documents and collections of congressional papers to analyze presidential influence in the Congress that was elected in 1952. But Reichard also employs the findings of research conducted in the early 1950s by political scientists who were primarily interested in advancing systematic empirical study of politics but who, in pursuing this end, gathered what now is invaluable historical data.

3. For a preliminary report, see John William Ellwood, ed., *Reductions in U.S. Domestic Spending: How They Affect State and Local Governments* (New Brunswick, N.J.: Transaction Books, 1982). On Reagan's domestic policy, see also John L. Palmer and Isabel V. Sawhill, eds., *The Reagan Experiment: An Examination of Economic and Social Policies under the Reagan Administration* (Washington, D.C.: Urban Institute Press, 1982).

4. Unless otherwise cited, my sources on Reagan's prepresidential career and his presidency are Lou Cannon's invaluable *Reagan* (New York: G. P. Putnam's Sons, 1982) and articles in *National Journal, Congressional Quarterly Weekly Report, Time, Newsweek, New York Times, Washington Post,* and *Wall Street Journal.* On Reagan's gubernatorial leadership, see the following instructive research report: Nicole Woolsey Biggart, "Management Style as Strategic Interaction: The Case of Governor Ronald Reagan," *Journal of Applied Behavioral Science* 17, no. 3 (1981): 291–308.

5. See also Richard P. Nathan, *The Administrative Presidency* (New York: John Wiley & Sons, 1983).

6. *Essays on Government* (Boston: Houghton Mifflin, 1897), p. 107.

7. Robert A. Dahl and Charles E. Lindblom, *Politics, Economics and Welfare* (New York: Harper, 1953).

8. David Braybrooke and Charles E. Lindblom, *A Strategy of Decision: Policy Evaluation as a Social Process* (New York: Free Press, 1963). Also Lindblom, "The Science of 'Muddling Through,' " *Public Administration Review* 19 (Spring 1959):79–88.

9. Yehezkel Dror, "Muddling Through: 'Science' or Inertia?" *Public Administration Review* 24 (September 1964): 154–56; Lindblom, "Contexts for Change and Strategy: A Reply," ibid., p. 157; and Dror, *Public Policymaking Reexamined* (San Francisco: Chandler, 1968).

10. Anthony King, "How Not to Select Presidential Candidates: A View from Europe," in Austin Ranney, ed., *The American Elections of 1980* (Washington, D.C.: American Enterprise Institute, 1981), pp. 303–28.

11. Ronald Reagan and Richard G. Hubler, *Where's the Rest of Me?* (New York: Elsevier-Dutton, 1965).

12. See, for example, Charles M. Hardin, *Presidential Power and Accountability: Toward a New Constitution* (Chicago: University of Chicago Press, 1974); "The Question of a Six-Year Presidential Term," *Congressional Digest* 51 (March 1972):68–96; Rexford G. Tugwell, *A Model Constitution for the United Republics of America* (Santa Barbara, Calif.:

Fund for the Republic, 1970); and Lloyd N. Cutler, "To Form a Government," *Foreign Affairs* 59 (Fall 1980):126–43.

13. James W. Ceaser, *Presidential Selection: Theory and Development* (Princeton: Princeton University Press, 1980).

14. Charles O. Jones, "Nominating 'Carter's Favorite Opponent': The Republicans in 1980," in Ranney, *The American Elections of 1980*, pp. 61–98.

15. Austin Ranney, "The Carter Administration," in Ranney, *The American Elections of 1980*, pp. 7–36.

16. Among other sources, my remarks on voter motivation in the 1980 general election draw on the various essays (notably that of William Schneider) in Ranney's *The American Elections of 1980;* Douglas A. Hibbs, Jr., "President Reagan's Mandate from the 1980 Elections: A Shift to the Right?" *American Politics Quarterly* 10:4 (October 1982):387–420; Warren E. Miller and Merrill Shanks, "Policy Directions and Presidential Leadership: Alternative Interpretations of the 1980 Presidential Election," *British Journal of Political Science* 12 (1982):299–356; and Paul R. Abramson et al., *Change and Continuity in the 1980 Elections* (Washington, D.C.: Congressional Quarterly Press, 1982).

17. Forty-seven percent of the national senatorial vote was Republican; 53 percent was Democratic. Hibbs, "President Reagan's Mandate from the 1980 Elections."

18. Rowland Evans and Robert Novak, *The Reagan Revolution* (New York: E. P. Dutton, 1981).

19. Ben W. Heineman, Jr., and Curtis A. Hessler, *Memorandum for the President: A Strategic Approach to Domestic Affairs in the 1980s* (New York: Random House, 1980).

20. Allen Schick, "How the Budget Was Won and Lost," in Norman Ornstein, ed., *President and Congress: Assessing Reagan's First Year* (Washington, D.C.: American Enterprise Institute, 1982), pp. 14–43.

21. William Greider, "The Education of David Stockman," *Atlantic Monthly*, December 1981, pp. 27–54.

2 Fiscal and Political Strategy in the Reagan Administration

Hugh Heclo & Rudolph G. Penner

The Reagan administration came into office possessing a detailed, comprehensive economic strategy that was to represent a radical departure from the economic policies of the previous fifteen years. Contrary to the views of most traditional economists, administration officials believed strongly that inflation could be conquered without imposing major short-run economic costs in the form of slow economic growth and rising unemployment. To them, inflation was a purely monetary phenomenon caused by an excessive growth in the money supply. Inflation could therefore be eliminated gradually by persuading the Federal Reserve System gradually to reduce the rate at which money was created. In an unusual intrusion into the business of an "independent" Federal Reserve System, a detailed monetary plan, including prescribed rates of growth for the money supply through 1986, was outlined in the administration's first budget document.

Although it was conceded that a shift to a more restrictive monetary policy might create a minor recession at the end of 1981, more severe costs were to be avoided by following a radically new fiscal policy. The administration believed that the unusually slow rates of productivity growth experienced during the 1970s were caused by excessive growth in government spending and in tax burdens. By reversing these trends,

21

it was thought that the economy could be made so productive that the negative effects of a tight monetary policy would be overwhelmed and that the United States would enter a prolonged period of healthy economic growth. Despite major tax cuts, the growth was assumed to be adequate, when combined with spending cuts, to bring in sufficient revenues to balance the budget by 1984.

It seems fair to say that no incoming administration had ever before staked so much on a specific, comprehensive economic program. In contrast, the administration of Franklin Roosevelt, with which Ronald Reagan and his supporters liked to compare themselves, was a hodge-podge of political expediency and unresolved economic theorizing. Observing the more recent experience of economic policy in the Nixon, Ford, and Carter presidencies, one might well have been justified in advising any new administration to avoid raising expectations about how far a president could control, much less improve, the functioning of the U.S. economy. External supply shocks, productivity slowdowns, and recurring combinations of both high unemployment and high inflation led many observers by 1980 to question whether anyone understood the rules of economic management. And yet the Reagan presidency committed its fortunes to an unambiguous promise and program for economic recovery. In this paper we seek to interlace economic and political analyses to understand how this programmatic commitment came about, how it worked in practice, and what it might portend. Of course, all of the results are not yet in, but enough evidence has accumulated to provide the basis for at least a tentative midterm assessment.

Creating "The New Beginning"

In strictly economic terms there were strong reasons to favor the main components of the Reagan strategy for economic policy. Accelerating money growth had clearly fueled accelerating inflation. The money supply (M-1), which had grown at an annual rate of less than 4 percent during the 1960s, grew at about 6 percent in the 1969–74 period and at about 7 percent between 1974 and 1979, partly as a response to the cost pressures resulting from world oil price increases. Federal outlays had grown from 18.2 percent of GNP in the 1955–59 period to 23.4 percent by 1980–81 (fiscal years) despite the fact that absolute defense spending remained roughly constant in real terms over the entire period. Since there was substantial agreement that the strength of the American military establishment was no longer adequate to carry out America's foreign policy by the end of the 1970s, strong upward pressures on total spending were likely to persist.

Total federal tax receipts had grown from 17.7 percent of GNP in 1955–59 to 20.6 percent by 1980–81. Over the same period the total deficit was also on a strong upward trend, rising from 0.5 percent of GNP in 1955–59 to 2.9 percent in 1980–81.

At the same time as average tax burdens were rising rapidly, the structure of the tax system was creating greater and greater impediments to productivity growth, particularly in the period after the Kennedy-Johnson tax cuts of 1964–65. After inflation began to accelerate during the Vietnam War, Congress passed periodic tax cuts to offset "bracket creep" in the personal income tax. However, the legislated tax cuts took a very different form from those that would occur in a tax system perfectly indexed for inflation. The legislature's cuts overcompensated the lower half of the income distribution for the effects of inflation, while those above the middle drifted into higher and higher tax brackets. By the early 1980s it was not uncommon for ordinary upper-middle-income families of four to face marginal income tax rates of about 40 percent—a level conceived of only for the very rich at the time of the Kennedy-Johnson reforms of the middle 1960s. The use of tax shelters was proliferating, and antagonism toward rising tax burdens grew at the federal, state, and local levels of government. Undoubtedly, this so-called tax revolt was an important factor in President Reagan's decisive electoral victory in 1980.

While the personal tax structure was clearly becoming less efficient as a result of inflation and legislative action, the effects of inflation on business taxation may have been even more destructive. Although the generosity of depreciation allowances had been increased in the early 1960s and again in the early 1970s, depreciation was still based on the original cost of an investment. As a result, inflation eroded the real value of the depreciation deduction. As recently as 1973 the U.S. Department of Commerce estimated that the depreciation deduction used by corporations for tax purposes had exceeded economic depreciation by $2.6 billion, but by 1980 it was insufficient by $14.4 billion, an amount equal to almost 8 percent of before-tax profits. In addition, corporations paid taxes on $45.7 billion of inflation-induced inventory profits in 1980 and investors were forced to pay capital gains taxes on equity holdings whose money value was inflated even if real values remained constant. Bond holders were also penalized because regular income tax rates were applied to the inflation premium embodied in interest rates. Borrowers could deduct those same inflation premiums from taxable income, but nevertheless, the effective tax rate on real corporate income rose significantly above statutory rates. Perhaps more important, the effective tax rate varied greatly from investment to investment depending on the nature of the investment and the characteristics of the investor's balance sheet. Not only was investment discouraged on average, but the allocation of that investment which did occur must have been badly distorted.

In short, the problems of the late 1970s provided strong justification for the major elements of what was later to become known as the Reagan economic strategy. Indeed, a number of policy shifts had already occurred in the Carter administration with a Democratic-controlled Congress. The Revenue Act passed by Congress and signed by President Carter in 1978 turned away from the approach of earlier tax cut legislation by skewing tax reductions more toward higher income brackets and by seeking to spur investment through major reductions in business and capital gains taxation. By the same token, in early 1980 the Carter administration, alarmed at mounting inflation and the negative reaction of financial circles to its initial budget proposal, collaborated with Congress to produce a much more austere spending program for fiscal year 1981. Perhaps the shift of greatest long-term importance occurred in the winter of 1979–80 when the Federal Reserve Board introduced a regime of strict restraint in the supply of money and credit. All of these changes indicated an important transformation in priorities, but the strategy of the incoming Reagan administration moved in more radical directions. In particular, the difficulties that eventually developed arose from the administration's extreme faith in the power of tax cuts to enhance the efficiency of the economy and to eliminate the pain usually associated with a shift from a proinflationary to an anti-inflationary monetary policy. The main reasons for the distinctive, self-confident optimism of the Reagan economic strategy had more to do with domestic politics than with the economics of policy-making in contemporary America.

We should begin by recognizing that Ronald Reagan was the first modern president to arise from what might be loosely termed a popular political movement. Dwight Eisenhower had already clearly emerged as a national figure before taking over leadership of the Republican party. John Kennedy pushed himself into the Democratic nomination in a few brief years through media exposure and primary victories while never challenging the ultimate authority of party organizations. Johnson, Nixon, and Ford were in this sense all creatures of the established Washington community. Like Jimmy Carter, Ronald Reagan enjoyed a strong regional political base as a former governor and compiled a string of successes in presidential primaries. But unlike Carter's, Reagan's candidacy represented the culmination of almost fifteen years of grass-roots political agitation and organization across the nation.[2] Following the Republican defeat of 1964, a multifaceted populism of the Right gradually evolved at the local level of American politics. It was a stream of political persuasions with many currents— of unabashed patriotism in a time of self-doubt about American power; of social conservatism alarmed at permissive "lifestyles"; of resentment against high taxes and high-handed bureaucrats. As the 1970s unfolded, it was a set of inclinations mobilized and sharpened by new direct-mail techniques and heavy investments in conservative media outlets and think tanks. Ronald Reagan certainly was not its sole leader, but he was one of the principal attendants and cultivators of this movement of opinion.

The fact that the Reagan presidency grew out of such a political agglomeration, and not simply from the virtuoso performance of a political entrepreneur (as with Kennedy and Carter) or from a long Washington apprenticeship (as with Johnson, Nixon, and Ford), had important implications for the incoming administration's economic approach. Economic policy positions were more than policy positions; they tended to become articles of faith during the long march to the White House. The validity of these positions depended on their ability, not to convince intellectuals and experts, but to resonate with the deepest yearnings and dissatisfactions of ordinary people. Thus, when compared with all other postwar contenders for the presidency, Ronald Reagan ended his long, drawn-out candidacy and entered the Oval Office with two unique predispositions: first, an explicit set of deeply held beliefs about the American economic order; and second, a willingness to be less than normally deferential to elite opinion, particularly that of the established economic profession.

At the same time, the community of economic scholars and financial advisers, which had largely dominated serious economic discussion and advice since World War II, was itself in considerable disarray. Chastened by the experiences of the past decade, liberal economists spoke with less confidence about the capacity to achieve rapid growth with price stability, and many accepted the inevitability of a recession that would result from the Carter administration's anti-inflation measures of 1979 and 1980. Mainstream conservative economists differed mainly by arguing for much more severe and sustained fiscal restraint to combat inflation. Adding to the confusion of this traditional cleavage in the profession was a self-consciously distinct monetarist school that had grown in strength in the 1970s. It gave little credence to any of the customary tools of fiscal policy.

The administration's faith that tax cuts would restore healthy economic growth was based on the work of yet another group of economists and economic commentators who eventually became known as "supply-siders." Supply-side economics was a peculiar addition to the economic scene of the 1970s in that it grew up outside mainstream economics and its propositions were debated in the popular press rather than in academic journals. The relevant theoretical work was done by economists such as Arthur Laffer, Craig Roberts, Robert Mundell, and Norman Ture, who eventually became an undersecretary of the Treasury. The work was popularized by Jude Wanniski, an editorial writer for the *Wall Street Journal*, and by Congressman Jack Kemp, who became an important adviser to Ronald Reagan during the election campaign.[3]

Supply-siders, who engaged in a quite conscious and effective campaign to mold public opinion, blamed almost all of the problems of the 1970s on rising marginal tax rates and argued that massive tax cuts would put the nation on the road to economic growth. Academic research provided a bit of support as scholars found the supply of labor and savings responded to tax cuts,[4] but the supply-siders greatly exaggerated the response. Some extremists even believed that general tax cuts would bring forth so much additional work, savings, and investment that tax receipts would actually rise rather than fall as a result of cutting tax rates. This proposition could not be disproved theoretically, but it had absolutely no empirical support in scholarly studies.[5] Nevertheless, the supply-siders managed to convince President Reagan of the validity of their views.

Considerably greater empirical support lay behind another strand of economic analysis devoted to the microeconomic effects of public policy. Beginning with R. H. Coase's paper, "The Problem of Social Costs," a host of economic analyses had accumulated to establish a strong case that much government regulation imposed excessive costs on the economy and promoted inefficiencies.[6] By the end of the 1970s the conservative movement had adopted these findings and generalized them into the policy principle that overregulation was a major cause of poor performance in the U.S. economy.

Since presidential campaigns are synthesizing processes it is not surprising that these various strands of economic thinking were woven together in the course of 1980. They were given expression in Ronald Reagan's September 9 speech in Chicago, which laid down the guidelines followed later in framing the new president's economic recovery program. For mainstream conservative economists there was the traditional stress on reduced government spending and balanced budgets. For monetarists there was a commitment to slower, more strictly controlled growth in the money supply. For deregulators there was the pledge to cut back government controls and regulations that could not be economically justified. Above all, Reagan enthusiastically endorsed the tax-cutting strategy of supply-side fiscal theory as the centerpiece of his economic program. The political attractiveness of this supply-side vision of growth is not difficult to understand. It seemed to allow the Reagan candidacy to escape the dismal prospect offered both by traditional Republican economics and by monetarism, a prospect of austerity and distributional conflict in the name of long-term solvency. Tax-induced "growthmanship" meant that there could be economic success without pain, as monetary policy held back inflation and faster growth in a private sector relieved of high taxes benefited everyone. As far as treating an ailing economy was concerned, supply-side theory was the equivalent of laughing gas when compared to the monetarists' and orthodox conservatives' devotion to chemotherapy. It is not difficult to convince people that the world would be a better place if their taxes were cut.

None of this, however, fully explains the incoming administration's remarkable confidence that in the initial economic recovery program announced in February 1981, it had discovered the guiding principles of successful economic management for the ensuing four to six years. After one month in office the new president's fortunes were publicly staked to a number of high-risk promises predicting lower unemployment and inflation rates, faster economic growth, and balanced budgets.

There was, of course, the euphoria and confidence initially created during the transition period by the unexpectedly large Reagan victory.[7] Added to this was a passive consensus that could be created among the different economic schools of thought contributing to the economic strategy, each of which tended to regard the others as tolerable because fundamentally irrelevant.[8] Monetarists dismissed supply-side theory and downgraded the balanced-budget goals of fiscal conservatives as cures for inflation. Fiscal conservatives worried about the irresponsibility of supply-side tax cuts, but also saw the advantage of reducing revenues as a permanent constraint on government spending. Hard-charging supply-siders were simply disdainful of everyone else's nostrums. The Reagan administration's disinclination to satisfy intellectuals by integrating the different strands of thought allowed each school to believe that its remedy was the one effective part of the Reagan package that would assure success. In effect, the array of offsetting advice from the economics profession created a kind of vacuum providing an opportunity for the political ideology of the Reagan administration to predominate. The economic course set by the White House in 1981 promised that all good things were compatible.

The ultimate reason for the Reagan presidency's confidence in its multiyear economic strategy lay in the fact that it was founded on a political, not economic, theory. Economic analysis alone was tentative and incomplete, changing as economic conditions changed. Not so the political analysis behind this economic strategy. Within the conservative movement two concerns, each identifying something real, had become inextricably linked: the problem of a malfunctioning economy and the problem of a malfunctioning big government. It was an act of political theory to link the latter as the chief cause of the former. Under this overriding concept, which lay at the heart of the movement and of Reagan's fifteen-year campaign, all strands of the Reagan economic program were fully compatible and mutually reinforcing. All were means of hemming in government so as to release the inherent forces of the market economy and thus create sustained economic growth. Hemming in government meant spending cuts to balance the budget, monetary restrictions to rein in the creation of money, deregulation to remove nonmarket controls, and, perhaps most important of all, a tax-cut tourniquet to restrict the flow of private productive resources into the maw of big government. Given this underlying rationale, any doubts expressed by economic experts, whose own ideological disarray often occasioned public ridicule, could be discounted. It was perhaps this feeling that prompted a quip by the president-elect questioning why he even needed a Council of Economic Advisers.

For all these reasons, therefore, it is unlikely that the Reagan administration's economic strategy would have been very different with or without what was perceived as a major electoral mandate. The idea of such a mandate did, however, help ensure that the new administration was rather quickly given the chance to put its strategy into practice. At that point, things began to go wrong for the new beginning.

The Strategy in Practice

Flaws in the Reagan economic strategy began to emerge when that strategy was translated into detailed legislative proposals.

The tax cuts advocated by the administration were massive. The initial proposal was for a 30 percent cut in personal marginal tax rates, to be implemented in three yearly installments of 10 percent each, beginning retroactively January 1, 1981. This was combined with an extraordinarily generous accelerated depreciation proposal, which, when fully implemented, would imply a negative tax rate on most equipment investment given the inflation- and interest-rate forecasts of the administration. The personal tax cut proposal was later modified to imply a 23 percent total cut implemented in three steps—a 5 percent cut in tax-withholding on October 1, 1981; a further 10 percent cut effective July 1, 1982; and a further 10 percent cut on July 1, 1983. The three reductions—5, 10, and 10 percent—add up to a total of only 23 percent because the last two reductions are cuts from a lower base. While the total marginal rate cut and the consequent revenue loss from this source were reduced, the administration agreed to various new congressional initiatives to provide additional savings incentives, increase incentives for charitable donations, and bring tax relief for married couples. The total revenue cost of the final package through 1984 was roughly equal to the cost of Reagan's original 30 percent marginal rate cut.

At the same time, the administration advocated nondefense spending cuts of $40 billion in fiscal 1982, growing to $100 billion in 1986. These were not cuts relative to 1981 spending levels. They were, instead, cuts relative to the levels to which spending was projected to rise under 1981 laws, if all programs were increased both to cover the growth in the number of those receiving entitlements and to compensate for inflation. Nevertheless, total spending, which had been growing faster than GNP, was now to grow at only about one-half the rate of GNP, while defense alone was to grow at an 8.6 percent real rate over the period. Total outlays were to fall from over 23 percent of GNP to 19 percent.

However, the administration did not project a falling ratio of outlays to GNP because they were advocating massive cuts in spending programs. In fact they wanted a huge increase in defense spending that largely offset desired cuts in nondefense programs. The projected ratio of outlays to GNP fell mainly because the administration projected a very high growth rate for GNP. Real economic growth was supposed to proceed at an average annual rate of 4.5 percent between 1981 and 1986 while inflation was expected to average 6 percent per year. Putting the two together meant that the growth in the money value of GNP would have to be almost 11 percent per year. This was not unreasonable relative to GNP growth rates during some recent recoveries. But earlier high growth rates had been fueled by a very rapid rate of growth in the money supply. The projected GNP growth rates were totally unreasonable given the monetary policy advocated by the administration, unless the amount of economic activity that could be financed by a given money supply grew at a rate far higher than anything experienced in past history.

It was possible to make the projections more consistent by assuming that inflation would come down much faster than the administration promised, but then taxable income would not grow as fast, taxpayers would not be pushed into higher tax brackets as rapidly, and receipts would be lower than expected. It would then become impossible for the administration to promise a balanced budget by 1984. Indeed it was clear that administration economists had chosen to project a high inflation rate so that projected deficits would be lower. More reasonable inflation assumptions led to deficits close to $100 billion for 1984 and 1985.

Of course, the current deficit outlook is much worse than that, and we shall later describe what went wrong. But before doing that, it is useful to step back and reflect on the merits of the Reagan plan as it existed in March 1981. Despite the fact that it implied very large deficits from the beginning, it could be rationalized as an appropriate strategy even if one believed that its merits were greatly exaggerated by the administration.

There was a broad consensus that the United States had to reduce inflation and to devote additional resources to defense and business capital formation. There was also a consensus that the tax system had become extremely inefficient. While the combination of tight money and large deficits would inevitably lead to high real interest rates, it was not unreasonable to believe that the latter's effect on business capital formation would be offset by the increased generosity of depreciation allowances. The negative impact of high interest rates would then be focused on housing and interest-sensitive consumer durables, and most American economists believed that we had been devoting too high a portion of the nation's resources to such goods in the past. Simultaneously, cuts in nondefense government spending would make room for a greatly enhanced American defense effort while allowing tax relief to overburdened taxpayers. Thus, despite large deficits, the program could be rationalized. Unfortunately, the strategy got out of hand for reasons to be explained in the next section.

What Went Wrong?

The Reagan administration clearly erred in thinking that spending and tax cuts would make it possible to conquer inflation while suffering only trivial costs. While a major recession was not inevitable, it was hard to believe that inflation could be reduced while the economy grew robustly. At a minimum, a period of slow and erratic growth seemed almost certain. However, it must be noted that the administration got far more of a monetary shock than it wanted. It had advocated a gradual reduction in the rate of growth of the money supply. Monetary growth turned out to be significantly lower than that recommended in the administration's plan. Moreover, for complicated technical reasons that will not be described here, the regulatory changes that allowed the invention of NOW accounts probably made the monetary growth that occurred less stimulative than it would have been otherwise. While a significant recession might have occurred even if the administration had obtained its preferred monetary policy, the greater-than-expected shock clearly intensified the problem.

The serious recession that emerged significantly increased the 1982 deficit, adding permanently to the interest costs, and also made it more difficult to cut social programs during the debate on the 1983 budget. Moreover, the recession implied that a rapid recovery was necessary to approach the administration's original targets, and it is not clear that this was possible without monetary accommodation. Such accommodation had occurred in all other postwar recoveries, but the Federal Reserve could not allow it this time if it hoped to achieve credibility against inflation in the long run.

The 1981–82 recession had an unexpectedly large impact on inflation, and it is now possible to project much lower price increases than were projected in the administration's original budget documents (see table 1). This should be regarded as a large success for the administration, and it is odd to include a description of falling inflation in a section that asks "what went wrong?" In fact, it is something that went right, but it has had a negative impact on the budget deficit because, as already explained, lower inflation rates depress total receipts. The legislated cuts in marginal tax rates were not offset by bracket creep to the degree expected, and the tax cut was, in fact, significantly larger than expected. Similarly, the depreciation reform

Table 1. Changes in the Administration's Budget Projections March 1981 to July 1982   (billions of dollars)

	Projections for Fiscal Year				
	1982	**1983**	**1984**	**1985**	**1986**
Outlay Projections					
As of 3/81	695.3	732.0	770.2	844.0	912.0
As of 7/82	731.0	761.5	812.5	874.7	932.7
Difference	35.7	29.5	42.3	30.7	20.7
Receipts Projections					
As of 3/81	650.3	709.1	770.7	849.9	940.2
As of 7/82	622.1	646.5	719.9	801.1	867.1
Difference	28.2	62.6	50.8	48.8	73.1
Deficit Projections					
As of 3/81	−45.0	−22.8	0.5	5.8	28.2
As of 7/82	−108.9	−115.0	−92.6	−73.6	−65.6
Difference	63.9	92.2	93.1	79.4	93.8

Sources: Office of Management and Budget, Fiscal Year 1982 Budget Revisions (Washington, D.C.: Office of Management and Budget, March 1982): 15, table 7; and Office of Management and Budget, Mid-Session Review of the 1983 Budget (Washington, D.C.: Office of Management and Budget, July 1982): 57, table 8.

has proved more generous than expected because the real value of the new depreciation deduction is being eroded less by inflation than was projected.

On the spending side, decelerating inflation tends to raise real outlays. The indexing of social benefits works with a time lag, with the adjustments in the current year dependent on last year's inflation rate. Real spending on indexed programs therefore rose more rapidly than expected as inflation decelerated in 1982. The real value of nonindexed programs was also higher than expected because past money appropriations assumed too high an inflation rate. Under the American system of budgeting it is hard to take money back from agencies once it has been appropriated.

Real spending will also be higher than the administration originally projected because Congress did not accept all of the nondefense cuts requested by the administration. The president asked for slightly more than $40 billion in cuts for fiscal 1982. Congress claims to have cut somewhat more than $30 billion. But this claim has to be examined critically. The policy changes in the summer of 1981 were so complex that it is difficult to get a proper accounting of all their effects. However, Congress made optimistic assumptions regarding savings resulting from program design changes and probably did not take proper account of the fact that cuts in one income-maintenance program often increase spending in some other program. For example, a cut in unemployment benefits may raise the demand for food stamps and AFDC (Aid to Families with Dependent Children). It is, in fact, quite possible that cuts were less than half the amount claimed.[9]

Another serious spending problem is related to interest on the public debt. A year ago one would have thought that if the economy were weaker than expected and if inflation lower than expected, there would be some reduction in projected interest because with that combination of events nominal interest rates would surely be lower than expected. Alas, the world has not worked the way it should, and the interest rate on ninety-day Treasury bills, projected in the original budget to average 8.9 percent in 1982, will actually average about 10.5 percent. This, combined with a higher-than-expected deficit, has caused interest costs to explode. The rise will exceed a reasonable estimate of all the budget cuts legislated in the summer of 1981. Interest has become a driving force in the budget.

While Congress did not accept all of the president's nondefense cuts, it did, much to the surprise of many observers, accept his defense program with only minor modifications. There may be cuts in the future, but the program enacted in 1981 initiated a number of expensive weapons programs that cannot easily be turned off.

Thus, America was put on a path of higher spending and a bigger real tax cut than the administration originally projected. With the policies in effect at the beginning of 1982, the implications for the deficit were frightening. Even if one assumed a significant economic recovery from the current recession, projected deficits would continue to rise in the long run if policies were held constant. With the president's defense program and other tax and spending laws as they existed at the beginning of 1982, the Congressional Budget Office estimated the 1985 deficit at $245 billion, or 5.9 percent of GNP.

A Midcourse Correction

Despite economic adversity, the president remained firmly committed to his economic strategy during the first half of 1982. He refused to contemplate any significant change on the tax side of the budget and attempted to close the deficit gap by constantly urging further cuts in nondefense spending. Those proposed cuts were highly concentrated because the president protected the elderly and disabled from any cuts in their social security benefits.

In February 1982 Reagan proposed total fiscal 1983 spending of $757.6 billion, of which $221.1 billion was for defense. Of the remaining $536.5 billion, $173.5 billion, or about one-third, represented the "untouchable" social security program and $96.4 billion, or about 13 percent, represented the net interest bill. Outlays, excluding defense, social security, and net interest, were to be $266.6 billion, but this amount could be obtained only by cutting more than $40 billion from other programs, an amount far higher than the cuts Reagan obtained in the summer of 1981 when he was at the height of his political power.

The proposed budget was generally thought to be politically unacceptable when it was first presented. But initially Congress had great difficulty formulating a viable alternative. Our decision-making processes were in considerable disarray.

However, things began to come together late in the spring. After intense bargaining between the administration and congressional leaders, and after several false starts once the bargaining failed to produce a bipartisan compromise, Congress finally passed a budget on June 23. That budget called for tax increases that were much more significant with respect to existing law than the relatively minor changes requested by the president. Spending cuts were also much less extensive. But, overall, the congressional budget turned out to be much closer to the president's initial February recommendations than anyone earlier thought possible.

After the budget finally passed, Congress faced the more difficult task of translating its recommended spending cuts and higher revenue projections into detailed legislation. Given that it was an election year and unemployment was at a post–World War II record, it was hard to be optimistic about implementation of the congressional budget.

However, Senator Dole, chairman of the Senate Finance Committee, exhibited extraordinary legislative skill and, with White House support, crafted a tax and spending-reduction bill that went a long way toward satisfying the requirements of the congressional budget passed earlier. Moreover, the bill was quite reasonably substantive, although not bearing much similarity to one that would be drafted by economists working in a world remote from political pressures. The bill had many provisions, but, in its most appealing sections, it corrected the depreciation reforms of 1981 to account for inflation being far less than expected when the original reforms were enacted.

Nevertheless, the bill was controversial. It would not have passed the House of Representatives were it not for the fact that the president gave it vigorous support. In doing so, he showed himself to be much more flexible regarding tax policy than he had been earlier in the year. While some accuse him of doing a policy flip-flop, this is an exaggeration. The tax bill is too important to be called a fine tuning of his overall fiscal policy, but it only offsets a relatively small portion of the 1981 tax cut and leaves in place more than a 5 percent cut in overall tax burdens relative to GNP between fiscal 1982 and fiscal 1983.

The tax and spending policy changes that occurred during the summer of 1982 are crucially important, for they take us off a path where deficits explode relative to GNP. They instead put us on one where the deficits stabilize, albeit at uncomfortably high levels, during the 1983–85 period. Absent a recession and assuming that the Federal Reserve Board continues its anti-inflationary strategy, it is probable that the deficit will average considerably more than 5 percent of GNP in 1983, 1984, and 1985, given the policies in effect at the end of fiscal 1982. This is far higher than official congressional and administration estimates, but the official estimates are based on extremely optimistic assumptions regarding the timing and strength of the recovery and on exogenous factors such as crop yields that determine spending on agricultural price-support payments.

What Went Right in Political Strategy?

Despite its economic difficulties, the Reagan administration has been strikingly successful in maintaining a united political front around its changing economic predictions and in retaining the initiative in the debate on national economic policy. This was true in passing the original spending and tax reduction program, and in returning subsequently to Congress for yet more cuts in domestic spending. It remained true as President Reagan was forced to embrace government deficits as the lesser of other evils, and as he reluctantly endorsed a 1982 program of raising federal tax revenues. While the president's policy change with regard to deficits and taxes was only a little more than fine tuning in economic terms, his earlier refusal to consider any change at all in the basic thrust of his 1981 policy made his vigorous support of the 1982 legislation seem like a political sea change. To those who hoped for a "Reagan revolution," the idea that accepting higher deficits and higher taxes did no violence to Ronald Reagan's original economic strategy seemed to require the sort of reasoning that would allow one to say, as Arthur Okun once put it, "the ship is fine except for two holes where the torpedoes hit." Whatever the rhetoric, policy did have to change to accommodate changing political and economic realities, and one of the most noteworthy achievements of the Reagan presidency in its first two years was its capacity to manage these changes without losing the political offensive or appearing indecisive.

Many reasons for this success in political management could be given. Ultimately they would all come back to one important fact: The Reagan presidency developed a capacity to deal with its economic ideology in a strategic rather than ideological manner. It would be difficult to exaggerate the significance of this factor. Without a capability for strategic management in this most ideological of administrations, the Reagan presidency would probably have quickly dissolved into a series of internal struggles reflecting the disarray in economic thought in the outside world. It probably would have gratuitously antagonized broad segments of public opinion and would almost certainly have fought with Congress in a self-defeating manner, as did the Nixon administration. Strategic management meant that the Reagan presidency self-consciously maneuvered to meet its opponents under favorable conditions, to thrust and parry depending on circumstances, and still to maintain an overall appearance of consistent commitment to its goals. Strategic management also meant that the basic political theory behind the Reagan economic policy—that of reviving the economy through retrenchment in goverment—was itself never open to question and debate. A typical script found the president enunciating some simple principle, followed by reports of the president resisting counterpressures with great stubbornness, then an eventual compromise sufficient for the president's proposal to win passage without the president himself appearing to engage in political bargaining, and finally a White House claim of victory.

The problem of the federal deficit as it emerged during 1981 and 1982 provides an excellent example of strategic management in the Reagan White House. As originally envisioned in the president's economic recovery program, there simply was no deficit problem; spending cuts in domestic programs would rein in budget outlays, tax cuts would revive growth and revenues, and monetary policy would reduce inflation. By 1984 or 1985 the budget would be in balance. But in August 1981, even as the administration was celebrating congressional passage of its budget and tax reduction program, some senior presidential advisers were worrying that the deficit projections were not unfolding as planned. It would be misleading to overschematize the policy discussions that occurred within the White House. What actually seems to have taken place was a continuous series of conversations and arguments spread over many months, occupying a handful of senior staff with occasional participation by the president. As one account aptly put it, the December 1981 *Atlantic Monthly* article on David Stockman "did not provoke a debate within the administration; it reflected it."[10] Then, as later, administration leaders were engaged in an endless effort to reconcile the major elements of the Reagan program as it had been broadcast in the first months of assuming office. Plans for the disappearing deficit were caught between constrictions in the scope for budget-cutting (given major defense increases and a political commitment to deal gently with "safety-net" programs) and a shortfall in revenues (produced initially by a failure of the economy to respond as expected to anticipated tax cuts and by the economic effects of highly restrictive monetary policies, and projected over the longer term by a three-year program of tax cuts and revenue indexing).

In essence the White House responded to the emerging deficit problem by carefully and gradually repositioning itself, without ever explicitly denying the merits of its original economic program.

One early device was to argue that doubts and criticisms were premature: the president's program had not yet taken effect. Even though the original selling of the program had made a considerable point of the expectations that would quickly change in advance of implementation, the appeal to patience could answer many critics during the latter part of 1981. Another tack was for the administration to make use of the deficit problem to serve its own purposes. Key administration strategists quietly welcomed the congressional and media alarums that greeted the periodically leaked projections of federal budget deficits.[11] This climate allowed the Reagan presidency to meet its opponents on quite favorable political terrain. To be alarmed at the projected deficits meant one had to either take the politically difficult step of supporting higher taxes and/or lower defense spending, or move toward the preferred Reagan approach of making still further cuts in federal civilian programs.

Notwithstanding these calculations, the real problem of a massive projected budget deficit persisted and grew even larger. The appeal to patience could not be counted on for long, and dissatisfaction with deficits had real and depressing effects in financial markets, the wellspring of the hoped-for Reagan recovery. Thus, during late 1981

the White House policy-makers seriously debated "revenue enhancement," launching the first trial balloons in a tentative manner always
well distanced from the president's own public positions. At the same
time the president also rejected the other logical possibility identified
by the strategists, a scaled-back program of defense increases. The
fact is that Ronald Reagan as well as his opponents were caught up
in the logic of a situation characterized by major tax cuts, a sluggish
economy, and the restricted scope for further spending cuts. One
approach to the deficit problem continually tried by the president
and senior staff in 1981 and the first half of 1982 was almost instinctive: to deny the value of economists' projections. This view could
suffice for Reagan-the-candidate, but it could not survive presidential
staff work in the Office of Management and Budget and Council of
Economic Advisers. Something had to be done. At the beginning of
1982, the next step was grudgingly taken in the president's budget
proposal and State of the Union message. Despite a lifelong commitment to balanced budgets, the president was led to argue that his
projected deficits were less undesirable than raising taxes or cutting
back on national security. More cuts in domestic programs would, of
course, be required, but here, too, the administration turned its la-
mented deficit problem into a strategic advantage. It did so by using
its dilemma as an offensive weapon and challenging those dissatisfied
in Congress and elsewhere to come up with a better formula. Given
the fragmented nature of legislative decision-making, it was a fairly
safe bet that no one else could produce a comprehensive package
without White House involvement. Hence, during 1982 the White
House managed to shift a good deal of responsibility for its economic
problems to Capitol Hill, while still setting the general terms of debate
(i.e., how to solve the deficit problem, or, as a practical matter, how
to come in with a fiscal 1983 deficit projection of around $100 billion)
and without losing its chance to help shape the detailed outcomes on
taxing and spending.

Ronald Reagan was constrained as well as helped by strategic management of his economic policy. Shifting the focus to Congress, with
active participation by White House aides in framing spending and
tax-increase proposals, meant that some of his own freedom of action
and initiative was being lost. It became more difficult for Reagan to
assume a stance of opposition to the Washington establishment.

By the summer of 1982 Ronald Reagan had taken the next grudg-
ing step in dealing with the deficit problem and accepted a tax increase
package worked out by Republican congressional leaders with the
active cooperation of senior White House aides. It was an idea the
president had rejected the previous winter when it was advanced by

his staff without the leverage of congressional backing. Passage of this tax program signaled the first major break in Republican ranks behind President Reagan's leadership, dividing antideficit fiscal conservatives from antitax supply-siders—among other cleavages. It is noteworthy, however, that the president himself was—until the very last moment when a public appeal was deemed necessary—not directly identified with the tax proposals and indeed reverted to his familiar antitax themes immediately following their passage.[12] There followed a number of highly dramatized presidential vetoes of congressional spending bills. Since these appropriation bills, which the White House labeled "budget busters," were generally within the president's agreed total spending target (but with different priorities), it seems safe to say that the chief motivation behind the presidential vetoes was to reassert the image of an antideficit, antitaxation presidency.

The deficit problem was only one of many examples of skillful policy management during the first two years of Reagan's term. There was, of course, no escaping economic realities, but the administration's capacity for strategic management allowed it to take advantage of its opportunities in the first year and to make the best of some difficult circumstances in the second. At least three factors help account for what appears—especially when compared with recent predecessors in the White House—to be a remarkable ability.

In the first place, Ronald Reagan and his immediate staff were willing to limit drastically the number of presidential priorities. There was, inevitably, a familiar need to deal with crises, usually of a foreign policy nature (e.g., Libya, the Falklands, the AWACS sale, the PLO in Beirut). But in terms of commitments of presidential time and effort, these were ad hoc and sporadic affairs. Likewise, defense policy issues, once the initial go-ahead for more spending was given, seemed to require little detailed presidential involvement. The economy was Reagan's first, second, and third priority. It was here that Ronald Reagan engaged in sustained struggles with Congress, launched his major public appeals, and put his personal reputation on the line. Nor was the president's commitment to all areas of economic policy broadly understood. The narrow compass of presidential priorities had little to say about industrial policies for particular economic sectors, about regional development, about industrial relations and wage bargaining (apart from air traffic controllers), or about international economic relations. The presidential priority in economic affairs was to reduce the role of government—its taxes, spending, and regulations—and then stand aside for an economic revival in the private sector.

All of this had a vastly simplifying effect on strategic calculations made in the White House. By drastically narrowing his priorities, the president appeared to rise above the prevailing complexities, most of which were obscure to the general public. The message to Washington contained in this presidential agenda was to the effect that there was a vast amount of government activity that was just not of any presidential interest, except as it might be cut back. Departmental bureaucracies found it difficult, if not impossible, to gain White House attention for their roles and missions. Any major national debate on social policy was sidestepped by subordinating social spending issues to the requirements of economic policy. In place of talk about policy trade-offs and arcane complexities there could be the appearance of simplicity and decision.

In short, the president's leadership was comprehensible even if, or rather because, it was narrowly focused.

In the second place, the president allowed his immediate staff broad scope to engage in strategic planning and coalition building. If that sounds a rather commonplace feature of the modern presidency, it is not. Recent presidents have been too hyperactive (as with Johnson), too suspicious (Nixon), or too bogged down in detailed decision-making (Carter) to create a White House atmosphere conducive to strategic thinking. Within the guidelines of an overarching economic ideology, Ronald Reagan expected his staff to think through possible contingencies and operational practicalities in producing a rolling game-plan for the administration's economic policy. It was this tolerance and expectation that allowed the continuing internal conversation on the deficit problem to occur and that produced a sequence of adaptations to control its political damage.

Finally, strategic management was made possible by the development of a small, rather close-knit group of policy managers in the White House. Future political scientists, and possibly psychologists specializing in small-group dynamics, will undoubtedly devote considerable attention to the internal groupings of the Reagan White House—the Deaver Luncheon Group, the Legislative Strategy Group, and the like.[13] The formal names are unimportant, and, indeed, overformalizing the description would obscure the very important informal qualities of what came to exist. In essence what evolved in the first two years of the Reagan administration was a working committee of the presidency, composed exclusively of senior staff, meeting on a continuous, daily basis, and responsible for meshing day-to-day tactics with longer-term goals. To put it most baldly, their loyalty was to the idea of a successful Reagan presidency rather than to any particular economic theory. This was a stance that infuriated true believers of the supply-side school, several of the most prominent of whom resigned in the second year of the administration. Well-known monetarists, as well as supply-siders, were absent from these inner councils, although their views were certainly taken into account. The more dogmatically oriented the presidential adviser, the less likely he was to gain entry into the ongoing circle of conversation that revolved around Deaver, Meese, and Baker.[14] Economic views from the Council of Economic Advisers were registered and deemed important, but the chairman of the CEA could resign in the summer of 1982 with little discernible impact on the process of top-level economic decision-making in the Reagan White House. By contrast, David Stockman probably survived the extremely embarrassing quotations in the December 1981 *Atlantic Monthly* because participants in this inner circle saw his strategic ability as essential to their efforts.

The existence of a relatively cohesive, strategy-conscious group in the Reagan White House meant that everyday decisions tended to be seen in reference to an evolving "game-plan," as it was known. At times this required that the president move into the forefront of confrontation with Congress; at other times events were allowed to run their course with the White House deliberately fading into the background. It meant that decisions were approached not only on the basis of immediate tactical advantage, but also with regard to calculations of longer-run consistency and/or the appearance thereof. None of this guaranteed success in dealing with economic policy in the first two years of the Reagan presidency. It did, however, vastly improve the odds for managing policy contradictions and disappointments in a politically productive manner.

What Next?

As this is being written the debate on the 1984 budget is beginning. More than any president in living memory, Ronald Reagan has staked his reputation on an ability to master economic policy. And we know that chances for delivering on this promise will depend on a continuing interplay of political calculations and only partially controllable economic developments. No one knows what the final results will be, but some interim predictions seem plausible.

The environment for making difficult decisions is more promising in 1983 than it was in early 1982. Legislators need not be obsessed by election-year politics; the economy should be recovering; and the new flexibility shown by the president will be conducive to easier bargaining. The debate on the fiscal 1984 budget should be better suited to foster progress in reducing projections of huge deficits.

On the other hand, the November 1982 congressional election gave many Republicans a good scare, and did not bode well for continued cohesion among Republicans such as had existed during 1981. Indeed, the cohesion had already begun to break down in the fall of 1981 when it proved impossible to get broad Republican support for the additional budget cuts desired by the president. Perhaps more important, Congress had already cut the programs that were relatively easy to cut politically, and in the summer of 1982 took back a substantial portion of the 1981 business tax cut.

In other words, the decisions that have to be made are progressively becoming more difficult. Spending growth will be dominated by growth in just three programs throughout the remainder of the eighties. There is a broad consensus that defense spending must grow at a rate far greater than GNP between now and 1990, although perhaps not as rapidly as the president wishes. Outlays for health services delivery systems, primarily Medicare and Medicaid, are also exploding. Together with interest, current projections suggest that defense, social security, and health will constitute about three-quarters of the federal budget by 1985. It would be impractical in the long run to attempt to offset their immense growth by cutting the other quarter of the budget, since even the most extreme conservative would admit there is a role for government in matters other than defense and social security.

And yet, despite strong public support for defense and social security, there is a fervent desire by the American people for lower taxes and lower deficits. These various goals are not compatible.

The American people still think the goals compatible because they have not yet become sufficiently well informed about the inexorable arithmetic of budget projections. The belief exists that taxes can be brought down by reducing welfare, waste, and inefficiency in the budget. Few realize that, in a few years, the annual increase in social security would be sufficient to finance the entire food stamp program and the entire Aid to Families with Dependent Children program, which, together with health care for the poor, constitute the core of the American welfare effort.

Unfortunately, American politicians, including the president, have done little to educate the public. They have played to the myths afflicting public opinion. But the basic problem will not go away. The options are limited. There either has to be a fundamental change in political attitudes toward defense, social security, and health, or taxes will have to be raised; or the United States will have to tolerate huge deficits far beyond anything experienced in post–World War II history.

There is, unfortunately, a fourth option that one hesitates to mention. Monetary restraint can be abandoned. Inflation can reduce the budget deficit. Although personal income taxes are scheduled to be indexed starting in 1985, inflation can still raise tax burdens. Indexing is far from perfect and, in particular, does not prevent inflation from raising the tax on capital income. Moreover, inflation can tax away the real value of past issues of government debt and the enormous interest bill associated with it. It is also unlikely that legislators would fully compensate for inflation in their appropriations for defense and other nonindexed programs. It is, thus, a way of slowing growth in spending.

Which path will the United States take? In today's volatile political climate, prognostication is dangerous. It is, however, reasonable to assume that a little will be chosen from each of the options. By the end of 1982, monetary policy began to reflect a new philosophy. It appears that less attention will henceforth be paid to controlling traditional measures of the money supply. This dramatic change has occurred without a word of protest from the monetarists within the administration. It may allow for a faster recovery than seemed possible under the administration's original monetary strategy, but it also raises the risk of reigniting inflation as the recovery proceeds.

In fiscal policy, it is probably safe to assume that the president will not get all of the defense spending he desires, but that defense will continue to absorb a rapidly growing portion of the total budget. Growth in social security benefits will probably be slowed in a minor way, and more of the 1981 tax cut will be taken back. But unusually large deficits will remain.

It is probably unwise to be any more precise than that, but the temptation is hard to resist. As time goes on and people become better educated regarding the quantitative dimensions of the budget dilemma, the voters may become more willing to accept further tax increases. This would seem to go against everything President Reagan stands for. But it should not be interpreted in this manner. Despite the fact that a considerable portion of the gargantuan tax cut of 1981 will be taken back, we are unlikely to return to the tax levels that existed when Reagan took office. Similarly, nondefense spending will have been brought significantly below the levels that would have prevailed if Reagan had not been elected. In addition, a sizable dent has been made in the inflation problem. That has occurred largely because this administration has been willing to "stay the course" longer, and to accept more costs in the form of higher unemployment, than has any other recent administration. It is not at all impossible for a substantial recovery to begin that, in the eyes of future economic historians, may make this administration appear to be a great success. Whether or not this happens is, of course, not just a matter of having selected the right policies; it will also require a lot of luck.]

Assuming that the wheel of economic fortune does not turn violently for or against the Reagan administration, its political future is probably neither as glowing as the believers in a Republican realignment predict nor as dismal as Democratic party leaders hope. In retrospect it is now clear that many observers in the 1970s underestimated not only Ronald Reagan but also the capacity of a conservative coalition to carry the costs associated with bringing down the inflation rate.] These costs have been measured in unemployment and in an immense loss of economic output brought about by idle or underutilized productive resources. But the Reagan administration has not been seriously threatened by the electoral power of the unemployed, and the loss of potential output decried by liberal economists has been just that, an abstract potential with little real political weight when compared with the mounting public fears of uncontrolled inflation that existed at the end of the 1970s. By this standard the Reagan administration had, at the end of its second year, dealt with the most salient public policy issue it had been elected to address.

And yet White House strategists should have cause to worry. In terms of the political management of economic policy, the Reagan administration had probably entered a new phase by the end of 1982. For one thing, there is the problem of maintaining the policy initiative once the battle against inflation is widely perceived as having been won. And that indeed was the perception by the end of 1982. Experience shows that the American political system is not motivated in any enduring way by the idea of gratitude, and success against inflation can easily become yesterday's battle, only to be replaced by the next topic of public concern. By midterm the Reagan administration was largely on the defensive regarding proposals for jobs, retraining, and industrial-assistance programs. Without fear of inflation as a motivating force, it will also become more difficult to subordinate social policy questions, including social security, to the requirements of economic policy. A major reduction of unemployment brought about by renewed economic growth in 1983 and 1984 would probably have the effect of shifting public attention back to "quality of life" issues such as the environment and public health. It remains to be seen whether the Reagan presidency, having staked out its position in an economic agenda hostile to government activism, will be sufficiently adaptable to move with the changing public concerns that constitute American politics. A few years from now it may well appear that the Reagan presidency spent the bulk of its intellectual capital in that first, brilliant year and a half of legislative successes.

A second problem for the political future is that the Reagan mandate, however conceived, has clearly become a depreciating asset. As noted earlier, the November 1982 congressional elections tended to undercut the basis for Republican cohesion. Taken as a whole, the results were ambiguous. They gave politicians no clear guidance as to whether to stay or stray the president's course. This in effect constituted a mandate for greater congressional independence, making policy management from the White House much more difficult. But in another sense the 1982 election result was unambiguous: it obviously did not give Reagan what the midterm election of 1934 gave Franklin Roosevelt, namely, a ringing endorsement of the president's first two years of stewardship. An administration that lived by the mandate myth in its first two years must expect to suffer from the myth of a lost mandate in the succeeding years.

Whatever the economic future holds, there is a final problem on the political horizon. By 1983, what we have called strategic management in the White House was producing clear disadvantages as well as advantages for the president. The task of senior Reagan staff, particularly those without long-standing personal attachments to Reagan (such as James Baker, David Stockman, and Richard Darman), had never been easy. Reagan's first principles provided an unchanging framework that was taken for granted and within which they had to operate—a commitment to retrenchment in civilian government, faith in the automatic working of private markets, a desire for more defense spending, and hostility to higher taxes. As economic facts accumulated in 1981 and 1982, it became increasingly difficult to square these principles with the day-to-day adaptations that had to be made in order to win in Congress and to maintain public faith in the White House's position on the economy. Presidential staff work became more aggressive with respect to the president's views. When their own advice was resisted, senior staff could be seen helping orchestrate congressional and public pressures on the president to cut defense increases, accept higher taxes, reduce expectations of economic recovery, and take deficit projections seriously. For example, such pressures, along with the arrival of the new CEA chairman Martin Feldstein, yielded more pessimistic White House projections of economic growth and deficits for fiscal year 1983 and the years beyond. This was a gain for White House credibility, but it conflicted somewhat with the president's personal optimism about the U.S. economy. Such efforts had the advantage of helping make key congressional leaders shoulder a good deal of responsibility for the nation's economic policy. But they also had the disadvantage of portraying the president as a somewhat detached, passive recipient of pressures—as if White House staff were maneuvering to change the title of the famous *Atlantic Monthly* article from "The Education of David Stockman" to "The Education of Ronald Reagan." In the jargon of social scientists, the danger to Reagan was one of being perceived as a dependent variable, something acted upon but not itself causing other things to happen.

This perception of a presidency crowding in on the president's personal leadership poses a special problem for Ronald Reagan. Every presidency has the problem of reconciling two faces. The public face demands the appearance of certainty, of confidence, of control, if a president is to have a chance of persuading others. The private face copes as best it can with inadequate information, conflicting advice, and events in an outside world that are more likely to distort than respond to the president's policy. But unlike most presidents, Reagan arose from a movement of opinion that was meant to be principled. The core of his supporters has little tolerance for discrepancies between the public and private faces of the presidency. To them, a strategic approach to economic ideology tends to be seen as an inherently corrupting enterprise. By 1983 many of the more ideologically inclined appointees had left the administration, adding weight to the potential sources of outside criticism in conservative circles in the years ahead. The administration's evolving position on deficits and taxes has already strained some of these relations, and the need to adapt to changing economic circumstances and public concerns will undoubtedly add new pressures in the future. Disappointing many of his friends will be part of the price Ronald Reagan will have to pay if he is to transform a movement of opposition into a party of government for the 1980s.

Notes

1. See, for example, Ellis W. Hawley, *The New Deal and the Problem of Monopoly* (Princeton: Princeton University Press, 1966), ch. 2; Arthur M. Schlesinger, Jr., *The Coming of the New Deal* (Boston: Houghton Mifflin, 1959), pp. 179–83; and *The Politics of Upheaval* (Boston: Houghton Mifflin, 1960), pp. 386–407.

2. Lou Cannon, *Reagan* (New York: G.P. Putnam's Sons, 1982); Sidney Blumenthal, "The Ideology Makers," *Boston Globe*, August 8, 1982, p. 88; Kevin Phillips, "Post-Conservative America," *New York Review of Books*, May 13, 1982.

3. A fuller description of the theory and the relevant cast of characters can be found in Jack Brooks, "The Annals of Finance (Supply-Side Economics)," *New Yorker*, April 19, 1982, pp. 96–150.

4. For an example, see Jerry A. Hausman, "Labor Supply," in *How Taxes Affect Economic Behavior*, Henry J. Aaron and Joseph A. Pechman, eds. (Washington, D.C.: Brookings Institution, 1981), pp. 27–83.

5. Don Fullerton, "On the Possibility of an Inverse Relationship between Tax Rates and Government Revenues," National Bureau of Economic Research, Working Paper no. 467, April 1980.

6. R. H. Coase, "The Problem of Social Cost," *Journal of Law and Economics* 3 (October 1960):1.

7. Dick Kirschten, "The Reagan Team Comes to Washington," *National Journal*, November 15, 1980, pp. 1924–26.

8. Gail Gregg and Dale Tate, "Reagan Economic Officials Put Differences Behind Them," *Congressional Quarterly Weekly Reports*, February 7, 1981, pp. 259–61.

9. John William Ellwood, ed., *Reductions in U.S. Domestic Spending: How They Affect State and Local Governments* (New Brunswick, N.J.: Transaction Books, 1982).

10. Sidney Blumenthal, "The Crisis of Reagonomics," *Boston Globe*, May 2, 1982, p. 11. See also the results of an investigation by Steven R. Weisman, in *New York Times Magazine*, October 24, 1982.

11. "Stockman on the Budget Outlook," *National Journal*, September 19, 1981, pp. 1665–67.

12. Thus the president's Saturday radio broadcast (of September 4, 1982) following his congressional victory on the tax bill was devoted to the theme of how current unemployment was due to the long record of high taxation.

13. Dick Kirschten, "Decision Making in the White House," *National Journal*, April 3, 1982, pp. 584–89; "Reagan's Legislative Strategy Team," *National Journal*, June 26, 1982, pp. 1127–30.

14. David Hoffman, "Reagan's Crusaders Fail to Find the Grail," *Washington Post*, July 4, 1982, p. 1.

3 The Reagan Presidency in Domestic Affairs

Richard P. Nathan

During the first year of the Reagan presidency, a lobbyist for education programs made a comment that shows how successful the Reagan administration was in taking over the reins of domestic affairs in 1981. In the midst of that intense period of budget cutting, the lobbyist said that he had obtained a good outcome on the floor of the House because an amendment was adopted for the funding of an education program that only cut it in half. This satisfaction with "half a loaf" in 1981 is a far cry from the mood of domestic policy-making in the sixties and seventies.

Not all of the credit for bringing about this changed mood in Washington should be assigned to Ronald Reagan. Retrenchment had been gaining strength in domestic policy since the mid-seventies. Its earliest manifestations were at the local level; many cities cut government spending and personnel as a reaction to the New York City fiscal crisis of 1975–76.

At the state level, retrenchment emerged as a major factor in 1978, when California voters approved Proposition 13, which lowered local property taxes. National policy began to change soon afterward. Jimmy Carter responded to the more conservative stance on domestic issues in the post–Proposition 13 period, but was much less successful than Ronald Reagan in his efforts to cut domestic spending. The Reagan presidency has produced a fundamental redirection in the domestic

48

policies of the U.S. government, both in the spending of the federal government and in the substance and purposes of its domestic programs.

Although other factors contributed to the austerity of the eighties, Ronald Reagan's domestic policies had a great deal to do with this shift. On coming into office, the Reagan presidency demonstrated an unusually high degree of decisiveness, clarity of purpose, and skill in the use of the powers of the presidency in the domestic sphere. Even those who disagree with the substance of the Reagan domestic program are likely to agree that it has been advanced rapidly and skillfully.

Moreover, the new austerity and mood of national policy in domestic affairs is likely to continue. Whether the Reagan presidency succeeds or fails—for example, because of the failures in other areas, such as economic or international policy—it has already marked a watershed in domestic affairs. The long cycle of growth in the role and activism of the national government in domestic affairs that began with FDR's New Deal ended with Reagan's New Federalism.

A second important generalization about the Reagan presidency in the field of domestic affairs relates to the means by which its program has been advanced. The Reagan program has been executed through a dual approach that involves both legislative and administrative actions.

The Dual Approach

It is customary in American government for new presidents to move quickly on the legislative front on domestic issues. The reason usually given for doing this is that, unless a new president takes advantage of the momentum of his election, he is unlikely to get major changes through Congress. Reagan followed his predecessors in this respect.

The administrative dimension of the presidency, on the other hand, has not been as important in the past. In contrast to the enactment of new legislation, it involves having appointed officials work to fulfill major policy objectives by implementing existing laws. Richard Nixon developed an administrative strategy for advancing his domestic policy aims, but it was aborted because of Watergate.[1]

The simultaneous pursuit of legislative and administrative domestic aims by the Reagan administration and its success so far in both pursuits is the major theme of this chapter. The chapter is divided into two main parts: the legislative objectives and accomplishments of the Reagan presidency, and the administrative tactics used to pursue the administration's objectives in domestic affairs.

Legislative Achievements and Proposals

The substance of the Reagan program in domestic affairs is best introduced by looking at the way in which issues have been conceptualized. ⌐Turning away from past emphasis on the definition and solution of public problems, the Reagan presidency focuses on limitations—limitations on the role of government, limitations on its ability to carry out its purposes, and limitations on its resources.

Three main themes of the Reagan administration in the field of domestic policy are:

⭑ 1. a commitment to the idea that the public sector should be smaller and less intrusive, and that the private sector should be strengthened and made more influential;

2. a theory of federalism that involves reducing the role of the federal government by devolving federal responsibilities to state governments; and

3. a concept of programs to aid the poor that consists of providing adequate benefits to the "truly needy," and removing from welfare able-bodied persons who can make it on their own.⌋

Two general points about this list need to be made here, one regarding what is on the list, the other regarding what is not.⌐The success of the Reagan administration in shifting the focus of domestic policy from problem solving to budget cutting turned out to be so closely ⭑ in line with the changed mood of the country that protest was relatively muted. The administration's 1981 cuts in social spending were not a major issue in the midterm congressional elections of 1982⌋ Concern about future cuts in social security benefits (which the administration stoutly denied it favored) kindled fires with better-off taxpayers. But ⌐cuts in antipoverty programs—most of which programs had their ⭒ roots not in FDR's New Deal but in Johnson's Great Society—caused hardly a murmur.[2] Cuts in antipoverty programs seemed to be widely accepted, even popular with the electorate.⌋

The second general point about the themes listed above concerns issues to which Reagan's most conservative supporters in the 1980 presidential campaign were emotionally and strongly committed but which never made it onto his legislative agenda. The three leading issues in this category are nonspending issues advanced in the form of proposals to amend the U.S. Constitution. They would permit

prayer in public schools, prohibit publicly funded abortions, and prohibit busing to achieve school desegregation. Reagan and his chief
lieutenants steered clear of these issues, while at the same time adroitly
avoiding confrontations with their conservative allies that could have
dissipated support for other legislative initiatives.\
The focus of domestic policy in Reagan's first year in office was
on the budget process. When Reagan came to office in January 1981,
the budget for fiscal year 1982 (October 1, 1981, through September
30, 1982) had already been transmitted to Congress by President
Carter. The debate within the Carter administration on this budget
produced an interesting dilemma. Political and substantive objectives
diverged. Politically, it was argued that Carter should submit a 1982
budget with significant cuts in order to limit the opportunities of his
more conservative successor to claim credit for the reductions he was
bound to propose. To have done so, however, would have required
Carter to abandon many programs Democrats have historically supported.

Little evidence of this debate appeared in the press. Few people
were interested in the lame-duck Carter budget. The result was a
standoff—a watered-down version of the two positions. Carter's proposed budget for fiscal year 1982 cut some domestic programs, held
others level, and proposed only a handful of initiatives. It showed a
deficit of $27.5 billion for fiscal 1982 and projected a $32 billion
budget surplus for 1984.

The playing out of the budget story for 1982 makes these original
Carter estimates unbelievable in retrospect. The actual budget deficit
for fiscal year 1982 reached $111 billion; a $208 billion deficit is
projected by the administration for 1983 and a $189 billion deficit
for 1984.[3] The reasons for these exploding deficits are well known—
a much deeper recession than anticipated and the enactment in 1981
of a $737 billion federal tax reduction over five years as the key
ingredient of Reagan's supply-side economic program.

Faced with fast-rising deficits, many politicians, including the president, called for the adoption by the Ninety-seventh Congress of legislation amending the U.S. Constitution to require that the federal
budget be balanced. The Senate passed the necessary enabling legislation in 1981, but the House (in this case because of effective tactics
by Speaker O'Neill) failed to do so despite attempts in both 1981 and
1982. The irony of the drive for a balanced budget requirement
coming at the very time that the budget was becoming increasingly
unbalanced did not go unnoticed. The *New Yorker* magazine saw
"something comical in this spectacle of people clamoring for a drastic

remedy for an abuse they themselves are engaged in at this very minute."[4] The editors likened it to a group of drunks "haranguing passersby about the evils of alcohol."[5]

Despite these longer-term budget frustrations, the spending cuts made in Reagan's first year were distinguished by the speed with which they were developed. Reagan used the budget-revision process to shape up his administration—identifying major policy purposes and calling for changes across the board.

/But even more notable than the speed with which these revisions were sent forward is the degree to which the administration succeeded in winning enactment for them in the Omnibus Budget Reconciliation Act, which was passed in August 1981\

One of the ironies of the story of the 1981 reconciliation act is that its passage depended heavily on a new interpretation of the procedures contained in the Congressional Budget and Impoundment Control Act of 1974. This act was adopted largely as a result of the efforts by liberal Democrats to curb the impoundment abuses of the Nixon administration. A provision of the act that was little noticed at the time was the basis for the budget changes made in fiscal year 1982. Section 310(c) of the 1974 act provides for a "reconciliation process." The basic idea was that changes in various laws had to be reconciled with the budget ceilings contained in the budget resolutions required to be established each fiscal year under the 1974 act. The reconciliation process was not defined in a precise way in the 1974 act, and it was not used at all until 1980. It was used for the second time by Reagan in 1981 for fiscal year 1982\

To simplify the explanation of what happened in 1981, the Reagan administration, under Budget Director David Stockman's able leadership, worked out reconciliation legislation in both the Senate and the House requiring nearly all authorizing and appropriations committees to take action on policy changes and spending cuts. These changes and cuts involved not just regular appropriations but also authorizations. The changes in authorizations affected both discretionary and automatic appropriations for entitlement programs, which do not require an annual appropriation. Forty percent of the funds cut in fiscal year 1982 were in these entitlement programs.[6] All of the cuts made in both houses were adopted in a single "up-or-down" vote in each on the 1981 reconciliation act. Members could either support the president or oppose him.\ When the dust settled, far-reaching substantive changes had been made in the domestic policies of the national government. Many of the main ideas of what came to be known as Reagan's New Federalism program were encompassed in this 1981 reconciliation act.

Reagan's New Federalism

White House officials maintain that President Reagan has never used the term "New Federalism" to describe his domestic program, and that it originated with the press. They acknowledge that some administration officials and documents have used the term, but say that the president prefers to speak instead of the administration's "federalism initiatives." A possible reason for Reagan's reluctance to take up the term New Federalism was that Nixon had used it. There are interesting differences between the two New Federalisms—Nixon's and Reagan's.

Both Reagan and Nixon embraced the idea of strengthening state and local governments. The formal term for this is "devolution," the transfer of responsibility and power from the central government to subnational governments. The word "decentralization" is often used to mean the same thing as devolution, although at other times decentralization is given a more restrictive meaning, referring to the transfer of administrative functions from the central government to states and localities. Devolution is not the sole preserve of Republicans. Some Democrats have the same proclivity, though usually with less intensity.

The main difference between the Reagan and Nixon views of devolution is that Reagan favors devolution from the national government to the states—not to localities—whereas Nixon was more pragmatic. He favored devolution to whatever type of government Congress would devolve responsibilities to. Nixon's attitude is understandable. He faced a Congress in which both houses were controlled by Democrats, whereas the Republican victory in the Senate in 1980 gave Reagan an important strategic advantage. Nixon probably would have failed to get new legislation for revenue sharing and block grants had he been unwilling to allow local governments to be their major beneficiaries. Local governments received the bulk of the funds distributed under the revenue-sharing program and the new block grants enacted in the Nixon-Ford period.

A second major difference between the Nixon and Reagan brands of New Federalism (which, like the first one, reflects differences in the political environment of the two periods) has to do with money. Nixon proposed block-grant legislation that provided new and additional funds referred to as "sweeteners," the purpose being to win the liberal votes needed for enactment. The community development block grant (CDBG) involved a bonus of 15 percent per year when enacted in 1974. The other major block grant enacted under Nixon was the Comprehensive Employment and Training Act (CETA), which also included a "sweetener." In sharp contrast, the Reagan block-grant proposals, advanced as part of the budget revisions for fiscal year 1982, proffered no sweeteners—only bitter pills in the form of budget cuts. The cuts were justified on grounds of efficiency. One result of creating new block grants, it was argued, would be to permit an appreciable reduction in the funding levels of the categorical grants "folded into" the new block grants.

Although in March 1981 Reagan proposed consolidating eighty-five existing categorical grant programs encompassing $16.5 billion into seven new block grants, Congress gave him only part of what he asked for. The reconciliation act passed later in 1981 created nine so-called block grants that affected fifty-four existing programs with total budget authority for fiscal year 1982 of $7.2 billion. Besides the lower dollar amounts, the result was more modest than Reagan's proposal in other ways. As shown in table 1, four of the new "block grants" contained only one established categorical program. Two of the programs included were already block grants (social services and community development); they were simply modified versions of earlier block grants. All nine, however, assigned administrative responsibility to the states. Hence, although Reagan did not get his full request, he

Table 1.   New or Changed Block Grants in the 1981 Reconciliation Act

Grant	Number of Programs Consolidated	Final FY 1982 Budget Authority (millions of dollars)
Social services	3	2,400
Home energy assistance	1	1,875
Small city community development	1	1,037
Elementary and secondary education	29	470
Alcohol, drug abuse, and mental health	3	432
Maternal and child health	7	348
Community services	1	348
Primary health care	1	248
Preventive health and health services	8	82
Total for nine block grants	54	7,240

Source: Published by permission of Transaction, Inc. from "Reductions in U.S. Domestic Spending" by John William Ellwood, Editor. Copyright © 1982 by Transaction, Inc.

did achieve a major objective, which can be expected to have important implications for the future of American federalism.)

The reconciliation act required states to accept funding under three of the nine block-grant programs covered by the legislation. States had the option of accepting or not accepting the other six block grants. If a state declines to accept responsibility for any of the six, the federal government under most circumstances continues to provide funds under the old categorical programs. Despite the availability of the choice to opt out, most states decided to take over the responsibility for most of the block grants in the reconciliation act.[7]

Unlike previous administrations, the Reagan team offered few domestic policy initiatives that added to the budget. The primary proposal designed specifically to benefit cities was the urban enterprise zones bill, based on a British program. It was advanced in the United States by Representative Jack Kemp (R-N.Y.), a Reagan supporter. The concept relies on tax incentives to attract businesses to distressed areas. The use of tax incentives, as opposed to the enactment of new expenditures, was reported to be a major reason the president went along with this plan during a period when the administration was not putting forward any major domestic initiatives that required new direct appropriations. The drafting process for the administration's urban enterprise zones bill took most of the first year of Reagan's presidency. The legislation was not seriously considered by the Ninety-seventh Congress. Its cost in lost federal revenue was estimated to average approximately $800 million per year in the first five years of operation. Although frequently featured in the president's speeches and in administration documents, this plan was criticized by liberals as a sop to the cities advanced only to deflect attention from urban ills.

Although the press and officials of the Reagan administration first used the term "New Federalism" to refer to block grants and the related proposals for fiscal year 1982, most observers think of this term in relation to the more sweeping "swap" and "turnback" proposals Reagan advanced in January 1982 (see discussion below). In fact, the first year's proposals, which were in large measure adopted, are likely to have substantial and sustained effects on American federalism, whereas the "swap" and "turnback" proposals were never even introduced in legislative form in the Ninety-seventh Congress. There are three main reasons for the substantial and sustained effect of the 1981 changes: (1) by withdrawing from domestic program areas, the national government challenged other governments (especially the states) to step in; (2) the 1981 package included proposals for fundamental changes in the structure and operations of welfare programs; and (3) the block grants enacted in 1981 portend major realignments in functions between states and local units.

Some observers saw the 1981 New Federalism changes, especially the block grants, as little more than a cover for cuts in social spending. Whatever the reason, the fact remains that cuts were indeed made affecting the lowest-income groups while those of Reagan's proposals that would have reduced spending on better-off citizens were much less successful. The prime example of this point is social security.

Social Security

In the heady days of 1981, with Stockman riding high on budget issues, the administration seemed confident that it could find a solution and win its way on the most nettlesome domestic issue of all, social security financing. The long-term financing problem was regarded as especially severe. By the year 2030, when the post–World War II baby boom reaches retirement age, the system is expected to face huge deficits unless basic changes are made. Despite the administration's yeoman efforts, its proposals in this area seriously backfired. The repercussions of the administration's several attempts in 1981 and 1982 to tame the social security trust fund became a major political liability in the 1982 midterm elections.

In May 1981, the Reagan administration suffered its biggest domestic policy defeat on social security when the Senate, by a vote of 96–0, passed a resolution explicitly rejecting administration proposals made a week earlier by Richard S. Schweiker, secretary of the Department of Health and Human Services. Opposition was immediate and widespread. Leaders of "Save Our Security" (SOS), a coalition of one hundred groups—including the AFL-CIO, the American Association of Retired Persons, and the National Retired Teachers Association—denounced the plan as "a calamity, a tragedy, and a catastrophe."[8] The administration, seeking to minimize the political damage caused by the Senate action, immediately backpedaled. In a letter to congressional leaders, the president acknowledged that "members of Congress on both sides of the aisle have alternative answers." He added: "This diversity is healthy."[9] The president asked Secretary Schweiker to meet with congressional leaders "to launch a bipartisan effort to save Social Security."[10]

The financial solvency of the social security system, both in the short and long terms, was the major concern of the Schweiker plan. This plan anticipated savings of $9 billion in fiscal year 1982, and savings of $46.4 billion for the five-year period between 1982 and 1987. The administration's package comprised eight proposals: Six were designed to save money, while the other two were intended to make the package politically more palatable. By far the most controversial proposal concerned early-retirement benefits. Workers who retire at age sixty-two currently receive 80 percent of the benefits that they would have been entitled to receive had they waited until age sixty-five to retire. The Schweiker reform package proposed that, beginning in January 1982, early retirees would receive 55 percent of their full benefits.

Of the five remaining cost-saving proposals, two were designed to reduce what was felt to be the "overindexing" of the social security system. The administration called for delaying the 1982 annual cost-of-living increase from July until October and revising the computation formula to reduce the benefits of future retirees. Other proposals would have substantially tightened up on the availability and amounts of benefits.

Two proposals included in the Schweiker plan involved added costs to balance out the package politically. Individuals who continued to work after age sixty-five were to be allowed to retain progressively higher amounts of earnings. Currently, benefits are reduced by one dollar for every two dollars earned in excess of $5,500 per year. The administration proposed that this ceiling be raised to $10,000 in 1983 and $15,000 in 1985, with no ceiling thereafter. The administration plan also recommended that the social security tax be lowered when the money in the trust fund reached 50 percent of the amount to be paid in benefits in the following year.

After being burned badly on social security in 1981, the president followed an age-old stratagem. He appointed a commission to study the financing of the social security system. The commission, chaired by Alan Greenspan, former chairman of the Council of Economic Advisers under President Ford, was charged to report after the 1982 congressional elections.

Despite these apparent political precautions, the social security financial dilemma emerged once more before the 1982 midterm congressional elections. When the 1983 budget was being debated, the administration, at a critical juncture in 1982, joined with the Senate Republican leadership in suggesting that a set of reforms of social security financing be included in the first congressional budget resolution. This plan, too, caused a political furor. Once again the administration retreated, deferring to its study commission, which, it reiterated, would report after the midterm elections.

Twice burned was enough. Thereafter, the administration's strategy was to make sure others were on board before taking a stand on social security financing issues. When the time came for the Greenspan commission to report, Reagan pressured its members to come up with a consensus plan that the administration could then accept. The commission's proposals, finally presented on January 15, 1983, were supported on a bipartisan basis by all but three members of the fifteen-person commission. Legislation closely following the commission report was enacted in 1983.

Changed Priorities

Despite the lack of success on social security financing in 1981, Reagan's first year in office produced an effect on the budget that got Reagan off to an impressive start in reordering spending priorities. Table 2 shows that the reordering of priorities, which began under President Carter in 1978, accelerated significantly under Reagan. In two categories—grants to states and localities for other than welfare purposes and direct federal operations—spending in current dollars is estimated to have declined under Reagan, even though overall government outlays are estimated to have increased by 10.4 percent (see top section of table 2). The second section of table 2 shows that when figures are adjusted for inflation total outlays in the seventies through 1978 (the year Proposition 13 was adopted in California) rose by 4.1 percent per year. Under Carter this rate was basically unchanged. Under Reagan the rate of increase is estimated to have fallen to 2.3 percent in fiscal year 1982.

The biggest impact by far of the Reagan budget cuts was on the poor. In fact, aside from this impact on the poor, the tendency in public discourse has been to overstate the size of the fiscal 1982 cuts. Both liberals and conservatives have reasons to exaggerate the size and scope of the cuts—conservatives because they want to take credit for the cuts and the shift from domestic to defense spending and liberals because they want to prevent further domestic spending cuts.

Other groups were also affected by the Reagan program, although not directly by the budget cuts. The chapter by Heclo and Penner in this volume discusses the effects of Reagan's economic program on aggregate employment. The "new poor" (that is, persons who became poor as a consequence of losing their jobs in the recession) were affected much more by Reagan's economic policy than by budget cuts.

Among people who were already poor, those who had some employment income—the "working poor"—were most affected by the budget cuts made in 1981. This is the group that Reagan has consis-

Table 2.   Growth Rates of Federal Outlays during the Carter Years

Type of Spending	FY1971– 1978	FY1978– 1981	FY1981– 1982 (estimate)
Annual Percentage Growth in Current Dollars			
National defense	4.9	15.0	17.4
Payments to individuals	14.9	15.4	11.0
Direct payments	(15.2)	(15.4)	(12.1)
Grant payments	(13.5)	(15.5)	(3.9)
Other state and local grants	17.5	1.9	−9.3
Net interest	13.4	24.8	20.8
All other direct operations	12.6	5.7	−6.5
Direct total outlays	11.5	13.6	10.4
Annual Percentage Growth in 1972 Constant Dollars			
National defense	−2.5	4.1	7.8
Payments to individuals	7.9	5.7	3.1
Direct payments	(8.2)	(5.7)	(4.0)
Grant payments	(6.7)	(5.6)	(−3.4)
Other state and local grants	9.3	−6.1	−16.6
Net interest	6.3	14.6	11.5
All other direct operations	4.1	−3.2	−11.2
Total outlays	4.1	4.0	2.3

Source: Published by permission of Transaction, Inc. from "Reductions in U.S. Domestic Spending" by John William Ellwood, Editor. Copyright © 1982 by Transaction, Inc.

Note: Average annual percentage growth rates calculated from outlay data are contained in Office of Management and Budget, Federal Government Finances: 1983 Budget Data (Washington, D.C.: U.S. Government Printing Office, February 1982), tables 10 and 11, pp. 59–70. Growth rate from fiscal year 1981 to fiscal year 1982 is based on the February 1982 OMB estimate of fiscal year 1982 outlays.

tently believed should be weaned from the welfare system. It consists of able-bodied persons of working age who have some earnings from employment and also receive welfare benefits, such as cash assistance under the Aid to Families with Dependent Children (AFDC) program, Medicaid (the medical care and hospital program for the poor), and food stamps. Many conservatives agree with Martin Anderson, Reagan's first domestic policy adviser, that these programs establish "a 'poverty wall' that destroys the financial incentive to work for millions of Americans."[11] Referring to the working-age, able-bodied welfare population, Anderson stated: "Free from basic wants, but heavily dependent on the State, with little hope of breaking free, they are a new caste, the 'Dependent Americans.' "[12]

*⌐This problem of growing dependency, often reflected in intergenerational welfare receipt, is hard to measure accurately, though most experts agree it is on the upswing⌐ Citing the reduction in income poverty brought about primarily through expenditures for welfare payments, economist John Bishop has stated: "We have not yet scored a victory over dependency, and reducing dependency is almost as important as reducing poverty."[13]

⌐There are essentially two approaches to reducing welfare dependency: reward and punishment. The people who favor the former tend to support plans, such as the negative income tax, that provide a cash incentive in the form of retention of a portion of welfare transfer payments by welfare recipients who go to work. The second approach emphasizes policies like "workfare" (discussed below) that deter people from ever getting on the welfare rolls. This is the approach favored by Reagan and his principal advisers on welfare issues⌐

Employed welfare recipients were affected by a number of important policy changes made in the 1981 Omnibus Budget Reconciliation Act.[14] While the impact is hard to measure, the evidence available so far indicates that the most notable impact of the reconciliation act was on this group.[15]

⌐The cuts in programs affecting the working poor took one of three forms. The first simply put a cap on benefits. For example, a ceiling was placed on payments from the AFDC program at 150 percent of the state's "standard of need⌐ The second change involved provisions that altered the character of the AFDC program. Under the previous eligibility rules, a family could keep thirty dollars per month of its earnings, plus one-third of its earnings above that amount, as an incentive to increase its earnings. The 1981 reconciliation act removed this "thirty-plus-one-third" exclusion after four months of eligibility. Both this provision and the 150 percent ceiling have the effect of removing AFDC families with earnings from the AFDC rolls. A third change has to do with the "categorical eligibility" for Medicaid coverage of families receiving any AFDC benefits (even relatively small monthly amounts). In many states, this medical and hospital insurance coverage for the poor is equal to, if not better than, the coverage many workers have in employment-related medical and hospital insurance programs. The loss of this protection for the parent and the children in a welfare family is in many cases more serious than the loss of the AFDC cash payment.

The reconciliation act contained still another important substantive change in welfare policy involving able-bodied welfare recipients of working age. Reagan has long supported the idea of "workfare," whereby a person receives a payment for work rather than a welfare check. Under most workfare arrangements, a welfare recipient works in some public agency at the minimum wage for the number of hours required to "earn" the welfare benefit for which the family or individual is eligible. The Reagan administration proposed that "workfare" be made mandatory for AFDC family heads on a comprehensive basis throughout the nation, with the stipulation that child-care arrangements be available or provided in all cases where this mandate is enforced. Congress balked at this comprehensive approach, and instead enacted provisions that require that at least one trial workfare program be established in each state.

Reagan's 1981 reconciliation victory was a historic piece of social legislation—not just a spending measure, but a major substantive change in national policies toward the poor. The Reagan philosophy is that marginally poor people should be weaned from welfare programs, because of what George Gilder calls "the overall moral hazard of the welfare state."[16] This, in essence, is the meaning of the Reagan concept that welfare programs should be a "safety net" for the "truly needy," that is, people who cannot work. If those who can work are exposed to welfare, it is feared that they will be drawn into the system and will become permanently dependent upon it. The remarkable event of 1981 was that this philosophy was enacted into law.

Although the fiscal 1982 cuts fell primarily on the poor, there is evidence that some officials of the administration, at least originally, had intended that the cuts in spending enacted in 1981 would be made on a broader basis, affecting all economic groups. In his dramatic article in *Atlantic Monthly* about David Stockman, William Greider quotes Stockman as expressing disappointment that what began as an effort to spread the pain evenly ended up falling almost exclusively on the poor. "Now, as the final balance was being struck, he [Stockman] was forced to concede in private that the claim of equity in shrinking the government was significantly compromised if not obliterated."[17] Besides his lament over the uneven distribution of the cuts, it was in this interview that Stockman made the point about the size of the cuts being exaggerated. "There was less there," he said, "than met the eye."[18] This observation reinforces the point made earlier about the politics of the cuts: Both conservatives and liberals have political reasons for exaggerating the size of the reductions.

To summarize, the cuts constitute an important change in direction, coming after a long period of growth in the domestic spending of the national government, but they cannot be said to constitute a deep penetration into the 1982 base of federal domestic spending.[19]

⌐Moreover, in the one area in which the cuts tended to be concen-
✱ trated, there is increasing evidence that the pain and dislocation predicted by many opponents of the cuts are not occurring to the degree
anticipated. Specifically, the return rate for families removed from
the welfare rolls due to the Reagan changes so far has been low—
about 10 percent on average. This estimate is based on information
from those states and local jurisdictions that had conducted studies
covering the first six months to one year of experience under the new
policies.[20]

These findings are preliminary; more data are needed. We need
to know whether people return to the welfare rolls in larger numbers
over a longer period of time and whether they receive other public
subsidies to substitute for lost AFDC and food stamp benefits. We
also need to know more about the work experience and living arrangements of the persons affected. Despite the low return rate, the
people affected are hurt; they have less money and a harder time
obtaining medical care than was the case before the changes.

Underlying these changes is a fundamental policy issue involving
work incentives, which has been at the forefront of social policy-
making for two decades. Liberals and conservatives who support the
idea of a negative income tax, or a plan such as Richard Nixon's to
reform welfare for families, argue that if able-bodied persons of working age can receive just as much or more money by being on welfare
as by working at the minimum wage, they will logically choose welfare.
The argument underlying this position is that the market works; poor
as well as rich people require an incentive to work.

It is in these terms that some observers predicted that Reagan's
policy of removing the working poor from the welfare rolls would
backfire—that the welfare rolls would actually increase rather than
decrease. According to these critics, what the administration did was
make it relatively more attractive financially to be on welfare than to
be employed.[21] But Reagan's policy was more than economic. It encompassed a philosophy of deterrence and an administrative strategy
based on that philosophy. In essence, the administration's position is
that, for their own good, people who can work should be prodded
into doing so.

Despite Reagan's success in obtaining passage of the reconciliation
act in August 1981, the combination of the very large tax cut, the
recession, and the refusal of Congress to cut spending as deeply as
Reagan's advisers had wanted led the administration to seek more
budget cuts in the fall of 1981. In a nationally televised, prime-time
speech in September 1981, Reagan asked Congress for further cuts.

By this time, it had become apparent that the fiscal 1982 federal deficit would be much larger than Reagan's original target of $45 billion. The president admitted that "in the euphoria just after our budget bill was approved this summer, we didn't point out immediately as we should that while we did get most of what we'd asked for, most isn't all."[22] In his speech, Reagan mentioned that Senate Budget Committee Chairman Peter Domenici had reminded him of Joe Louis's comment about one of his opponents: "He can run, but he can't hide."[23] The president said he agreed with Domenici that this was true of the budget. "We have to face up to it," said Reagan.[24]

Despite these fighting words, the administration's position on domestic budget restraint grew weaker, not stronger. Several factors contributed. One was an event in November—the early release of the *Atlantic Monthly* article based on the Stockman interviews with William Greider. Few magazine stories have had such a dramatic impact. Stockman was compromised. The consensus was that he had burned out; his role thereafter was decidedly less important and more low-key and technical. The administration's success rate on budget issues diminished at the same time.

There are other explanations besides Stockman's problems for the weakening of the administration's position on domestic spending. The biggest was the fact that the recession that began late in 1981 turned out to be much deeper and longer lasting than most economic forecasts had predicted. The administration's standing on all economic policy issues declined, and along with it its ability to continue to win enactment of domestic spending cuts and related policy changes.

The responsiveness and subtlety of the nation's political process are illustrated by these events. As the administration's standing declined, the victory achieved in fiscal year 1982 began to disintegrate. Both in the regular and supplemental appropriations that followed the August victory on the reconciliation act, Congress began to restore some of the cuts previously agreed to. The pattern is interesting. Cuts in programs affecting welfare recipients were not restored; however, cuts in a number of programs affecting generally better-off citizens were restored. One illustration of this point, reflective of the strength of the lobbying groups involved, concerns grants for college students. A substantial part ($217 million) of the cuts made in aid for students in higher education in the omnibus reconciliation act was restored in the 1982 supplemental appropriation, which was enacted over a presidential veto. Welfare recipients, notable for their lack of an effective lobby, proved to be politically much more vulnerable.

The 1982 Reagan Program

The failure of Congress to enact all of Reagan's proposed spending cuts for fiscal year 1982, its approval of tax cuts in excess of those initially proposed, and the recession all combined to create deficits larger than anticipated. In Reagan's second year in office, this problem undermined much of the support he had enjoyed in 1981.

Partly in response to the deficit problem, Reagan's budget for fiscal year 1983, sent to Congress on February 8, 1982, recommended new and deep cuts in many domestic programs. However, unlike the administration's earlier budget revisions, the 1983 program projected very large budget deficits.

When Reagan proposed his 1983 budget, the deficit for fiscal year 1982 was estimated to be a shade under $100 billion, and that for 1983 $91.5 billion.[25] The end result for 1982 was more than a doubling of the deficit that Reagan had projected in March 1981. Despite Stockman's earlier espousal of even-handed cuts in fiscal year 1982, the new budget for fiscal year 1983 spread the pain unevenly from the outset. Reagan's program continued the trend of the previous year: It called for giving defense programs a larger slice of the pie and social programs a smaller one. An analysis by the Congressional Budget Office (summarized in table 3) showed defense rising from one-quarter to one-third of total federal spending over the five years from 1981 to 1985. Social security was also projected as rising in proportion to other federal outlays. Welfare payments to individuals (i.e., not counting social security, as in line 4 of table 3) and other nondefense spending (line 5) were predicted to fall as a share of the budget. Throughout the discussion of the formulation of the 1983 budget, the president strongly resisted proposals for tax increases in 1982 or the idea of rolling back the two tax cuts that had been enacted in 1981.

The new budget also contained further federalism initiatives. The president proposed consolidating forty-nine programs into seven new block grants, involving $6.8 billion in outlays in fiscal year 1983. The largest new block grant, that for welfare administration, was tied to a radical new proposal (discussed in more detail below) that would have assigned the responsibilities for the AFDC and food stamp programs to the states. The administration proposed to combine and cap federal grant-in-aid funds for administering the AFDC, food stamp, and Medicaid programs at 95 percent of the 1982 levels, and to create a block grant for this purpose.

As in the prior year, the newly proposed grant consolidations placed

Table 3.   Composition of Federal Outlays, Fiscal Years 1981–
85   (percentage distribution)

	Actual	Budgeted	Administration Estimates		
	1981	**1982**	**1983**	**1984**	**1985**
1. National defense	24.3	25.9	29.2	31.4	33.6
2. Social security	21.0	21.3	22.9	23.4	23.3
3. Net interest	10.5	11.4	12.7	12.2	11.6
4. Other payments to individuals	27.2	27.1	25.4	24.4	23.9
5. Other nondefense	17.1	14.2	9.8	8.6	7.6
Total (percentage)	100.1	99.9	100.0	100.0	100.0
Total (billions of dollars)	678.2	745.0	773.3	820.2	879.4

Source: Congressional Budget Office, An Analysis of the President's Budgetary Proposals for Fiscal Year 1983 *(Washington, D.C.: Congressional Budget Office, February 1982), table 2.6.*

administrative responsibility at the state level. Yet the 1983 budget was not entirely negative for localities. It recommended keeping unchanged two of the biggest federal aid programs that provide funds directly to local units: the general revenue-sharing program and the community development block-grant program.

The Reagan program, as originally laid out for fiscal year 1983, had three main parts: (1) further cuts of $12 billion in welfare programs (i.e., entitlement programs other than social security); (2) cuts of $14 billion in discretionary domestic spending; and (3) modest increases in user fees yielding $2.5 billion in 1983 and $10 billion over the three-year period from 1983 through 1985. This time the administration was much less successful than in fiscal 1982. The outcome was partly deliberate. Unlike the first year, the administration was much less aggressive on Capitol Hill in pushing its program. It took a pragmatic approach, as Reagan has often done when there has been heavy pressure to modify his principles. In 1982, Reagan chose to pull back and let congressional priorities prevail to a much greater degree than he had been willing to do the year before.

The net result was that Congress, eventually with administration support, achieved most of the deficit reduction accomplished in 1982 through tax increases rather than expenditure cuts. For fiscal 1983, taxes (primarily business and excise taxes) were raised by $18 billion;

the three-year cumulative increase in taxes passed in 1982 was $98 billion. Entitlement programs were cut by $3.6 billion (mostly for Medicare) in fiscal 1983 and by a total of $17 billion for the three-year period from 1983 through 1985. This is one-third of what the administration had originally sought. Other cuts in domestic discretionary spending were proportionately even smaller—about 20 percent of what the administration had originally requested. Overall, the steps taken in fiscal year 1983 to reduce the federal deficit fell much more evenly on all groups than had either the measures enacted in 1981 for fiscal year 1982 or the administration proposals originally made for fiscal year 1983.

The last gasp of the Ninety-seventh Congress came in the frustrating December 1982 lame-duck session. Called to act on the appropriations, as well as a number of other key issues, Congress passed few bills. The main drama was created by recriminations over a Senate filibuster conducted by conservative Republicans. The issue was a five-cents-a-gallon increase in the federal gasoline tax to help refurbish the nation's transportation system and create an estimated 320,000 jobs. This measure was eventually enacted when the Senate finally closed off its deliberations and members sped out of Washington for the Christmas holidays. Four appropriations were passed in the lame-duck session for a total of seven out of the required thirteen; funding for the other six appropriations was provided under a continuing resolution.

Much unfinished business remained at the adjournment of the Ninety-seventh Congress on December 23, 1982. Some unfinished business on the calendar—for example, important immigration reforms, which had been arduously crafted—came within a hair's breadth of passage. Other measures, such as the federalism reforms that the administration announced with great fanfare in January 1982, made no progress at all.

The Grand Design of Reagan's Federalism

Reagan used his January 1982 State of the Union message to recommend far-reaching changes in domestic policy in the form of federalism initiatives. Some observers called this his "*New* New Federalism." The new plan was to go into effect over seven years, between 1984 and 1991; it involved $46.6 billion in program realignments.

The central features of the new plan were what the president called "swaps" and "turnbacks." These proposals harked back to ones Reagan had made in New Hampshire in his 1976 primary campaign against Gerald Ford, when he called for the elimination of $90 billion in domestic programs, on the condition that state governments be assigned the revenue sources to pay for the functions involved. The highly critical responses to this sweeping proposal, which as it turned out had not been carefully developed, were costly for Reagan in 1976.

The bold New Federalism plan that Reagan advanced eight years later as president was developed more carefully, but in the final analysis suffered from the same vagueness in critical areas. The "swap" part of Reagan's 1982 plan called for the federal government to assume responsibility for Medicaid, which is administered by state and local governments. In exchange, Reagan proposed that the states assume responsibility for AFDC and food stamps. This represented a fundamental shift, not only for American federalism but for Ronald Reagan. In his 1982 budget revisions and indeed for a long time before that, Reagan had advocated that the Medicaid program be devolved to the states, in essence as a block grant. Now, Reagan was proposing that Medicaid be taken over by the federal government.

The proposed swap also broke new ground in the way it treated AFDC and food stamps. Since the New Deal, the main impetus for social programs had been to increase the responsibility of the national government—in both policy-making and financing—for income-transfer programs. In 1972, the federal government, through the Supplemental Security Income (SSI) program, took over responsibility for the state and local programs that aided the aged, blind, and disabled. Also during the Nixon years, the food stamp program expanded and became a uniform national program, fully funded by the federal government.

Reagan's proposal to devolve the food stamp program to the states was the most radical shift for Americal federalism advanced in the 1982 State of the Union speech. The food stamp program, from its inception, has been primarily a national program, whereas the AFDC program has been a divided responsibility. States and some counties play a major role in financing and administering AFDC.

The Reagan plan to devolve the food stamp program was short lived. In April 1982, three months after this proposal had been put forward, Reagan abandoned the idea of turning the food stamp program over to the states in response to strong opposition from state and local officials.

Reagan's proposal to have the national government take over the Medicaid program, on the other hand, pleased many state and local officials. Medicaid has been by far the fastest-growing federal grant-in-aid program. Because about half the cost of this program is paid by the states, and some localities, the problem of controlling expenditures has put many states and some local governments in a difficult financial bind. Although the news that the federal government would take over this responsibility was welcome, state officials and health experts expressed concern about the administration's failure to spell out what medical services the federal government would provide and who would be eligible.

Shortly after Reagan's grand design for federalism was unveiled in January 1982, the discussion, not surprisingly, turned from political theory to money. State and local officials claimed the savings from the swaps were inflated, because AFDC and food stamp costs were calculated under the assumption that the cuts proposed in the 1983 budget would be adopted.

The finances of this plan were further complicated by the fact that the swap was only part of the plan. It also called for establishing a trust fund to finance turnbacks, i.e., programs that would be devolved to the states. The forty-four programs listed in the 1983 budget as "illustrative" of those to be turned back to the states included 125 separate grants. Besides revenue sharing, the major functional areas affected were education, employment and training, social services, public health, transportation (though not interstate highways), and community development.

Finally, certain federal taxes were to be relinquished to the states to help finance the programs to be turned back to them. These taxes included the alcohol, tobacco, and telephone excise taxes; two cents per gallon of the gasoline tax; and a portion of the windfall profits tax on energy resources. These federal taxes are scheduled to be terminated eventually; however, in the meantime the money was to be distributed to the states. Each state's portion of the relinquished taxes was to be equal to the difference between its 1979-to-1981 share of the funds previously allocated for the turnback programs and what each state gained or lost under the *swap* part of Reagan's plan. The basic goal was that no state would gain or lose from the swap and turnback initiatives taken together. After 1987, it was proposed that the federal taxes assigned to the trust fund would be reduced by 25 percent each year, and, in 1991, the trust fund would go out of existence. As might be expected, this turned out to be one of the most controversial features of the Reagan plan, namely, that beginning in 1987 states would pick up the taxes being phased out.

The most basic issue posed by Reagan's 1982 grand design of federalism initiatives, as with Nixon's New Federalism, involved transfer programs for able-bodied poor people and their children. This group (covered by AFDC and food stamps) has always been the most controversial welfare population. A major argument made against the Reagan approach of turning over the prime responsibility for welfare programs for the working-age poor to the states is that, in a national economy with high mobility among regions and places, transfer programs (both cash and in-kind) should be uniform. Working-age poor people, it is argued, should not be inhibited from moving to other states where a new job or a better job might be available because of fears about lower welfare support (if they need it) and more stringent welfare eligibility requirements.

The conservative argument in favor of devolving AFDC to the states is grounded in the belief that welfare payments contribute to dependence and inhibit initiative. According to George Gilder, "All means-tested programs (designed exclusively for the poor) promote the value of being 'poor' (the credential of poverty), and thus perpetuate poverty."[26] To the extent that the proposed swap would have provided incentives for the states, particularly those that are fiscally hard pressed, to hold down and even reduce welfare benefits, many conservatives would have regarded it as a type of competition that would have the desirable effect of causing the reduction of or even suppressing welfare benefits. Such an outcome, according to this viewpoint, would tend to reinforce self-support values and encourage economic independence.

For reasons having to do with both finance and philosophy, reactions to the president's proposed 1982 federalism initiatives were cool, although they varied from state to state. The administration, in response, said it was flexible, and that its plan was meant to be the basis for discussion. The White House aide in charge of intergovernmental relations, Richard Williamson, directed lengthy negotiations to work out a version of the Reagan plan that would be acceptable to state and local government officials. Despite literally hundreds of hours of discussion, agreement was slow in coming. One reason for this lack of consensus was the emergence of internal disagreement, unusual for the Reagan presidency, about the purposes and main features of the Reagan grand design for federalism. David Broder called attention to what he termed "the lack of discipline and the degree of disorganization of the Reagan administration" on this issue.[27] Other accounts appeared in the press of disagreements between conservatives led by Stockman and Robert Carleson in the White House who opposed the administration's 1982 New Federalism plan and its architect, Williamson. The necessary enabling legislation to implement Reagan's swaps and turnbacks was not transmitted to the Ninety-seventh Congress, which ended in 1982.

Early Effects of the Reagan Domestic Program

Although it is early to assess the effects of Reagan's domestic policy initiatives, it is possible to indicate some of the initial effects of the spending cuts and related domestic policy changes made in fiscal year 1982. In the results of field research conducted in fourteen states and fourteen large cities for the first quarter of federal fiscal year 1982, five points stand out:

First, the cuts that were made in federal domestic spending in fiscal year 1982 affected the "working poor" more than they affected the treasuries of state and local governments. Although there were exceptions, state and local governments as a rule did not replace lost federal aid for the poor with their own revenues.

Second, other fiscal problems—the worsening recession, legal limits on spending and revenues, and the effects of earlier tax cuts—were of more immediate importance to most state and local governments than were the federal aid cuts. State and local governments were preoccupied with these problems and were largely unable to replace lost federal funds, even in those cases where they wanted to do so.

Third, the block grants, which tended to have high public visibility in the first year of the Reagan administration, did not result in the announced 25 percent cuts in spending in the early period, although there are indications that over time the cuts will have greater effects on spending and programs, and could produce important institutional changes. The early budgetary effects of the block grants tended to be muted for a variety of reasons.

Fourth, nonprofit organizations (particularly community-based organizations) have been among the major victims of the cuts made in 1981. Although there is some early evidence of greater efforts on the part of philanthropic organizations such as the United Way, the administration's intent that the voluntary sector play a larger role in dealing with social needs has not come anywhere near compensating for the cuts in social programs.

Fifth, the rapid pace of the process for making budget cuts in 1981 and its constantly shifting character created confusion and uncertainty in the domestic public sector. Under these conditions, the early responses of state and local governments and nonprofit organizations were necessarily hurried and short-term accommodations. It is possible, as the Reagan administration has claimed, that its program in the future will produce increases in the efficiency of the domestic public sector.[28]

Administrative Tactics

A central theme of this chapter is that one needs to understand not only the legislative agenda but also the administrative approach of the Reagan administration in order to assess its role in domestic affairs. Having considered the legislative agenda and some of its early effects, we turn now to the question: How does a president succeed in having his policy objectives advanced in the administrative processes of government? How does he penetrate the federal bureaucracy? The Reagan approach is founded on the appointment of loyal and determined policy officials as the key to achieving this goal. This, of course, is not a new idea. Every president pays lip service to this objective. The difference is that Reagan's administration has in substantial measure carried it out.[29]

The Appointments Process

Six months before the 1980 presidential campaign was officially under way, steps were taken by Reagan's close advisers to set up a system for filling cabinet and major subcabinet posts with persons ideologically in tune with Ronald Reagan. This process was designed by Edwin Meese III, who became counselor to the president, and E. Pendleton James, a White House personnel aide to Nixon, who became director of personnel in the Reagan White House. Although under steady fire from the Republican right wing, James served until mid-1982, during which period he had an office in the White House, held a level II appointment (cabinet officers are level I), and had regular access to the president. According to G. Calvin MacKenzie, James "provided an unprecedented thread of consistency throughout the entire staffing of the Reagan administration" as "the most stalwart protector . . . of a policy of centralized control of presidential appointments."[30]

The evidence suggests that candidate Reagan, with his experience as a governor, was committed to putting his management philosophy into effect at the very beginning of his administration. Speaking to the International Business Council in Chicago in September 1980, he said: "Crucial to my strategy of spending control will be the appointment to top government positions of men and women who share my economic philosophy. We will have an administration in which the word from the top isn't lost or hidden in the bureaucracy. That voice will be heard because it is the voice of the people."[31] On the night before the election, Reagan is quoted as having said it was his intention to bring about "a new structuring of the presidential cabinet that will make cabinet officers the managers of the national administration— not captives of the bureaucracy or special interests they are supposed to direct."[32] Admittedly, such statements do nothing more than suggest presidential intent. The key criterion is the outcome of the appointments process.

Compared with other recent administrations, the Reagan administration took a long time to fill approximately 2,500 appointive positions. The delays were a function both of new procedural steps—e.g., additional steps in the conflict-of-interest clearance process—and of the care taken to find talented, committed Reaganites who would accept federal salaries, which inflation had seriously eroded by 1981. Nevertheless, by mid-1981, Howell Raines was able to write in the *New York Times* about "a revolution of attitudes involving the appointment of officials who in previous administrations might have been ruled out by concern over possible lack of qualifications or conflict of interest, or open hostility to the mission of the agencies they now lead."[33] Raines cited the following examples:

- In appointments, regulatory jobs important to business were filled months ago, while key positions in agencies aimed at guaranteeing the rights of minorities, consumers, workers and union members have been filled only in the last few weeks or remain vacant.
- In regulatory agencies, most appointees are former employees or financial beneficiaries of the concerns whose activities they are supposed to police. But appointees to agencies that guard individual rights often have records of little or no experience, philosophical neutrality or proven opposition to the missions of the agencies they direct.
- Stewardship of natural resources on Federal lands has been turned over to former employees of mining, timber and oil companies, while environmental quality jobs have gone to advocates of increased use of coal and nuclear power and of lower water and air quality standards for industry.[34]

In addition to presidential appointments (cabinet and subcabinet posts), there are some 2,000 lower-level political jobs in the national government. In the Reagan administration, the White House exercised strong control over presidential appointments. Cabinet officials were consulted and involved in the selection process for subcabinet appointees, and, in exchange for their involvement in this area, White House officials insisted that they be consulted on political appointments that did not involve presidential designation. This includes about 700 Senior Executive Service noncareer appointments and 1,300 Schedule C appointments of aides and assistants.[35]

The result of these supervisory efforts and consultative processes is that not only are Reagan's cabinet and subcabinet officials ideologically in tune with their chief, but many of them in the domestic agencies also have managerial experience and a willingness, if not a desire, to apply this experience in government. Reagan's appointees have taken advantage in an unprecedented way of the considerable administrative discretion available under many existing laws to change the character of domestic programs. At the outset of the administration, orders were issued on a comprehensive basis for administrators of many large spending programs to put all pending Carter projects on hold. Review processes were launched that resulted in shifting contracts and grants away from previously identified recipients in favor of recipients felt to be in agreement with the administration's conservative policies. Some major projects with a liberal cast developed under Carter were disapproved. The funds recouped were used in other ways or simply allowed to lapse. (In the latter case, the law requires that a rescission be approved by Congress; some reprogramming decisions also require congressional approval.)

Although Reagan created cabinet councils, which met frequently on various aspects of domestic policy, the changes made in domestic affairs appear to be much more the result of the ties of cabinet and subcabinet appointees to the Reagan philosophy than of a White House control system. Indoctrinating newly appointed officials with the idea that they were selected by the president and are *his* appointees has been a major activity of the Reagan White House. Periodic meetings have been held to build and maintain the ties of subcabinet officials to the president.

Judging from interviews with White House and other administration officials, the Reagan method for dealing with domestic affairs appears to be working harmoniously and efficiently. Part of the reason is the fact that the administration is ideologically based. It has a clear direction. There are, according to one aide, "few pragmatists floating around."

Deregulation

In addition to gaining control over spending decisions and related policy issues, deregulation was a major announced aim under Reagan, as it had been under Carter. The difference was that, while Carter achieved legislative successes in this area, his appointees did not pursue this objective on an intensive and comprehensive basis through administrative action. Under Reagan, federal regulatory changes—particularly the removal of existing regulations and the relaxation of their enforcement—were used as an important instrument of policy redirection. The main arena of regulatory change for the Reagan administration was the private, rather than the public, sector. Deregulation has been used primarily to remove rules and red tape that restrict business activities. To a more limited extent, deregulation has also been used as an instrument for devolution in the area of domestic policy, especially to remove "strings" on state and local governments under grants-in-aid. In this area, the establishment of block grants through legislative action has been the more important approach, but there have been important cases, in the welfare sphere particularly, where the Reagan administration has increased regulation of states and localities as a means of putting its domestic policies into effect.[36]

Personnel Management

A third type of administrative leverage used skillfully by many of Reagan's cabinet and subcabinet appointees involves personnel management. Reagan's appointees have been adept in taking advantage of opportunities to transfer and remove career officials felt to be unsympathetic to the administration's objectives. "Reductions in force" (RIFs) were carried out in many domestic agencies.

In the Labor Department, for example, a notice of a reduction in force was sent to the entire staff of the Employment and Training Administration. After the required notice period had elapsed, many staff members were "terminated." The dividing line in seniority for these layoffs was fifteen years of service. Persons with less than fifteen years' service were laid off. Many who stayed on were reduced in grade, with the result that some twenty-year veteran managers were assigned to routine tasks with no substantive authority.

In the case of the Commerce Department's Economic Development Administration, where the authorizing law had expired and the Reagan budget proposed abolishing the agency, the administration sought to eliminate the agency's entire staff. The result was that when Congress appropriated a limited amount of money for the Economic Development Administration in fiscal year 1982, barely keeping it alive, its staff was dispersed and discouraged, and the program languished as a result.

The Civil Service Reform Act of 1978, hailed by Carter as a management advance, turned out to be an effective instrument in Reagan's hands for achieving his administration's management goals. Under this new system, career officials with the new "senior civil service" status can more easily be reassigned, or even demoted. While some proponents of the reform saw Reagan's actions as a perversion of the new system, it can be argued that the new law is working well—despite the pain for many old-line bureaucrats—in facilitating greater executive control over the bureaucracy.

Agency Examples

Increasingly, media and public comment have been taking the administrative approach of the Reagan administration seriously. The *Wall Street Journal*, at the end of Reagan's first year, said the administration "has found a way to reshape the federal government without necessarily changing laws. It is called *Reaganizing*."[37] The article defined Reaganizing as "the transformation of departments and agencies by appointed officials devoted to President Reagan's vow to 'curb the size and influence of the federal establishment.' "[38]

There are many examples in which Reagan appointees have successfully taken on the bureaucracy in order to pursue Reagan's conservative domestic policy goals. An almost competitive relationship has existed in this respect between Interior Secretary James G. Watt and Anne Gorsuch, administrator of the Environmental Protection Agency. The result has been that the environmental policies of the past fifteen years have been substantially diluted under Reagan through administrative actions. Watt, for example, opened up federal lands to coal and timber exploration and recreational uses and sharply increased contracting for offshore oil drilling. Gorsuch cut the budget and staff of her agency and relaxed the enforcement of federal air and water pollution regulations, some of which she changed.[39]

Early in the term, Watt came across as especially heavy handed. When he characterized Washington as divided between "liberals and Americans," a corporate lobbyist active in Democratic politics who criticized the secretary's remark was removed from his position, according to the *New York Times*, as a result of Watt's intervention.[40] Gorsuch was less visible at the outset, but got headlines for proposing drastic budget cuts for her agency and producing what critics termed a "talent hemorrhage." The *National Journal* reported that the agency might lose about 2,500 full-time employees through voluntary departures over a two-year period.[41] She began to get even bigger headlines in December 1982, when Congress started a series of investigations into the EPA's handling of the clean-up of dangerous hazardous-waste sites that ultimately led to her resignation March 9, 1983.[42]

Other Reagan appointees, particularly at the subcabinet level, behaved in the same way, but with less fanfare. In the Labor Department, Assistant Secretary Albert Angrisani, who kept out of the limelight, took control of the department's employment and training programs in an unprecedented way. On taking office, he suspended all grants and contracts in the pipeline and allowed no existing or new projects to go into effect without his personal approval. He drastically cut the number of employees in the Employment and Training Administration, the largest operating unit in the department and one that in the past has had high-level funding and been assigned major social-policy objectives. Angrisani transferred and downgraded veteran staffers and, in countless strong actions, asserted his ideas throughout the agency. A former banker, he dismissed the past record of employment and training programs as "seven years of mismanagement practices." He sought to make manpower training programs, in his words, "lean and mean."[43]

Angrisani's actions are typical of the steps taken by Reagan subcabinet appointees, who have tended to be more doctrinaire Reaganites than their cabinet superiors. This is an interesting strategy. Many subcabinet officials have much closer ties to Meese than their cabinet superiors do. This use of lower-level personnel to teach and extend the gospel is the same approach Reagan used as governor of California.[44] Reagan's cabinet officials, on the other hand, tend to be more conciliatory than these subcabinet appointees. Hence, media attention to encounters between Reagan appointees and the bureaucracy is more subdued than it would be if the more visible cabinet members— Watt is an obvious exception—were involved in intense efforts to discipline the bureaucracy.

In the welfare field, a triumvirate of former California Reagan aides appointed to key posts below the cabinet level came to play a dominant role both in policy and administrative processes. While Secretary Schweiker is supportive of their activities, he also tends to act, and to be portrayed in the press, as more of a moderate. Robert Carleson, a White House aide, is the intellectual leader of the group. The other two are David B. Swoap, undersecretary of the Department of Health and Human Services, and John A. Svahn, commissioner of the large and powerful Social Security Administration. Each of the three had served earlier as Reagan's welfare director in California. A newspaper article on the influence of this trio stated: "Not only do they have a long and close working association with Mr. Reagan and one another but also, by virtue of their work in California and later with Federal welfare agencies and welfare committees on Capitol Hill, they tend to have a more detailed bureaucratic knowledge about social programs than does Mr. Schweiker, a former Senator from Pennsylvania."[45]

Carleson, Svahn, and Swoap get major credit for the dramatic changes in welfare policies contained in the 1981 budget reconciliation act, especially the removal of many of the working poor from the welfare rolls. They have also been very successful in efforts to influence administrative decision-making, procedures, and personnel assignments in the welfare area.

Similar, though less aggressive, efforts were made to assert control over the housing and community development programs of the Department of Housing and Urban Development. Regulations under the agency's large and important block-grant program for community development (over $3 billion per year) had been tightened under Carter to target these funds on distressed neighborhoods and the poor. Under Reagan in 1981, changes were made in the law to loosen these restrictions. But, more important than these legal changes, Reagan's HUD appointees reduced the department's oversight activities and staff, in effect returning to the "hands off" policy that had prevailed under Gerald Ford when this block-grant program was first enacted.

The net effect of these and similar efforts to tame the bureaucracy was a decided change in tone in "official Washington." Morale in the agencies plummeted as jobs were cut and changed. The threat of being terminated or downgraded, with the strengthened oversight by appointed officials, had a pervasive effect throughout the federal establishment. Career officials were required to clear all decisions with their appointed superiors. They were prohibited from discussing policy matters with outside groups. The most decided change in tone and mood, as one would expect, was in the domestic agencies.

Concluding Comments

What explains the success of this dual approach—both legislative and administrative—in the early period of the Reagan presidency in achieving a marked turn to the right in domestic affairs? One would expect that a president who seized the bureaucratic reins to advance his policy goals would come into sharp conflict with Congress and the "iron triangles" in the legislative arena. The literature of public administration contains many examples of close ties between high-level agency officials for a particular function, the heads of the interest groups concerned with that function, and the ranking members of the appropriate congressional committees and subcommittees. Yet Reagan's appointed officials in the executive branch have in many cases been able to circumvent this traditional power structure.

Four explanations of this success appear to be especially cogent at this juncture. One involves the Congress. Republican control of the Senate was a major asset, as was the availability of the budget reconciliation process for revising the fiscal year 1982 budget by obtaining a single up-and-down vote in each house on what can be characterized as omnibus domestic-policy legislation in 1981. The administration's effective handling of congressional relations in 1981 under an experienced hand, Max L. Friedersdorf, was an important contributing factor to the success achieved. A second explanation for the success of Reagan's dual approach in domestic affairs relates to management. Ronald Reagan has proved to be skillful in the selection of his principal subordinates, in the structuring of his relationships with them, and in the use of his own time and energy. Another explanation for the success of the administration in domestic affairs is the change in national attitudes toward issues in this field. Retrenchment gained acceptance steadily in the seventies, beginning at the local level in the mid-seventies and moving up the governmental ladder. A fourth explanation of the success of Reagan's domestic program has to do with the tax policy encompassed in the administration's supply-side economic policy. The huge tax cut enacted in 1981 put pressure on the federal budget that made it easier to win the necessary support in Congress for large cuts in domestic spending.

This chapter on the success in the field of domestic affairs in the early period of the Reagan administration began with a prediction that the results, regardless of what happens in other areas, will be enduring. The Reagan administration seized the moment in 1981. Under the impetus of budget revisions, the administration achieved a major change of direction in national policy for domestic, and particularly social, programs. The decay rate of the administration's legislative success in this area has been commented upon, as illustrated by the erosion in the fall of 1981 of some of the gains made in the summer, the lack of success in enacting the budget changes proposed for fiscal year 1983, and the quiet demise of the administration's legislative swap and turnback program in the fall of 1982. However, in my view, these events do not have as much importance as do the fundamentally changed tone and approach to domestic policy-making and its execution that were brought about under Reagan. Reagan's conservative movement, I would argue, has had its greatest success in the field of domestic policy.

Notes

1. Richard P. Nathan, *The Administrative Presidency* (New York: John Wiley & Sons, 1983).

2. Samuel H. Beer argues that Reagan's domestic policy was aimed at reversing policies of the Great Society rather than those of the New Deal. He argues: "The main object of attack of the Reagan administration during its first year in office was the Great Society." See "Foreword," *Reductions in U.S. Domestic Spending: How They Affect State and Local Governments*, ed. John William Ellwood (New Brunswick, N.J.: Transaction Books, 1982), p. xv.

3. Executive Office of the President, Office of Management and Budget, *Budget of the United States Government, Fiscal Year 1984* (Washington, D.C.: U.S. Government Printing Office, 1983), p. M11.

4. "The Talk of the Town," *New Yorker*, August 2, 1982, p. 25.

5. Ibid.

6. Ellwood, ed., *Reductions in U.S. Domestic Spending*, p. 28.

7. Ibid., p. 340.

8. Warren Weaver, Jr., "President Proposed Negotiating a Plan on Social Security," *New York Times*, May 22, 1981.

9. Ibid.

10. Ibid.

11. Martin Anderson, *Welfare: The Political Economy of Welfare Reform in the United States* (Stanford, Calif.: Stanford University, Hoover Institution Press, 1978), p. 43.

12. Ibid.

13. "The Welfare Brief," *Public Interest*, no. 53 (Fall 1978), p. 175.

14. This is the summary act referred to earlier that included most of the budget cuts made in 1981.

15. See Richard P. Nathan, Philip M. Dearborn, Clifford A. Goldman, and Associates, "Initial Effects of the Fiscal Year 1982 Reductions in Federal Domestic Spending," in Ellwood, ed., *Reductions in U.S. Domestic Spending*, pt. 3.

16. George Gilder, *Wealth and Poverty* (New York: Basic Books, 1981), p. 111.

17. William Greider, "The Education of David Stockman," *Atlantic Monthly*, December 1981, p. 50.

18. Ibid., p. 51.

19. For a fuller discussion of the magnitude of the Reagan cuts, see Ellwood, ed., *Reductions in U.S. Domestic Spending*, pt. 1, ch. 4.

20. Based on a telephone canvass of field research associates for the Princeton study of the effects of the Reagan domestic program and of state and local officials. The findings of the Princeton study are discussed later in this chapter.

21. See Tom Joe, "Profiles of Families in Poverty: Effects of the Fiscal Year 1983 Budget Proposals on the Poor," Center for the Study of Social Policy, Washington, D.C., February 25, 1982 (processed). This report includes an analysis of the fiscal year 1982 proposals. This analysis, in calculating marginal welfare-benefit reduction rates, assumes that all AFDC family heads receive an amount in earnings equal to the average earnings of working AFDC family heads in the state. A higher assumption for working family heads, e.g., full-time work at the minimum wage, would produce lower marginal welfare-benefit reduction rates.

22. *New York Times*, September 25, 1981.

23. Ibid.

24. Ibid.

25. Executive Office of the President, Office of Management and Budget, *Budget of the United States Government, Fiscal Year 1983* (Washington, D.C.: U.S. Government Printing Office, 1982). The 1982 deficit ended up at $111 billion; Reagan's March 1981 estimate was $45 billion.

26. Gilder, *Wealth and Poverty*, p. 111.

27. David S. Broder, "Reagan's Bold Stroke Went Wild," *Trenton Times*, August 11, 1982, p. A9. Other press commentary in this period stressed infighting between Baker and Meese. See for example, Jack Nelson, "Infighting Racks Reagan Advisors," *Los Angeles Times*, August 15, 1982, pt. 1, p. 1.

28. See Ellwood, ed., *Reductions in U.S. Domestic Spending*, pp. 315–77; passage quoted, pp. 318–19. This research is continuing. For information on the effects of the Reagan cuts for the full 1982 federal fiscal year, see Richard P. Nathan and Fred C. Doolittle, and Associates, *The Consequences of Cuts: The Effects of the Reagan Domestic Program on State and Local Governments* (Princeton, N.J.: Princeton Urban and Regional Research Center, Princeton University, 1983). Additional field observations are planned for fiscal years 1983 and 1984.

30. G. Calvin MacKenzie, "The Reaganites Come to Town: Personnel Selection for a Conservative Administration" (Paper presented at the 1981 meeting of the American Political Science Association), p. 5.

31. Transcript reprinted in the *New York Times*, September 19, 1980.

32. *New York Times*, March 8, 1981.

33. "Reagan Reversing Many U.S. Policies," *New York Times*, July 3, 1981.

34. Ibid.

35. The Senior Executive Service is made up of the top cadre of federal officials below the presidential appointment level, who are in the top General Schedule grades and the lower levels of the Executive Schedule. Schedule C was created by President Eisenhower. Its posts are exempt from competition, because their appointees will have confidential relationships with political appointees. The schedule ranges from GS 15 down and includes not only managers and staff assistants, but also such personal aides as drivers.

36. For a discussion of this subject, see Catherine Lovell, "Federal Deregulation and State and Local Governments," in Ellwood, ed., *Reductions in U.S. Domestic Spending*.

37. Burt Schorr and Andy Pasztor, "Reaganites Make Sure That the Bureaucracy Toes the Line on Policy," *Wall Street Journal*, February 10, 1982, p. 1 (emphasis added).

38. Ibid.

39. Reagan's "mixed environmental record" is discussed in ch. 21, "The Westerners," in Lou Cannon, *Reagan* (New York: G.P. Putnam's Sons, 1982), p. 351.

40. Phil Gailey, "Democratic Lawyers Finding Interior Cold," *New York Times*, February 2, 1982.

41. Lawrence Mosher, "Move Over, Jim Watt, Anne Gorsuch Is the Latest Target of Environmentalists," *National Journal*, October 24, 1981, p. 1900.

42. Anne Gorsuch married in 1983 and now uses the name Anne McGill Burford.

43. William J. Lanouette, "Life After Death—CETA's Demise Won't Mean the End of Manpower Training," *National Journal*, February 6, 1982.

44. William J. Lanouette, "Reagan Plays Chairman of the Board . . .," *National Journal*, July 19, 1980, pp. 1177–82.

45. Robert Pear, "Three Key Aides Reshape Welfare Policy," *New York Times*, April 26, 1982, p. B8. David Swoap left the Reagan administration in December 1982 to

become the head of Human Services under the new Republican governor of California, George Deukmejian. He was succeeded as undersecretary of Health and Human Services by John Svahn. There was also a widely publicized change in the department in January 1983 when Secretary Schweiker departed and was succeeded by Margaret M. Heckler, former Republican congresswoman from Massachusetts.

4 The Defense Policy of the Reagan Administration, 1981–1982

Samuel P. Huntington

Conventional wisdom has it that U.S. defense spending goes through recurring cycles of feast and famine. On this point, the conventional wisdom is, generally speaking, correct, but it is also incomplete. The ups and downs in defense budgets are also related to changes in American strategy, to shifts from more conservative strategies of military pluralism appropriate for the upside of the budget cycle to more radical, more selective, and less costly strategies appropriate for the downside of that cycle.[1]

The Third Phase of the Third Cycle

Each strategy-budget cycle tends to go through five phases:

1. The development by a relatively small group of people of new strategic concepts and approaches (an upside strategy) in response to new perceptions of threat and need;

2. One or more triggering events that create public support for and a political environment favorable to a larger defense effort;

3. A defense buildup reflecting the concepts and priorities of the new strategy;

4. Increasing concern about the impact of the defense buildup on other social needs, followed by a leveling off and decline in the defense effort; and

5. Formulation of new strategic concepts (a downside strategy) appropriate for a reduced military effort.

The first two years of Reagan administration defense policy reflect the cresting of the defense buildup in the third phase of the third cycle in American defense policy after World War II and the beginning of transition to the fourth phase.

The first cycle began with the growing concern among government officials in 1948 and 1949 over the intentions of the Soviet Union and the weakness of American defenses following the massive U.S. demobilization of 1946–47. These concerns were heightened by the Soviet atomic explosion in August 1949 and the completion of the Communist conquest of China a few months later. The overall rationale for a buildup and its general broad outlines were developed in a basic strategy paper, NSC 68, prepared by a joint State-Defense team under the chairmanship of Paul Nitze. This group reported its recommendations for tripling the U.S. defense effort to President Truman in April 1950. Two months later the North Korean attack across the 38th parallel made this strategy politically feasible. Between 1950 and 1953, real spending for defense tripled (see figure 1). Only a small portion of this was directly related to the conduct of the war in Korea. The bulk of it was designed, first, to broaden the U.S. mobilization base and prepare the United States to fight a prolonged, major war in Europe if that should be necessary and, second, to bring into existence the active forces necessary to deter such a war. In two years a major expansion of U.S. military power occurred:

	June 1950	June 1952
Army divisions	10	20
Army regimental combat teams	11	18
Marine divisions	2	3
Navy ships	671	1,130
Air force wings	48	95
Total military personnel	1,461,000	3,636,000

During the same years the Strategic Air Command was rejuvenated,

Figure 1. U.S. Defense Outlays in Constant Dollars

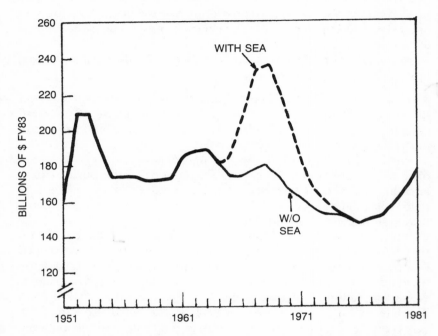

Source: *Adapted from Caspar W. Weinberger, Secretary of Defense,* Annual Report to the Congress, Fiscal Year 1983 *(Washington, D.C.: U.S. Government Printing Office, 1982), p. I–20.*

Note: SEA = additional expenditures for Vietnam War.

acquiring new jet bombers (the B–47), a substantial number of overseas bases, and large numbers of improved fission bombs.

By 1952, however, the achievements of the buildup, the stalemate in Korea, and increased concern with the domestic economy all led to a slackening in the defense effort and a stretch-out or postponement of those goals, such as a 143-wing air force, that had not yet been achieved. In the spring of 1952 this attitude was reflected in

the harsh treatment which Congress gave the Administration's request for $50.9 billion in the defense budget for FY 1953. Alarmed over the prospects of a substantial deficit, continued high taxes, waste and duplication in the Defense Department, and the relatively large carry-over ($38 billion) of unobligated funds, Congress cut $4.3 billion from the President's estimate, absolutely and proportionately the largest cut in the military budget between 1946 and 1961. . . . The low level of the Administration's strategic effort between 1946 and 1950 had created a gap between military policy and foreign policy. By 1952 the high level of its strategic effort had eliminated that gap but was creating another one between the military goals of the Administration and the domestic goals popular in both the Administration and Congress.[2]

In 1953 a new administration reconsidered the U.S. position, stressed the importance of a sound economy for national security and the need to be prepared for the "long haul," and elaborated a downside strategy of massive retaliation, cutbacks in conventional forces, and 25 percent reductions in defense spending, reductions which remained in effect for the rest of the decade. So ended the first cycle.

In the middle and late 1950s civilian and military strategic analysts began to develop new concerns over continued U.S. reliance on nuclear weapons (strategic and tactical) at a time of growing Soviet nuclear capabilities. The need, they felt, was for a broad spectrum of capabilities, from paramilitary and special forces at one end through substantial conventional forces to nuclear forces and deliverable fusion weapons at the other. This would make possible an upside strategy of graduated and flexible response at appropriate levels to whatever challenges the Soviets or other Communist states might pose. The Soviet space and missile achievements of 1958–60, the Berlin crises of the same years, Khrushchev's fulminations about the growth of Soviet power, and the election of a new president dedicated to "getting this country moving again," combined to make possible a significant increase in U.S. military capabilities in the early 1960s. The number of army combat divisions went up from eleven to sixteen and air force tactical wings from sixteen to twenty-one. Marine Corps manpower increased from 175,000 to 190,000 and army manpower by 100,000. The Special Forces were strengthened and airlift expanded. The readiness of general purpose forces was enhanced. At the same time, massive investments were made in the development and production of the Minuteman and Polaris missile systems.[3]

These increases in military power were financed by only a 13 percent increase in real defense spending between 1960 and 1962, owing in large part to the centralization of power and effective management systems that Robert McNamara introduced as secretary of defense. In 1964 and 1965, military spending dropped modestly and then moved into its second phase of expansion as a result of U.S. involvement in Vietnam. In 1968 it was 30 percent greater than it had been in 1965. This second expansion, however was directly related to the conduct of the war and did not have positive effects on other U.S. military capabilities. In some respects, indeed, it had a negative impact to the extent that equipment and forces were diverted to Vietnam from other missions, while the priority necessarily accorded combat needs in Vietnam meant that other programs were cut back or abandoned. As Secretary Weinberger observed many years later, in the 1960s the United States failed to replace World War II capital equipment that was becoming obsolete. "Such a reinvestment program for conventional forces was indeed begun under President Kennedy, but it was interrupted by the Vietnam War."⁴ In 1950 the Korean War had made rearmament possible; in 1964 rearmament made the Vietnam War possible and the war aborted that rearmament.

By 1968 increasing opposition to the war and to the military establishment generally halted the expansion of the defense effort. The following year a new administration inaugurated a new downside strategy, more appropriate for straitened circumstances and the antimilitary environment. This strategy fostered and exploited the opening to China and the shift from two-and-a-half wars to one-and-a-half wars as the basis for military planning, placed increased reliance on allies and friends for regional security (the Nixon Doctrine), and attempted to limit and channel the arms competition with the Soviet Union through arms control agreements. Real military spending declined steadily for eight years. Except for the MIRVing of U.S. ballistic missiles, few improvements were made in the strategic forces after 1970. The conventional forces were cut back to levels below those of 1964; overall military manpower was reduced to its lowest level since 1950. So ended the second cycle.

The first phase of the third cycle got under way in the mid-1970s as defense analysts focused on the new interests and vulnerabilities of the United States and its allies in the Persian Gulf, the sustained expansion of Soviet military spending at a rate of 3–4 percent a year from the mid-1960s, the strengthening of Soviet forces in Europe and along the Chinese frontier, the development by the Soviets of air and naval power projection capabilities that had become evident in the Angolan crisis of 1975–76, and the development and deployment of new generations of Soviet missiles that would, in due course, pose a major threat to U.S. ICBMs. In late 1976 these concerns were reflected in the "Team B" alternative assessment of Soviet intentions and capabilities commissioned by the Ford administration and in the creation of the Committee on the Present Danger. The new upside strategy emphasized three key needs: the modernization of U.S. strategic forces to maintain parity with Soviet forces, the strengthening of NATO conventional and theater nuclear forces to reestablish an effective European deterrent, and the creation of new military capabilities to deter or to defeat military threats in the Persian Gulf.

In comparison with the previous cycles, however, the process by which these new strategic concerns were translated into a defense buildup was slow and halting. Each of the earlier defense buildups had taken about three years. The third buildup has been strung out over at least six years. The principal reason is the absence of a single dramatic triggering event (as in June 1950) or a clustering of lesser triggering events (as in 1959–61). The buildup got off to a modest start with the advent of the Carter administration, which in its first year undertook an extensive assessment of the trends in the overall balance of power, formulated a general statement of strategic goals and policies, and committed itself to a 3 percent annual increase in real defense spending. Overall, however, the administration was deeply divided over the nature of the Soviet threat and the nature of the responses that should be made to it. As a result there was no sustained impetus to push forward vigorously with a defense buildup.

Events of the fall of 1979, most notably the invasion of Afghanistan, led the administration to conclude that "the defense program must be substantially increased over the next five years, and . . . we must begin the effort now."[5] Four percent annual increases in defense spending were projected, and the overall level of defense spending for fiscal years 1980–84 was set 15 percent higher than it had been the previous year. At the same time, the administration was also elaborating the "countervailing" strategy to guide its nuclear weapons policies and the concept of the "three strategic zones" toward the defense of which the conventional buildup was directed. In its last policy statement in January 1981, the administration projected defense spending increases of about 5 percent per year.

At this point in the cycle the Reagan administration entered the scene. As a result of its far greater unity on strategic issues, plus the additional triggering impact of the Polish crisis, it moved swiftly to increase the prospective rate of defense buildup to more than 7 percent per year. It thus accelerated what its predecessor had begun in a much more modest and uncertain fashion. The crucial questions are:

1. What strategic purposes has the Reagan administration pursued in its first two years?
2. What has happened and is likely to happen to the defense buildup designed to achieve those purposes?

3. If the available resources are or will be insufficient to implement the Reagan upside strategy, will this gap be closed by redefining strategy in a downside direction (as occurred in the first two cycles), or by some other means?

Upside Strategy: Implementation and Elaboration

Almost everyone who was not in the Reagan administration during its first eighteen months criticized it on the grounds that it lacked an overall strategy, that it was "throwing money at the problem of national defense" while neglecting the need, as former defense secretary Schlesinger put it, that there be "a vision and explicit strategy along with expenditures."[6] This criticism was voiced by Democrats (Sam Nunn, Gary Hart, Les Aspin), Republicans (Melvin Laird, Henry Kissinger), neoconservative Reaganites (Walter Laqueur), journalists (James Fallows, Leslie Gelb), and military experts (Maxwell Taylor, John Collins). The prevailing picture was of an administration wildly spending money on almost everything with little or no idea as to why it was doing so. "The most important theme of President's Reagan's proposals for defense," Fallows wrote, "has little to do with military strategies or concepts, but rather with sheer quantities: the budget stands for *more*." In a similar vein, Collins argued that "we've got a national military strategy called M-O-R-E. We've got a request for $1.5 trillion over the next five years with no policy behind it."[7]

The administration's inactions and words during its initial year invited these criticisms. Coming in at the beginning of either an upswing or downswing in the defense cycle, the Eisenhower, Kennedy, Nixon, and Carter administrations had all launched major reviews in efforts to determine the broad outlines of the upside or downside strategies the times demanded. These studies resulted in the identification of new priorities, new departures in policy, new concepts, and, in due course, in the formulation of administration directives providing general guidance for strategic planners. In its first year the Reagan administration consciously avoided this pattern. It put its emphasis on more money and better management rather than new strategy.[8] Indeed, it quite explicitly rejected the desirability of attempting to formulate a strategy during its first months in office. We have a "philosophy," not a "totally articulated strategy," said Deputy Secretary Carlucci. "We knew little was to be gained," Secretary Weinberger added, "by an early enunciation of some elaborate 'conceptual structure,' a full-fledged Reagan strategy." In the past, he argued, such pronouncements "prejudged and oversimplified reality; they put blinders on our vision."[9]

Both the administration and its critics misstate the case. The administration did have a strategy, but it could not admit that it did. Its strategy was essentially the upside strategy the Carter administration had outlined. The foreign policy–defense failures of the Carter administration, its responsibility for the "years of neglect" of American military strength, had, however, been central themes in Reagan's campaign. Hence, from the administration's viewpoint it was less embarrassing to plead no strategy than admit to a Carter strategy. Yet, in fact, the new administration accepted the strategic framework that had been laid down by its predecessor and the general prescriptions that had been embodied in Carter directives: PD-18 (overall strategy, NATO buildup, rapid deployment force), PD-41 (civil defense), PD-50 (arms control and defense policy), PD-53 (C^3 and telecommunications), PD-57 (mobilization planning), PD-58 (continuity of government), PD-59 (nuclear targeting and employment of nuclear forces), PD-62 (Persian Gulf regional security framework), and PD-63 (elaboration of PD-18 military priorities). It also accepted the Carter emphasis on the importance of conventional forces in an era of strategic equivalence and the need to strengthen European defenses through the Long-Term Defense Program and the two-track policy on theater nuclear force modernization. It accepted the concept of the "three strategic zones" (Western Europe, East Asia, and Southwest Asia) and hence the need to develop, through a rapid-deployment force, at least a one-and-two-half-wars capability—although it publicly repudiated the war-counting approach. At the strategic nuclear level, it accepted the essentials of Harold Brown's "countervailing" strategy and the Carter administration's goal that the United States "must be able to respond at a level appropriate to the type and scale of a Soviet attack."[10] Apart from the SALT II agreement, no broad military concept or policy of the Carter administration was rejected by the Reagan administration. In addition, no significant military program approved by the Carter administration was canceled by the Reagan administration, although several programs that its predecessor rejected or never considered won its approval: B-1, two nuclear carriers, and battleship conversions. Overall, however, and particularly for its first year, the Reagan administration carried forward the broad strategic policies of the administration it had displaced.

There was, however, one crucial difference. Far more than the Carter administration ever did, the Reagan administration attempted to make its strategy a reality. The divisions within the Carter administration over the need for a defense buildup, the demands of domestic programs and constituencies, the absence—at least until Afghanistan—of a politically powerful triggering event, and, last but not least, the president's own ambivalent attitudes toward military force all meant that Carter strategies outlined in state papers often went unrealized in practice. Two specific examples illustrate the point. In the summer of 1977 the president directed the Pentagon to create a rapid-deployment force of several light divisions supported by sufficient air- and sealift to deal with Third World contingencies, particularly in Southwest Asia. Only in the fall of 1979 and after Iran and Afghanistan did this force begin to become a reality. Similarly, in September 1978 a presidential directive declared civil defense to be a component of U.S. nuclear strategy and directed that plans and preparations be made for the relocation of urban population in a crisis. The very modest sums required to implement this directive were, however, never forthcoming. The fate of the RDF and civil defense are symbolic of the much broader failure of the administration to follow through on the policies it had adopted.

The Reagan administration attempted to do exactly this. "The principal shortcoming of the defense budget we inherited," Secretary Weinberger explained after six weeks in office, "is not so much that it omitted critical programs entirely in order to fully fund others, but rather that it failed to provide full funding for many programs it conceded were necessary but felt unable to afford." The administration confronted, he added a few months later, a situation of "great urgency," in which "there was literally nothing we did not need."[11] As a result, the Reagan increases in the FY 1981 and FY 1982 budgets were generally spread across the board and necessarily involved acceptance of the basic strategy underlying the existing allocation of funds. Such a broad-gauged, pluralistic distribution of defense increases also did not differ greatly from what occurred during the first and second defense buildups, even though those had been accompanied by explicit strategic formulations by the Truman and Kennedy administrations. In those cases, as in 1981–82, a rising tide of defense spending lifted all boats. While undoubtedly there were differences in emphasis, increased funding was provided for virtually all significant defense programs: land, sea, and air; conventional and nuclear; investment and operations.

Insofar as there were significant modifications in the inherited strategy and programs in the first months of the Reagan administration, these were primarily due to the administration's effort to decentralize decision-making within the Defense Department. As a result, the services had a relatively free hand as to which programs would receive the marginal dollars. These increases, particularly for conventional forces, "tended to follow the program preferences of the service chiefs and their staffs, rather than recommendations of the Office of the Secretary of Defense." They were primarily "a selection from what the military services already had on their lists of priorities but failed to obtain in the original budgets for fiscal years 1981 and 1982."[12] As a result, the relation between spending patterns and the distribution of power in the defense establishment reverted in part to that which had existed in the pre–McNamara era. Before 1961, increases in defense spending had been accompanied by a loosening of central authority in the Pentagon while cuts in the military budget had gone hand-in-hand with efforts to centralize authority, most notably in 1949, 1953, and 1958. McNamara reversed this pattern and increased the budget while centralizing authority. Laird maintained the relationship but shifted the direction; authority was decentralized while expenditures dropped. The course adopted in the Reagan administration thus resembles that of Forrestal in 1947–48 and Marshall and Lovett in 1950–53, with the services getting both more money and more leeway, within carefully defined limits, to determine how that money should be spent. By proceeding as he did, McNamara achieved a major increase in conventional and nuclear capabilities for a relatively modest 13 percent increase in real defense spending over two years. Whether the Reagan administration, by proceeding as it has, will achieve a comparable increase in capability for the much larger increases in spending it wants is an open question.

By the end of its first year the administration began in several areas to move beyond Carter strategy not just in funding but also in concepts and emphasis. These modifications and innovations were reflected in

Table 1. Trends in Defense Spending and Decision-Making

| | Decision-Making | |
Defense Spending	More Centralized	More Decentralized
Up	McNamara	Weinberger
Down	Wilson	Laird

three major statements of administration policy during the first six months of 1982: Secretary Weinberger's annual report presented to Congress in February; the FY 1984–1988 Defense Guidance, completed in March and leaked to the press in late May; and a National Security Decision Directive on national strategy, approved by the president on May 21, and described by his national security adviser, William P. Clark, and other officials shortly thereafter. The first two of these statements are regular annual productions of the Defense Department. They were, however, the first to bear the full imprint of the Reagan administration. The NSDD, on the other hand, was in effect the belated, Reagan administration equivalent to the Eisenhower administration's NSC 162/2, the Nixon administration's NSSM 3, and the Carter administration's PD-18. When he took over as national security adviser, Clark said he found the strategy "which had been developed during this Administration's first year in office" to be "a collection of departmental policies. . . ." In their place, the president wanted "a well thought through, integrated strategy for preserving our national security."[13] As a result, a major study was launched in which the NSC staff played the leading role, under the leadership of former Secretary of the Air Force Thomas C. Reed, who was brought aboard for this purpose. Nine interagency groups were apparently formed to draft individual segments of the study, all of which were reviewed by the president. After three months effort, an eight-page directive was produced—twice the length of Carter's PD-18—outlining the political, economic, diplomatic, informational, and military components of a comprehensive national strategy.

The military portion of the paper was largely based on Secretary Weinberger's annual report and the FY 1984–88 Defense Guidance. Commentary on the NSDD tended, however, to highlight possible differences in emphasis between them. Clark's exposition of the NSDD tended to play down the idea of "horizontal escalation" and to stress the inability of the United States to fight simultaneously on a number of fronts. The paper was also interpreted as an effort to assert White House leadership in the national security area, to rebuff criticisms of the president that he had been neglecting foreign policy, and to bring about a "diminution of Mr. Weinberger's previously unquestioned authority to establish defense doctrines himself."[14] Certainly during the administration's first year Weinberger had had relatively free rein to act as he wished on defense policy and often to involve himself in a commanding manner on foreign policy issues. As an even older friend of the president's than Weinberger, Clark could be expected to exert considerably greater influence in the national security area than had Richard Allen. A natural way to assert his role was through an interagency policy review and a presidential directive on strategy. Secretaries of defense are not normally enthusiastic about White House directives on military policy. Consequently, the strategic review, the resulting directive, and the differences in nuance between it and Department of Defense policy statements, all can be taken as signs of an effort to set a framework around the previously free-wheeling Weinberger.

The strategy embodied in these 1982 documents of the Reagan administration reaffirms the three-pronged focus on strategic nuclear force modernization, European defense buildup (theater nuclear and conventional), and power projection capabilities for the Persian Gulf. It also brings to the fore a number of concepts and emphases that constitute distinctly Reaganite emendations and supplements to the original upside strategy. These can be grouped under four headings.

Economic Warfare

By the end of the 1960s Soviet economic performance was lagging and the regime was beginning to be confronted by the need to reform the economic system, which might weaken its political control, moderate its military buildup, or cut back the growth of consumption. To postpone or to avoid altogether this hard choice, the regime pursued economic détente, increasing imports of capital, technology, and food from the West. As a result of this new pattern of economic relations, the Nixon, Ford, and Carter administrations all attempted, in varying ways, to influence Soviet behavior by manipulating economic carrots and sticks. They also discovered that bureaucratic and congressional interests, American socioeconomic groups, and the differing perspectives and interests of the allies made this a very difficult task. In the Carter administration in particular, while the president endorsed the idea of economic diplomacy vis-à-vis the Soviets, no consensus on it existed among his advisers, and the use of economic leverage to influence Soviet behavior with respect to either human rights or foreign policy was spotty and inconsistent.

Even more explicitly than its predecessors, the Reagan administration began with the view that the Soviet economy was in crisis. The Soviet Union, it was repeated again and again, is "an economic basket case."[14] The United States should capitalize on this situation, but in a very different manner than had been attempted under Nixon, Ford, and Carter. It should pursue not a policy of economic diplomacy but one of economic warfare; it should attempt not to modify Soviet behavior but to lessen Soviet strength. Leverage, Secretary Weinberger argued, will not work because "it is the Soviets who do the manipulating—and with considerable success—in spite of their inherently weak bargaining position." They have, indeed, been successful in bringing into existence "powerful interests in the West which now press for even more generous trade policies toward the Soviet Union." If, however, the "economy of the Soviet Union is propped up," the Soviet Union will be "enabled to divert more of its resources to its military buildup." In the long run, "no defense policy, no strategy" can succeed unless we pay attention to this fact.[16] Hence, the West must make every effort to ensure that its resources, credits, and technology are not exploited for this purpose. This argument had two implications for policy.

First, the argument logically implied that there should be a complete severing of economic relations between the West and the Soviet Union. Weinberger never explicitly carried his logic that far, but he also took advantage of every opportunity to eliminate or to reduce the supply of Western credits and technology to the Soviet Union. The United States promoted a redrafting of the regulations of the Coordinating Committee for Multilateral Export Controls (COCOM); a major campaign was launched to curb unauthorized exports to the U.S.S.R. and to curb Soviet industrial espionage; the Defense Department vigorously opposed U.S. underwriting of Polish credits; and it was in the lead in pressing for a tough position on the gas pipeline. While the president did not approve the Defense Department's position in every instance, he did seemingly share the policy assumptions and predispositions that underlay that position.

A second element in the policy of economic warfare went beyond simply cutting the supply of credits and technology to the Soviet Union and involved shaping U.S. military policies and programs so as to maximize the economic burden they placed on the Soviet Union. The United States, it was said, should invest in weapons that "are difficult for the Soviets to counter, impose disproportionate costs, open up new areas of major military competition and obsolesce previous Soviet investment."[17] It is not clear to what extent or in what cases the administration implemented this policy. It was, however, a significant innovation in declaratory military policy in that it set as a guideline for decisions on U.S. programs not just their military usefulness to the United States but also the economic burdens they could impose on the Soviet Union.

In its first two years the Reagan administration had relatively little success in carrying out its strategy of economic warfare or economic denial. This was owing principally to skepticism among key elements in Congress and the executive bureaucracy and to the almost unanimous resistance to it by U.S. allies, manifested most notably in their vigorous opposition to the administration's efforts to extend the pipeline sanctions in mid-1982. This opposition, in turn, led to the administration's backing off and attempting to enlist the allies in a broader and longer-term formulation of appropriate policies to govern the supply of credit and the export of technology to the Soviet Union.

Arms before Control

The Reagan administration made arms control an integral part of defense policy, a course which Carter had approved in theory but never implemented in practice. Both before and after coming into office, leading figures associated with Reagan repeatedly said that the new administration was not interested in negotiating new arms agreements until it had taken measures to create a more satisfactory arms balance. The Reagan administration thus endorsed the utility of bargaining chips to influence Soviet policy on arms at the same time it rejected the usefulness of economic leverage to influence other aspects of Soviet foreign policy. Having staked out this position, the new administration moved very slowly to define and to clarify its arms control goals and policies, preferring to wait until it had made its own decisions on strategic arms (which were announced in early October 1981). More important, it was also desirable in the administration's view to wait still further until those programs had been authorized by Congress and were in the process of being implemented, so as to place more pressure on the Soviets to adopt an accommodating position.

Prior decisions and European politics did not, however, allow the administration to postpone theater nuclear force (TNF, or, later, INF) negotiations for as long as it would have liked. According to administration logic, serious negotiating should only begin when U.S. cruise missiles and Pershing IIs were in the process of being deployed in Europe. According to NATO's December 1979 two-track decision, however, negotiations were to be undertaken while preparations went ahead for deployment, and only if the negotiations failed to produce progress toward satisfactory agreement would the deployment then proceed. In addition, in the summer and fall of 1981 several large anti–nuclear weapons demonstrations took place in Western Europe and it became clear that European politics made serious negotiations a prerequisite to any possible deployment. After much debate within the administration, the president set forth in November a "zero-option" proposal that the United States would forgo modernization of its theater missile forces if the Soviets would eliminate their theater nuclear forces (SS-4s, SS-5s, and SS-20s). Paul Nitze was appointed negotiator for this purpose, and by the end of the year the theater nuclear force talks had gotten under way in Geneva.

Through 1981 neither prior commitments nor domestic politics led the administration to move quickly on strategic arms negotiations. The SALT II treaty was, in Reagan's view, "fatally flawed" because it legitimized Soviet heavy missiles that could in theory destroy the U.S. ICBM force in a surprise attack. In its force programs the administration did not (see pp. 99–101) pursue any "quick fixes" to reduce this vulnerability. In its arms control policies, however, it gave heavy emphasis to attempting to achieve this result through diplomatic negotiations, despite the failure of similar efforts by three previous administrations. By delaying negotiations until the United States had moved firmly ahead with the MX, B-1, cruise missile, Trident II, and strategic C^3I programs, however, the administration claimed that it would be able to produce more forthcoming participation on the part of the Soviets. The section on arms control in the February 1982 annual report of the secretary of defense was indicative of the administration's priorities: In three pages there is much discussion of the false hopes generated by previous arms control efforts and of the dangers of the Soviets violating arms agreements. Totally lacking is any reference to the possibility of future strategic arms control talks.[18]

At this point once again domestic politics interfered; this time U.S. domestic politics. The administration was subjected to increasing criticism from congressmen, the media, and others for its failure to move ahead on the strategic front. Democrats began to talk about reviving the SALT II treaty. Most important, in the winter and spring of 1982, the nuclear freeze movement gained momentum, eventually reaching the point where in July a freeze resolution was barely defeated in the House of Representatives. In these circumstances, the administration had no choice but to give higher priority to strategic arms control. Rapid action was, however, made all the more difficult by the strong desire within the administration to change the units and focus of strategic arms control. The previous agreements and talks had focused almost entirely on the limitation of strategic launchers. Within the administration, however, strong sentiment existed to focus on warheads—and thereby get at the problem of U.S. ICBM vulnerability, as well as potential Soviet ICBM vulnerability, if the United States built the MX—and on throwweight, where the Soviets had a substantial advantage. After much intra-administration negotiation, agreement was finally reached on a proposal unveiled by the president at Eureka, Illinois, on May 9, 1982. Under this plan, U.S. and Soviet missile warheads would be reduced to 5,000 apiece—roughly a one-third cut—with no more than one-half of these based on land. A second phase would involve negotiating a reduction to levels of throwweight less than the current U.S. level. U.S. officials also said that in addition to discussing these two proposals—both of which would require significant concessions on the part of the Soviets—the United States would also be willing to discuss possible limits on bombers and cruise missiles. The START negotiations got under way in Geneva at the end of June.

The administration thus made the success of its arms control strategy depend on its ability to create the bargaining chips needed to induce Soviet concessions. Its policy became hostage to the politics of antinuclearism in Western Europe and the United States. Arms control agreements require that both the United States and the Soviet Union simultaneously see it in their interests to negotiate such agreements. As time went on, however, the dynamics of politics in the Western democracies tended to increase the incentives for the United States to want an agreement and decrease the pressure on the Soviet Union to be interested in one.

Modernization / Readiness

Force programs can be divided between those for the strategic nuclear forces and general-purpose forces, on the one hand, and between those for force modernization and force readiness, on the other. This produces the four types of programs set forth in table 2 and indicates the priorities assigned to them by the Reagan administration.

"The modernization of our strategic nuclear forces," Clark declared, "will receive first priority in our efforts to rebuild the military capabilities of the United States."[19] Other administration spokesmen have made similar statements, and the allocation of funds in the FY

Table 2. Reagan Administration Force Program Priorities

	Modernization	Readiness
Strategic nuclear	1st	4th
General purpose	3rd	2nd

1983 budget is evidence of this point. In marked contrast to the proposed increases in the Carter budget the previous year, which had emphasized general purpose forces, the FY 1983 increases provided for a more than one-third rise in the strategic forces budget, with general purpose funds going up only 13.5 percent (see table 3).

Among strategic programs, the administration "accorded the highest priority to a survivable strategic C^3I system."[20] The other elements in its program included production of 100 B-1B bombers, installation of cruise missiles on B-52s, development of the advanced technology "stealth" bomber, production and deployment (in some mode) of the MX, production of one Trident submarine a year, development and production of the Trident II (D-5) missile, installation of cruise missiles on attack submarines, intensified research and development on ABM systems, improved air defenses, and an expanded civil defense program. Of its eleven major components, eight were carry-overs from Carter plans, while three (the B-1, air defenses, and SLCMs) were Reagan administration innovations. All in all, the program involved a massive investment in strategic forces, easily comparable to those which had taken place in the two earlier buildups of 1950–53 and 1961–63.

Second priority in budget allocations, administration officials claim, was to be given to the readiness of the general purpose forces. This meant improvements in manning levels, training, and maintenance and acquisition of larger supplies of spare parts, fuel, and ammunition, with a view to creating a minimum sixty-day combat supply of

Table 3. Reagan Administration Funding Changes

	Percentage Changes Recommended	
	Reagan FY 1982/ Carter FY 1982	Reagan FY 1983/ Reagan FY 1982
General purpose forces	18.2%	13.5%
Airlift and sealift	17.2	2.3
Strategic nuclear forces	11.3	34.3
Intelligence and communications	10.0	21.6
Total defense budget	9.1	13.3

Source: Adapted from Secretary of Defense Harold Brown, Department of Defense Annual Report Fiscal Year 1981 *(Washington, D.C.: U.S. Government Printing Office, 1980); Secretary of Defense Caspar W. Weinberger, March 1981; Weinberger,* Annual Report to the Congress Fiscal Year 1983 *(Washington, D.C.: U.S. Government Printing Office, 1982).*

these items.[21] According to defense officials, emphasis was also being placed on greater sustainability of conventional forces, improved command and control, and additional mobility. It remains to be seen, however, whether readiness will receive the same emphasis in practice as it does in policy declarations. Much of the funding for improved readiness is included in the operations and maintenance category of the military budget. The administration proposed a 14.5 percent real increase in O&M funding in FY 1983 over the level of two years earlier, compared with a proposed 27.6 percent real increase in the defense budget as a whole and a 63.5 percent real increase in procurement. One would expect increases in O&M appropriations (which are reflected almost immediately in outlays) to lag behind increases in procurement appropriations (which are spent over several years). At the same time, however, limits on defense spending are also likely to have their principal immediate impact on O&M appropriations and outlays. Readiness programs, consequently, are likely to face a crunch, and in the fall of 1982 it was reported that "all of the military services will fail to achieve their minimum combat readiness this year because operations and maintenance funds have been siphoned to pay for new tanks, missiles, planes, and ships."[22]

The procurement of new weapons and equipment for the general purpose forces, according to the administration, was given "lower priority" than enhancing the readiness of existing forces. The administration, it was said, does not contemplate "a wholesale cancellation of programs now ready for production." But, "in the context of limited defense dollars," it will be "considering modernization in light of other priorities before starting new developments."[23] The administration does, however, have in mind a major shipbuilding program. "The most significant force expansion proposed by the administration," Secretary Weinberger said in his FY 1983 annual report, "centers on the Navy, particularly its offensive missions." Over a six-year period the administration proposed to build 152 new ships as compared with a total of 98 in the Carter program. These, plus conversions and reactivations (including four battleships), would cost $93 billion in 1983 dollars.[24] A principal issue is therefore the extent to which the administration will in fact pursue this major program, which its secretary of the navy wants and to which it was initially favorably inclined.

The administration obviously proposes to maintain existing U.S. strategic nuclear forces at their usual high levels of combat readiness. Nonetheless, in a broader sense this issue received low priority in the administration's program, in that the administration made no serious effort to deal with the "window of vulnerability" opening on U.S.

land-based intercontinental missiles in the early and mid-1980s. This omission in the administration's program is all the more striking because many of Reagan's most active supporters had played major roles in focusing public attention on this issue in the latter years of the Carter administration. In 1981 and 1982, Reagan administration officials continued to warn of the dangers posed by the "window of vulnerability." The mid-1980s, Weinberger asserted again and again, constitute "a period of substantial danger," "our most vulnerable period," and he agreed that on coming into office the administration "assigned the highest priority to closing the so-called window of vulnerability." He also alleged that "parts of this [strategic forces] program are especially designed to secure additional strength for the near term."[25] The programs he cites, however—cruise missiles, B-1, deployment of MX missiles in existing silos—while increasing U.S. nuclear strength, do nothing to reduce the vulnerability of U.S. silos and air bases to a surprise first strike. In 1979 and 1980, ardent supporters of the Reagan approach, including the Committee on the Present Danger, had come up with a significant number of "quick fixes" that could be used to reduce this vulnerability in the short term. In March 1982, however, the committee regretfully reported that "the administration has adopted no quick fixes to close the 'window of vulnerability.' Over the next five years, the window will open wider due to the administration's decisions. . . . The net result of these actions and inactions will be increased strategic force vulnerability."[26]

In 1961 Kennedy administration officials came into office alarmed over the "missile gap" and discovered that it really did not exist. They nonetheless went ahead with massive ICBM and SLBM programs as if it did. In 1981 Reagan administration officials came into office alarmed over the window of vulnerability, continued to assert that it still existed, and yet took no significant action to meet this imminent threat. Why should this be the case? One answer might be found by asking who entered the Reagan administration where. Five leading figures of the Committee on the Present Danger took administration posts, none of them, however, in the Defense Department. William R. Van Cleave, an active member of the committee, served as head of the defense transition team but did not get along with Weinberger and his associates and was conspicuously not given a Defense Department job. Neither was Scott Thompson, who had been associated with Van Cleave in dramatizing the window of vulnerability issue.*

---

* Conversely, one could say that the appointment to high Defense posts of Francis J. West, Jr., and John Lehman ensured an emphasis on naval forces, Fred Iklé an emphasis on defense mobilization, and Richard Perle on East-West economic relations.

Those who did occupy Defense posts may have accepted the window arguments intellectually but may not have felt passionately gripped by them. In addition, defense officials may have believed that while it was important to have a high degree of readiness for conventional war, the possibility of nuclear war or nuclear confrontation of any kind was sufficiently remote that the window issue could be placed on a back burner. There is also the possibility that officials thought that undertaking the quick fixes recommended by Van Cleave and others would be a signal to Americans, our allies, and the Soviets that the administration believed nuclear confrontation was imminent, a perception that would tend to contribute to that imminence. In any event, the low priority accorded strategic force vulnerability made it possible for many to think with James Fallows that *"the President does not believe that 'vulnerability' really matters. If he did, he could not in conscience have made this choice."*[27]

Space–Time Escalation

For a quarter of a century U.S. strategy vis-à-vis the Soviet Union was based on the premise that deterrence before or during a conflict required the explicit or implicit threat of escalation to the nuclear level. With Soviet achievement of nuclear parity in the early 1970s, this threat became less and less credible, and it was last used in the Middle East crisis of 1973. At the same time, U.S. interests and, eventually, commitments were extended to include the Persian Gulf. The need thus arose for new forms of deterrence against new possibilities of attack. American strategy gradually groped toward solutions to this problem in the late 1970s. A comprehensive resolution of the issue, however, had to await the Reagan administration. In what was probably its most significant strategy innovation, the Reagan administration consciously and formally substituted the threat of escalation in space and time for the threat of escalation in weapons. The Soviets would be deterred not by the prospect of nuclear devastation but rather by the prospect of conventional counterattacks on major Soviet interests and/or the prospect of a long conventional war in which American and allied economic strength would be a decisive factor. "Horizontal escalation" and "prolonged war" emerged as two central concepts in administration military thinking.

In their public statements, administration officials always indicated that it was "in the interest of the United States to limit the scope of any conflict" and that the United States must have "adequate military capability to defend our vital interests in the area in which they are threatened." Clark stated, however, that a "capability for counteroffensives on other fronts" was also "an essential element of our strategy."[28] The Defense Department also emphasized horizontal escalation. This approach commended itself early on to Secretary Weinberger and was included in the revisions the new administration made in the FY 1983–1987 Defense Guidance in the late spring of 1981. "We will not restrict ourselves to meeting aggression on its own immediate front," Weinberger said at that time. "If we are forced into war, we must be prepared to launch counteroffensives in other regions and try to exploit the aggressor's weaknesses wherever they exist. If aggression by superior forces cannot be reversed where it occurs, we should not be confined to that particular arena." This theme was reiterated in Weinberger's FY 1983 annual report, subsequent speeches, and the FY 1984–1988 Defense Guidance. The latter document explicitly identified Cuba, Vietnam, and North Korea as potential points of conventional retaliation. It also, however, pointed to the need to "develop more effective linkages with the people of East Europe so as to deny Soviet confidence in the reliability of her allies" and to have special operations forces prepared to operate in Eastern Europe. The United States and its allies should also be prepared to launch conventional attacks on "the Soviet homeland."[29]

Horizontal escalation was thus an appropriate response to any single Soviet attack that could not itself be defeated directly through conventional forces. Conceivably, several attacks or contingencies could arise simultaneously. How could these be dealt with? Should and could the United States deal with them simultaneously or would it have to deal with them sequentially? The military planning objective of the upside strategy of the 1960s was, in theory, to be able to fight two major wars against the Soviet Union and China and to deal with one small contingency at the same time. The capabilities to implement the strategy were never realized, and the Nixon administration's downside strategy shifted the planning objective to one major war against the Soviet Union and a "half-war" in Korea or elsewhere. In 1977, the Carter administration's upside strategy in effect posited that the United States should be prepared to fight one major war in Europe plus two half-wars, one in Korea and one in Southwest Asia. The administration fell far short, however, of developing the capabilities to do this.

The Reagan administration accepted the Carter commitments to the three zones but rejected what it called the "mechanistic assumptions" of the war-counting approach. The United States, it argued, must be prepared for a global conflict with the Soviet Union and should be ready to fight wherever the Soviets might attack and to take advantage of Soviet weaknesses wherever they might occur. It explicitly recognized that "U.S. forces might be required simultaneously in geographically separated theaters."[30] Conceivably a restructuring of reserves, pre-positioning of equipment, and improved air- and sealift could enable the United States to meet such multiple contingencies without a major expansion in its regular standing forces.[31] Administration spokesmen, however, argued that it was neither necessary nor possible for the United States to "have the capability to successfully engage Soviet forces simultaneously on all fronts." Instead, "priorities for sequential operations" were necessary, including an order of regional priorities for "general planning in the event of a worldwide war with the Soviet Union." First priority went to the defense of North America, second to Western Europe and the North Atlantic lines of communication (LOCs), third "to ensuring access to the oil in Southwest Asia," and fourth to "defense of U.S. Pacific allies and the LOCs for the Indian and Pacific oceans."[32] In keeping with these priorities, the administration endorsed NATO's Long-Term Defense Program and the need for the United States to be able to deploy six army divisions and sixty air force tactical squadrons to Europe within ten days. It increased the funding for the airlift and tankers that might eventually make this possible. It also carried forward and greatly expanded the Carter plans for a rapid-deployment force for Persian Gulf contingencies, creating a new unified command for that area of the world, and providing for assignment to that command of five army divisions, two marine amphibious forces, ten air force tactical wings, two air force B-52 wings, and three navy carrier battle groups. Most significantly, of course, a strategy of horizontal escalation plus the possibility of multiple, even if sequential conflicts, provided the rationale for the administration's plans for a major expansion of U.S. naval capabilities.

Horizontal escalation almost necessarily implies temporal escalation also. The Reagan administration, as Secretary Weinberger put it, "abandoned the dangerous fallacy of a 'short war'—that any conventional war would necessarily be short because the aggressor would retreat or the war would quickly escalate to the nuclear level." The United States must instead be prepared "to fight a prolonged major conventional war." U.S. readiness to fight such a war is, the administration argued, particularly critical to the deterrence of aggression in areas like the Persian Gulf. Hence the emphasis on improving the sustainability of U.S. forces, and hence also a new stress on the importance of mobilization planning, the expansion of stockpiles, and general enhancement of the capability of American industry to move quickly into war production. As Secretary Weinberger noted, both

U.S. wars since World War II were "of long duration."[33] What he did not note was that while the American military establishment can be prepared to fight a long war, it is difficult to prepare the American people to do so.

Resources: Buildup and Slowdown

The upside strategy devised by the Carter administration and significantly revised and extended by the Reagan administration clearly required greatly increased resources for defense. The Carter administration did not secure significant increases in congressional appropriations, which declined very slightly in real terms in FY 1978 and FY 1979 and increased by 2.5 percent in FY 1980. Drawing upon more substantial increases in total obligational authority (TOA) that occurred under President Ford in FY 1976 and FY 1977, the Carter administration did, however, increase real outlays in FY 1979 and FY 1980 by 3.9 percent and 3.8 percent, respectively. As we have seen, in reaction to Afghanistan Carter proposed a major rise in TOA in FY 1981, and in his last Five-Year Defense Plan he set forth a proposed program involving roughly 5 percent average annual increases in TOA and outlays from FY 1981 through FY 1986.

The Reagan administration came into office after a campaign in which it had denounced the incumbent administration for being weak on defense. Politics as well as strategy thus dictated that it spend more on defense than its predecessor. It quickly moved to do this. On March 4, 1981, the administration unveiled its proposals for an increase of $33.4 billion in the Carter estimates for TOA for FY 1981 and FY 1982, including amendments to the FY 1982 budget that would raise it by some 13.2 percent. For the longer term the administration proposed an ambitious program involving TOA for FY 1982–86 of $1,460.2 billion, an increase of 14.4 percent over Carter's proposed five-year estimate of $1,276.1 billion. In real terms TOA would increase by over 14 percent in FY 1982 and thereafter by about 7 percent a year, for an average of more than 8 percent as compared with the Carter average of about 5 percent for the same period (FY 1982–86). In FY 1986, defense spending would have been about 6 percent of GNP under the Carter plan and would be about 7 percent of GNP under the Reagan proposals.

⌐The Reagan administration thus proposed major increments to an already substantial Carter buildup of defense monies. In the spring of 1981 the time was ripe for such actions. During the late 1960s and early 1970s a plurality of the American public had favored reductions in defense, and these had occurred. In the mid-1970s, a plurality favored maintaining defense spending at its existing level. In September 1979, for the first time since the early 1960s, a plurality, albeit a small one, favored an increase in defense spending. By December 1979—after the hostage seizure but before the invasion of Afghanistan—this plurality had become a 51 percent majority favoring an increase, with only 9 percent of the public supporting a decrease. After Afghanistan and through 1980 and early 1981, more than 60 percent of the public wanted defense spending increased.[34] The Carter administration had adapted its plans accordingly, and the Reagan administration clearly felt that it could and should do more. In this environment, the changes it proposed in the FY 1981 and FY 1982 budgets sailed through Congress relatively unscathed. In May, for instance, the Senate approved the FY 1982 military authorization bill of $136.5 billion ($1 billion less than the administration requested) by a vote of 92–1, with only Mark Hatfield opposing it and with such frequent critics of defense as Edward M. Kennedy, Paul Sarbanes, and Paul Tsongas all voting in favor of it. "The vote," the *New York Times* reported, "taken after two days of desultory debate in which few questions were raised about the size of the military budget, appeared only to underscore the widespread support in Congress for increased military spending."[35]

⌐Very shortly thereafter, however, concern about the levels of defense spending in relation to the economy began to manifest itself in both Congress and the executive branch, most notably in the Office of Management and Budget (OMB). Confronting massive tax cuts, a faltering economy, and the looming prospect of unprecedented deficits, David Stockman and others began to press for cutbacks in the proposed increases in defense spending. In July the president approved a $3.4 billion reduction in outlays spread across the FY 1982, 1983, and 1984 budgets. The battle continued, however, and over the summer OMB circulated a variety of plans for possible drastic cutbacks of up to $58.8 billion in defense spending over the next three years. These were vigorously resisted by the Defense Department, and eventually in September the president approved a modest reduction of $13 billion in proposed outlays: $2 billion in FY 1982, $5 billion in FY 1983, and $6 billion in FY 1984.[36] Meanwhile, members of Congress had also become concerned about the effect of rising defense spending on the economy, as well as the accuracy of Defense Department cost estimates and the ability of the department to spend the large sums it was getting without wasting them. As a result, there was renewed debate over the final appropriations for FY 1982, with $206.9 billion in TOA eventually being approved in December. This was still only a modest 3.4 percent reduction from the administration's final request.

Defense Secretary Caspar Weinberger and OMB Director David Stockman had squared off over the latter's efforts to reduce the defense increases. They could agree, however, on Stockman's desire to give primary emphasis in planning the FY 1983 budget to controlling outlays rather than TOA. For Stockman, of course, this made sense since outlays (minus tax revenues) determined the size of the federal deficit. To Weinberger, it was useful since the FY 1983 budget would feature a major increase in procurement funds for both nuclear and conventional weapons systems. He could readily accept a lower level of outlays provided he could get higher levels of TOA for these purposes, the bulk of which would not be reflected in outlays for several years. This could, of course, create great problems for Stockman or his successor in FY 1985 and FY 1986, but that was not Weinberger's worry, and it did not seem to trouble Stockman either. As a result, in February 1982 the administration proposed FY 1983 outlays of $215.9 billion, down from the $221.1 estimated in March 1981, and TOA of $258 billion, up from $254.8 estimated the previous March. It is even reported that in the final budget review in December, the TOA figures approved exceeded by $6 billion what the military departments themselves had requested in October, a dramatic departure from the usual practice.[37] As it was, the administration's FY 1983 figures involved an 18 percent increase in outlays and a 20.4 percent increase in TOA over FY 1982.

The 1982 struggle over defense spending went on for twelve months and was fought on at least five fronts: the overall budget resolution; the military authorization bill; the FY 1982 supplemental appropriation; the continuing resolution; and the Defense Department appropriation bill. The battles on the first two fronts were over by midsummer, and in them the administration was substantially able to secure its objectives. The budget resolution set defense spending for FY 1983 at $209 billion—a figure which the administration accepted. It also set figures for the FY 1984 and FY 1985 defense budgets, to which the leading figures in Congress thought the administration had agreed. In midsummer, however, the White House announced that the president would not feel bound by these figures, an announcement that apparently was designed to reassure Reaganauts on the right, but which certainly outraged Republican senators—including both Howard Baker and Mark Hatfield—in the middle. With respect to the military authorization bill, members of Congress were not as tractable as they had been the previous year, but the dominant forces in both houses were still ready to go along with the administration. Various efforts to eliminate or drastically to reduce funds for the MX, B-1, Pershing II, and C-5B were all voted down, although in some cases narrowly. The House of Representatives also defeated by a vote of 348–55 an alternative motion by Congressman Dellums of California to provide $126.1 billion for defense instead of the $183.4 billion requested by the administration. In the end, Congress approved an authorization of $178.0 billion, sharply reducing or deleting administration requests in only three areas: civil defense, nerve gas production, and ballistic missile defense.

Meanwhile, however, changes were occurring in the climate of opinion in which defense spending was discussed. The public majority in favor of increasing defense spending that had formed in the fall of 1979 disappeared in the fall of 1981. Through 1982 its replacement was a substantial plurality (36–47 percent) favoring maintenance of the current level of defense spending. In the winter and spring of 1982, criticism of the administration's defense plans became much more widespread.[38] While the administration won the major battles over the military authorization bill in Congress, members of Congress were also much more active in challenging its proposals and attempting to limit or condition its spending programs. In August the chairman of the president's Council of Economic Advisers resigned with a blast at the "horrendous deficits" caused by the administration's failure to curb military spending.[39] In September, as unemployment went over the 10 percent mark, increased opposition to the military buildup was reported to exist in various parts of the country. "I find almost unanimous support for my position which is that we need to trim defense spending," reported Congressman Tom Tauke, a moderate Iowa Republican, on his constituency. "When Reagan went in to office there was public support for increasing defense spending. But I think that support is eroding rapidly. The nuclear freeze movement has something to do with it, but I believe the biggest factor is going too far, too fast."[40]

The shifting political balance was reflected most dramatically in the battle over the FY 1982 supplementary appropriation bill. The bill was rewritten in the House to remove $2 billion the administration wanted for defense and to add $918 million it did not want for social programs. This action was undoubtedly in part stimulated by the president's announcement that he did not feel bound by the ceilings for FY 1984 and FY 1985 that Congress had approved in the budget resolution. When the revised bill was approved by Congress, the president's veto of it also antagonized congressmen who thought there had been at least an implicit deal that he would approve it in return for Democratic support for his tax increase proposals. In the end, Republicans running for reelection joined with Democrats to override the veto, handing the president the most clear-cut legislative defeat of his administration. In the meantime, the FY 1983 defense appropriation bill was tied up in subcommittee with Senator Ted Stevens and Congressman Joseph Addabbo negotiating with Secretary Weinberger on where cuts should be made to bring it within the approved budgetary ceiling. As the fiscal year expired, neither house had voted on the appropriation measure, and after intense three-way lobbying among House, Senate, and Defense Department, a continuing resolution was agreed to authorizing spending at an annual level of $228.7 billion TOA with the proviso that no funds could be spent on projects (such as the MX, B-1, nuclear carriers) that had not been funded in FY 1982. When Congress resumed after the elections, the House deleted from the FY 1983 appropriation bill $988 million for production of the MX missile and directed the administration to come up with a reconsidered basing plan for the missile by March. In the end, Congress appropriated $232 billion for defense for FY 1983, about $17 billion less than the administration's final request. This would, it was estimated, permit defense outlays for FY 1983 of about $200 billion.

The decisions on the FY 1984 defense budget will be made by a Congress and in an atmosphere that are considerably less favorable to large increases in defense spending than those dating from early 1980 until mid-1982. Defense outlays increased by 15.5 percent (3.8 percent real) in FY 1980, 17.5 percent (4.1 percent real) in FY 1981, and 17.1 percent (7.7 percent real) in FY 1982. The administration's plan called for a 10.5 percent real increase in defense outlays in FY 1983, but it appears unlikely to achieve that goal. It has, indeed, been suggested that the real increase in defense outlays in FY 1983 is likely to be about 6.5 percent.[41] The peak rate in the expansion of the defense sector was undoubtedly reached in 1981 and 1982. Defense spending will probably continue to rise in real terms, but it will do so at less than anticipated rates. Hard choices will increasingly have to be made. Some procurement programs could be eliminated entirely and others stretched out, among them navy shipbuilding and the air-defense buildup. Nonprocurement programs are, however, likely to bear a heavier share of the budget revisions. The increases in TOA in FY 1981 ($26.8 billion; 19.2 percent) and FY 1982 ($30.8 billion; 17.5 percent) are dramatically increasing the carryover of appropriated but unexpended funds. As of October 1, 1981, these amounted to $86 billion; they rose to roughly $110 billion by October 1, 1982.[42] These funds are, of course, heavily concentrated in the procurement accounts. In 1983 and 1984, as the administration and Congress both attempt to lower the federal deficit, they will necessarily focus on holding down defense outlays. The natural impetus will be to cut back on TOA and outlays for operations and maintenance in order to preserve the planned expenditure of the already appropriated procurement funds.

One other factor could come into play as the administration attempts to limit its budget deficit by reducing spending. About 76 percent of the total federal budget consists of relatively uncontrollable funds impervious to administration budget-cutting efforts. Almost two-thirds of the defense budget (which is about 25 percent of the total budget) consists of controllable funds, and defense funds also make up two-thirds of all controllable funds in the total budget. In 1981 and 1982 the public mood was very supportive of the defense buildup. As that mood changes to opposition, the relative vulnerability of the defense accounts will make it feasible to make big cuts there relatively quickly.[43]

In September 1982 the administration came under attack from right-wing critics on the grounds that it was spending no more and, in some respects, less than Jimmy Carter had proposed to spend on defense. This was indeed the case. In FY 1981 the Reagan administration spent $1.5 billion less than Carter had proposed, and in FY 1982 it was spending only $2.8 billion more (out of a budget of $182.8 billion). This fact, however, did not exactly justify criticizing the administration for "a defense buildup that really isn't."[44] The implication of such a comment is that Carter had not proposed a buildup, when, in fact, of course, he had set forth a rather substantial one. The Reagan administration, to be sure, had wanted to do more, but it was still doing something if its spending approximated the targets outlined by Carter. Members of Congress and others were, indeed, increasingly critical of it for attempting to do too much. Anyone familiar with the Carter administration knows full well that if it had remained in office it never would have achieved the defense-spending goals it set forth as it left office. The Reagan administration is much better equipped to realize these goals, and it would score a major success if it did so. Thus in 1983 and 1984 the administration may paradoxically find itself attacked from the right for not doing more than Carter wanted to do, while defending itself against antimilitary Democrats on the ground that it is only trying to do what Carter wanted to do. In February 1983 the president began to do just exactly that, informing a group of newspaper editors that President Carter had "recognized" the need for a major military buildup and noting that "we are now adding only about $3 billion a year to what their plan was."[45]

The Fourth Phase
of the Third Cycle

By the end of 1982 the third phase of the third postwar strategy-budget cycle was clearly drawing to an end. Its termination was signaled by the increased attention being given to the gap opening up between strategic needs and available resources. Even though the Reagan administration had increased military spending considerably, many outside critics, including former supporters, argued that it was not doing enough to meet defense requirements. The administration, the Committee on the Present Danger argued, had reduced U.S. strategic capabilities and failed to improve conventional ones. At best, the administration's program was "a minimal one. It will not halt the unfavorable trends in the U.S.-Soviet military balance, let alone reverse them."[46] Other critics joined the committee in warning that the administration was falling far short in developing the forces necessary to implement its strategy of "global conflict" with the Soviet Union. "Conditions could arise," wrote one well-informed military analyst, "in which the need to reinforce more or less simultaneously in such disparate and distant areas as Europe, the Persian Gulf, and Korea would appear urgent. Under these conditions, the active-duty forces would be too few in number to cover all three theaters; reserves would not be sufficiently ready to make up the deficits; and airlift would fall far short of demand." Others spoke of the "abyss separating the administration's strategy and resources."[47]

The recognition of the strategy-resources gap was not confined to those outside the government. To implement the administration's strategy, the Joint Chiefs of Staff estimated, would require a more than 50 percent expansion in military force levels (e.g., twenty-two

instead of thirteen carrier battle groups, twenty-five instead of fourteen active army divisions, thirty-eight instead of twenty-four tactical
air wings) by 1991. These force levels were considerably higher than
the relatively modest expansion the administration hoped to achieve
by 1988 (fourteen carrier battle groups, sixteen army divisions, twenty-
seven-and-one-half tactical air wings). Achieving them, it was estimated, would require spending by 1988 $750 billion more than the
$1,600 billion the administration proposed to spend.[48] Moreover,
administration leaders themselves admitted that their buildup was not
enough to support their strategy. In early 1981 Weinberger reportedly argued that a 9 percent rather than a 7 percent average annual
increase in spending would be necessary to reach this goal. A year
later Undersecretary Iklé in effect confirmed from within the administration what the Committee on the Present Danger had been saying
on the outside. Even more money than the administration asked for,
he told the Senate Armed Services Committee, "would not close the
gap in accumulated military assets between the United States and the
Soviet Union until the early 1990s. This is a bleak outlook, implying
either a further deterioration in our security or a need for a defense
increase considerably greater than what the administration now proposes." The Defense Guidance issued that year admitted the shortfall.
"Because of funding constraints, production lead times, and the urgent need to ensure the current forces' responsiveness and fighting
capabilities, meeting our planning goal during this five-year program
period [FY 1984–88] is probably infeasible." Hence, it remains necessary, the Guidance continued, to work out some way "in the longer
term to blend force capabilities and strategy into agreement."[49]

Administration officials thus seemed to agree that they would be
lacking not only the resources to provide optimum security in the
1980s but also the resources necessary to implement the particular
strategy they had adopted. They also saw little likelihood of those
resources becoming available in the future when, if anything, the
pressures would all be in the other direction. They were, in short,
confronting the distinctive challenge of phase four in the strategy-
budget cycle. How could this be met? There were three possibilities.

First, the advent of the fourth phase could conceivably be resisted
and strenuous efforts made to continue or even to expand the growth
of the defense sector. Such efforts would fly in the face of all the
natural tendencies among politicians and public to feel that the military had gotten theirs, that physical limits (material shortages, industrial bottlenecks) dictated a slower rate of growth, and that the
time had come to emphasize other priorities (balancing the budget,

domestic programs, economic recovery). This defense buildup had, moreover, continued longer than either of its predecessors (setting aside the force increments directly related to the Vietnam War) and had already invalidated the conventional cliché that real defense spending never increased for more than three consecutive years. The other buildups, moreover, had occurred during periods of economic expansion. Real economic growth had been 16.6 percent between 1950 and 1953 and 12.9 percent between 1960 and 1963; it was nonexistent between 1979 and 1982. In such circumstances, it seemed remarkable that the buildup had continued for as long and gone as far as it had. In the absence of a major new Soviet challenge or other international crisis, it also seemed highly improbable that it could continue on course much longer.

Second, strategy and resources could be brought into line by redefining U.S. commitments and goals. Confronted with a comparable challenge and a diplomatic opportunity in 1969, this was what the Nixon administration had done in concluding that it was no longer necessary to maintain the unrealizable goal of preparing for a major war with China as well as with the Soviet Union. This was also what Senator John Tower suggested in 1982 when confronted with the administration's pessimistic picture. The time has come, he said, when Congress must "identify which commitments we will no longer be able to honor." Well, indeed, responded Weinberger a few weeks later:

> . . . what should we give up? Should we give up defense of the Central Front in Europe? Should we give up the Caribbean? Should we give up any attempt to defend the oil fields, so vital to Europe and Japan? Should we give up our defense of Northeast Asia? Should we give up any other vital interests?[50]

A few outside critics were ready to rush forward with suggestions to abandon one or more of these commitments, most particularly perhaps the defense of Europe. Such a revolution in U.S. foreign policy would, however, in all probability require an even greater political upheaval and battle than that necessary to increase resources.

A third way of bridging the gap and that most popular in past cycles has been to find new ways of maintaining the same commitments with fewer resources; that is, to devise a less expensive downside strategy. Downside strategies typically stress several elements:

1. Greater reliance on allied military forces (e.g., the Nixon Doctrine), supported by U.S. economic and military assistance, rather than on U.S. military forces. Such an emphasis has already been latently

present in the Reagan administration emphasis on greatly expanded arms sales and military assistance and its efforts to get Japan and the European allies to increase their military strength.

2. Greater reliance on nuclear weapons and lowering the nuclear threshold (e.g., massive retaliation) instead of much more expensive conventional forces. Such a shift would reverse the major thrust of Reagan administration strategy on the need to prepare for a long conventional war. By the latter half of the 1980s, however, the modernization of U.S. strategic and theater nuclear forces could make such a shift more attractive. One can imagine the question being raised: Why do not hundreds of U.S. theater nuclear weapons in Europe, together with British and French nuclear forces, suffice to deter a Soviet attack? Why are a quarter-million U.S. ground forces also necessary?

3. Greater reliance on reserve forces rather than active forces. Recurring efforts have been made in the past to develop more militarily effective and combat-ready reserves, but they have never generated the results their proponents hoped for. The Reagan administration to date has placed great stress on the readiness of the active forces; greater reliance on reserve forces would involve a significant shift in emphasis.

4. Greater emphasis on selectivity, offense, and retaliation rather than on across-the-board defenses. The administration's horizontal escalation strategy contains the germs of such an approach. Weinberger's articulation of it indeed parallels (presumably consciously) John Foster Dulles's formulation of massive retaliation. This would, however, mean being less prepared to fight anywhere and more prepared to take the offensive in a few key spots (e.g., Cuba) in retaliation against Soviet action elsewhere.

In criticizing the administration's approach, the *New York Times* opined, "The right strategic question is not how much to spend for defense, but what kind of defense the United States needs. The reluctance to address it is dangerous."[51] The administration had addressed it, however, and concluded that the United States needed a defense it now appears unwilling to pay for. That is useful enough on the upside of the cycle. Now, however, the administration—or its successor—needs to reverse the sequence; to start with what the country is willing to pay, and to put together a downside strategy appropriate to those limits.

Notes

I am indebted to Christopher Meyerson for his able research assistance in connection with my writing of this paper.

1. On the interrelations among strategy, budgets, and diplomacy, see Samuel P. Huntington, "Radicalism and Conservatism in National Defense Policy," *Journal of International Affairs* 13, no. 2 (1954):206–22.

2. Samuel P. Huntington, *The Common Defense: Strategic Programs in National Politics* (New York: Columbia University Press, 1961), pp. 63–64.

3. Alain C. Enthoven and K. Wayne Smith, *How Much Is Enough? Shaping the Defense Program, 1961–1969* (New York: Harper and Row, 1971), p. 167.

4. Secretary of Defense Caspar W. Weinberger, *Annual Report to the Congress Fiscal Year 1983* (Washington, D.C.: U.S. Government Printing Office, 1982), p. I–6.

5. Secretary of Defense Harold Brown, *Department of Defense Annual Report Fiscal Year 1981* (Washington, D.C.: U.S. Government Printing Office, 1980), p. 2.

6. *Newsweek,* June 8, 1981, p. 28. See also *New York Times,* March 22, 1982, p. 1, and April 21, 1982, p. 18.

7. James Fallows, "The Great Defense Deception," *New York Review of Books,* May 28, 1981, p. 15; John Collins, *Newsweek,* June 8, 1981, p. 30.

8. See, for example, the interview with Secretary Weinberger, *U.S. News and World Report,* November 23, 1981, p. 30.

9. Caspar W. Weinberger, "The Defense Policy of the Reagan Administration," Address, Council on Foreign Relations, New York, N.Y., June 17, 1981, p. 2; Frank Carlucci, *Newsweek,* June 8, 1981, p. 30.

10. Brown, *Annual Report Fiscal Year 1981,* p. 66.

11. Caspar W. Weinberger, Hearings before the Committee on the Budget, United States Senate, 97th Cong., 1st sess., *First Concurrent Resolution on the Budget—FY 1982;* vol. I: National Defense; April 2, 1981: "The Administration's Defense Program," p. 121; Weinberger, Address, June 17, 1981, p. 2.

12. Herschel Kanter, "The Reagan Defense Program in Early Outline," *Strategic Review* 9 (Summer 1981): 27; William W. Kaufmann, "The Defense Budget," in Joseph A. Pechman, ed., *Setting National Priorities: The 1982 Budget* (Washington, D.C.: Brookings Institution, 1981), p. 137.

13. William P. Clark, "National Security Strategy," Address, Center for Strategic and International Studies, Georgetown University, May 21, 1982, p. 2. See also *New York Times,* May 22, 1982, p. 1; May 25, 1982, p. 16; May 31, 1982, p. A8, and May 30, 1982, p. 1.

14. Steven R. Weisman, "Reagan Moves on Military Priorities," *New York Times,* May 25, 1982, p. 16.

15. Thomas C. Reed, "Banquet Address," *Signal,* August 1982, p. 25; *New York Times,* May 22, 1982, p. 15; *Boston Globe,* May 22, 1982, p. 4.

16. Weinberger, *Annual Report Fiscal 1983,* p. I-23.

17. FY 1984–1988 Defense Guidance, quoted in *New York Times,* May 30, 1982, pp. 1, 12.

18. Weinberger, *Annual Report Fiscal 1983*, pp. I-19–I-22.

19. Clark, "National Security Strategy," p. 7.

20. Ibid., p. 7; Reed, "Banquet Address," p. 25.

21. Weinberger, *Annual Report Fiscal 1983*, pp. I-12–I-13.

22. *Chicago Tribune*, October 11, 1982, p. 1.

23. Reed, "Banquet Address," p. 25.

24. Weinberger, *Annual Report Fiscal 1983*, p. I-30; Herschel Kanter, "The Reagan Defense Program: Can It Hold Up?" *Strategic Review* 10 (Spring 1982): 26–27.

25. Hearings before House Subcommittee on Department of Defense of the Committee on Appropriations, 97th Cong., 1st sess. *Department of Defense Appropriations for 1982*: pt. 9, Weinberger, October 5, 1981, p. 110; Weinberger, *Annual Report Fiscal 1983*, p. I-39; Weinberger, *U.S. News and World Report*, November 23, 1981, p. 29.

26. Committee on the Present Danger, *Is the Reagan Defense Program Adequate?* (Washington, D.C.: Committee on the Present Danger, March 17, 1982), p. 13.

27. James Fallows, "Reagan's MX Surprise," *Atlantic Monthly*, December 1981, p. 14 (emphasis in original).

28. Clark, "National Security Strategy," p. 12.

29. *New York Times*, June 26, 1981, p. 11, and May 30, 1982, pp. 1, 12; *Boston Globe*, July 17, 1981, p. 3; Caspar W. Weinberger, Address, June 17, 1981, p. 5; *Washington Post*, June 2, 1982, p. 7.

30. FY 1984–1988 Defense Guidance, quoted in *New York Times*, May 30, 1982, pp. 1, 12.

31. Kaufmann, "Defense Budget," in Pechman, *Priorities 1982*, pp. 173–75.

32. Clark, "National Security Strategy," p. 11; FY 1984–1988 Defense Guidance, quoted in *Washington Post*, June 2, 1982, p. 7.

33. Weinberger, Address, June 17, 1981, p. 3, and "United States Defense Policy," Address, Council on Foreign Relations, New York, April 20, 1982, p. 3. See also Weinberger, *Annual Report Fiscal 1983*, pp. I-16–I-17; *Los Angeles Times*, June 6, 1982, p. 4; *New York Times*, August 22, 1982, p. 17.

34. Alvin Richman, "Public Attitudes on Military Power, 1981," *Public Opinion* 4 (December/January 1982): 44–46.

35. *New York Times*, May 15, 1981, p. 15.

36. Kevin N. Lewis, *The Reagan Defense Budget: Prospects and Pressures* (Santa Monica: RAND Corporation, p-6721, December 1981), pp. 3–5.

37. *Boston Globe*, January 17, 1982, p. A16.

38. *New York Times*, March 22, 1982, pp. 1, B11.

39. *Boston Globe*, August 27, 1982, p. 1.

40. *New York Times*, September 8, 1982, p. A17.

41. *New York Times*, July 15, 1982, p. A11.

42. *New York Times*, July 13, 1982, p. A22; William W. Kaufmann, "The Defense Budget," in Joseph A. Pechman, ed., *Setting National Priorities: The 1983 Budget* (Washington, D.C.: Brookings Institution, 1982), p. 54.

43. Lewis, *Reagan Defense Budget*, pp. 9–13.

44. *Washington Times*, September 8, 1982, pp. 3, 10.

45. *New York Times*, February 15, 1983, p. A20.

46. Committee on the Present Danger, *Is the Reagan Defense Budget Adequate?*, p. 34.

47. Kaufmann, "Defense Budget," in Pechman, *Priorities 1982*, p. 169; Jeffrey Record, "A 3-War Strategy," *Washington Post*, March 22, 1982, p. A15.

48. *Washington Post,* May 27, 1982, p. 1; Kanter, "Reagan Defense Budget: Can It Hold Up?", p. 34.

49. *New York Times,* March 22, 1982, p. B11, and July 13, 1982, p. A22.

50. Weinberger, Address, April 20, 1982, p. 6.

51. *New York Times,* April 29, 1982, p. 18.

5 The Evolution of Reagan Foreign Policy

I. M. Destler

The Reagan foreign policy story is at least two stories, intertwined in practice but needing some separation in their telling. The first—that of internal politics and procedures—is one of unique chaos in year one, followed by unusual improvement through leadership shifts at the National Security Council and the State Department. The second—that of policy—revolves around the continuing tension between the campaign commitment to fundamental change—the Reaganite program—and the pressures for compromise that the real world dependably brings.

Linked to each story is a mandate Reagan could plausibly claim. One is a mandate for coherence, reflecting the near-universal bipartisan judgment that Carter foreign policy-making had been a mess. The second, more controversial, concerns policy content, belief in the need for a militant, robust campaign against a worldwide Soviet/Communist threat. The policy story is the more important, yet it was both disrupted and postponed by the personality clashes of the first seventeen Reagan months. Thus the internal political account will be presented first here.

The Promise of Coherence

The present Administration has been unable to speak with one voice in foreign policy. This must change. My administration will restore leadership to U.S. foreign policy by organizing it in a more coherent way.

An early priority will be to make structural changes in the foreign policymaking machinery so that the Secretary of State will be the President's principal spokesman and adviser.

The National Security Council will once again be the coordinator of the policy process. Its mission will be to assure that the President receives an orderly, balanced flow of information and analysis. The National Security Adviser will work closely in teamwork with the Secretary of State and the other members of the Council.

This promise was Point One of Reagan's foreign policy address of October 19, 1980. It was part of a speech aimed at foreign policy reassurance, reaching for the center, rebutting the notion of Ronald Reagan as a threat to peace. It was an easy promise because it played upon broad dissatisfaction with Jimmy Carter and Zbigniew Brzezinski, and because it reflected the standard prescription of specialists in foreign policy-making.[1] But for those who had studied Ronald Reagan as a political executive, it also seemed a plausible one. He had been, to paraphrase Lou Cannon, the great delegator,[2] one who set goals but gave trusted aides considerable leeway in deciding how these goals could best be accomplished. He was most unlikely to immerse himself in policy detail in the Carter—or Kennedy—manner. Thus he would need a Dean Acheson, a strong secretary of state whose primary allegiance would be to the president, but who was willing and able to take on a large share of the leadership burden. This need became all the more clear as the president-elect determined to give overriding priority to economic policy during his first year, a goal that would preoccupy his personal staff as well.

The man he named secretary, Alexander Haig, seemed a plausible choice. He was a tested veteran of several administrations, with his controversial White House staff service to Kissinger and Nixon followed by success in the diplomatically demanding post of NATO commander. His known views, hewing to the hard line, qualified him to be Jesse Helms's candidate to head off George Shultz. It did not hurt Haig on the right when Richard Nixon was quoted in admiration: "The meanest, toughest s.o.b. I ever knew, but he'll be a helluva secretary of state." And this was nicely balanced by the European connections and ties to other experienced Kissinger protégés.

Haig therefore seemed a good bet to press for Reaganite goals substantively and to be responsive to presidential needs politically. He seemed almost certain to play, astutely, the strong hand he was initially given. Instead, he became the central player in a curious, unantici- pated public drama, and engaged in running battles with virtually all his senior colleagues, with the president seeming not to know or care.

Haig's impulse toward self-destruction was evident from the start. His sound performance at the marathon Foreign Relations Committee confirmation hearings was undercut by his brittle, confrontational style and the personal anxiety it exposed. More important was his mishandling of White House relations. Haig's connection to the pres- ident was new and thin. He had impressed Reagan in two long, pre- election conversations. But they had—it appears—very little serious communication on either substance or process between the election and Inauguration Day, when Haig delivered to the hands of White House aides Edwin Meese and James Baker a soon-to-be infamous draft presidential memo, through which Reagan was to grant him and the State Department unparalleled formal authority over the other foreign affairs agencies.

The precedent was a secret memo Henry Kissinger had done twelve years before. The crucial difference was that Richard Nixon had asked for it, and approved it privately *before* others were brought in. Reagan, by contrast, operated collegially. When Meese consulted the other senior foreign policy players, including Secretary of Defense and long- time Reagan intimate Caspar Weinberger, the reaction was predict- able, as were the press leaks. Meese then brokered a curious com- promise. Haig, Weinberger, and CIA Director William Casey were given coordinating responsibility within their spheres, but no senior person (short of Reagan) had any clear means of coordinating *them*. Meese then developed an even more curious mechanism: a crisis man- agement committee headed by a man who was not a full-time foreign policy player—Vice-President George Bush.

Having initiated in January a game he could not win, Haig pro- ceeded in March to raise the stakes. On a visit to Capitol Hill, he publicly criticized the crisis committee Reagan was about to announce. He was rewarded by an equally public White House rebuff. Reagan quickly approved a terse press statement not only affirming the Bush chairmanship but omitting any mention of the secretary of state and insisting that "management of crises has traditionally—and appro- priately—been done within the White House."

Seldom had a secretary of state been so visibly humiliated by the president upon whose confidence he depended. And just six days later, in the wake of the attempt on Reagan's life, Haig did himself enormous further damage with his nervous White House declaration, "I am in charge here." In the fifteen months that followed, Haig seemed to be fighting intermittent (and usually inconclusive) skirmishes with almost everybody else: Weinberger, national security assistant Richard Allen, ambassador to the United Nations Jeane Kirkpatrick, the ambassador to Saudi Arabia, and the White House trio of Meese, Baker, and Michael Deaver, not to mention Jesse Helms on Capitol Hill.

Haig's peremptory, combative, "politics of exclusion" style seemed as out of place in the Reagan administration as it had been in place under Nixon and Kissinger. Taking a phrase from Paul Nitze's 1960 testimony to Senator Henry Jackson's subcommittee on national policy machinery, he upset key presidential aides by dubbing himself Reagan's foreign policy "vicar," and being so crowned on the cover of *Time*. He seemed unable to grasp the notion that the way to build Reagan's confidence was to work with, not against, the man's trusted aides.

Yet Haig hung in there, fought battle after policy battle, and won a surprising number. He never attained either the clear leadership mandate he so coveted, or the Presidential confidence that was its prerequisite. Yet he was still the most important single foreign policy figure in the administration through the spring of 1982, Ronald Reagan included.

For if the president had trouble doing with Haig, he had difficulty also doing without him. One reason was that Reagan had delivered on the other half of his October promise of "structural changes," by cutting back on the role and visibility of the assistant for national security affairs. Meese got the prestigious, Kissinger-Brzezinski corner office, while Richard Allen was moved downstairs to the Bundy-Rostow basement and placed under Meese in White House organization charts.

There was much to be said for this formal downgrading. The high-profile willful assistant had become a major foreign policy problem, causing McGeorge Bundy to write during the transition that Reagan was "entitled to the comfort of knowing that there is one place where less would be more—in the job of Assistant for National Security Affairs."[3] The problem was that the low-profile prescription presupposed a strong secretary of state with presidential confidence. It also required that the person holding the White House national security job be (1) primarily a manager with (2) a direct operational relationship with the president and (3) the trust of the other senior policy players.

Richard Allen satisfied none of these criteria. His governmental experience had been limited and unimpressive: a few unhappy months on the 1969 NSC staff, being pushed aside and labeled a right-wing ideologue by Henry Kissinger (a period in which Haig was making himself Kissinger's trusted aide), and a brief tour as deputy assistant to the president for international economic policy two years later. Though Allen had served as Reagan's chief campaign adviser for foreign policy in 1980 and 1976 (and indeed as Nixon's in 1968), he had never really penetrated the Reagan inner circle. In giving him the job, Reagan and Meese were following the path of least resistance, rewarding a faithful servant and—by extension—the campaign entourage. But the choice made no operational sense. In fact, it was an egregious blunder once Haig was designated secretary. Was there any reason to believe that the requisite trust could develop between Allen and a man who helped to ease him out twelve years before?

Allen did not reduce the size of the NSC staff (Bundy had suggested a 60 percent cut). His support group of substantive professionals numbered, like Brzezinski's, in the upper thirties. But it was almost universally judged the weakest since the Truman administration, a mixture of ideologues like Harvard historian Richard Pipes, conservative academics, and career military and civilian officials. With a few exceptions, it was not a staff that seemed well suited to the task of interagency process management, and its weakness was compounded by Allen's secretive operational style, his reluctance to share information. At times the staff's main function seemed to be to offer a sympathetic hearing for conservatives who found administration foreign policy not Reaganite enough.

With Allen's weak presidential connection, Haig on shaky probation, and the president and his political aides preoccupied with economic policy, the stage was set for protracted, visible infighting that made the Carter administration look orderly by comparison. Secretary of Defense Caspar Weinberger was more active on foreign policy than any of his predecessors since Robert McNamara—and took unilateralist and Arabist lines at sharp variance with Haig's Europeanist, pro-Israel stances. By the end of the year, Brzezinski could credibly label the Reagan system "the worst ever," a blend of "chaos and confusion."[4] Frequent but unfocused National Security Council discussions angered Haig, but did not unduly constrain him. The White House trio intervened selectively on issues with political implications—

like grain sales to Russia—and on those causing presidential embarrassment. Told in October by *New York Times* correspondent Leslie Gelb that other officials saw an issue reaching the White House as akin to its entering a black hole, Meese responded, "Exactly. That's the way we like it." Few shared his satisfaction.

Haig had filled key subordinate positions at State, in the main, with conservative establishment professionals: some, like Lawrence Eagleburger, Thomas Enders, and John Holdridge, from the career foreign service; others, like Richard Burt and Chester Crocker, from the broader policy community. Jesse Helms and his ideological allies cried betrayal, and Helms fought a delaying action at several stages of the confirmation process against many of the appointments. He succeeded in slowing action in the White House, the Senate Foreign Relations Committee, and on the Senate floor, as neither Reagan, Foreign Relations Chairman Percy, or Majority Leader Baker showed any zest for taking him on. Yet in the end, Haig generally prevailed.

The Defense Department, however, had a stronger sprinkling of ideological hard-liners. Weinberger had insisted on seasoned professional manager Frank Carlucci as his deputy, rebuffing transition defense specialist (and Evans and Novak hero) William Van Cleave in the process. But with Fred Iklé as undersecretary for policy, John Lehman as secretary of the navy, and Richard Perle, arch-foe of détente, as assistant secretary for international security policy, the dominant civilian view at Defense was strongly disposed toward confronting the Soviets and shaking up the allies. The Joint Chiefs of Staff became, by comparison, a moderate voice, particularly on arms control and the need to retain SALT II constraints on Soviet strategic weaponry. The Arms Control and Disarmament Agency, for its part, became home to three prominent SALT II critics with overlapping mandates and an uncertain relationship: Director Eugene Rostow, START negotiator Edward Rowny, and Intermediate Nuclear Force negotiator Paul Nitze.

The weaknesses in the system were illustrated by the handling of the AWACS sale to Saudi Arabia, which a series of blunders made into Reagan's most visible foreign policy venture of 1981.[5]

After considerable Saudi pressure and air force advocacy, the proposal to sell advanced surveillance aircraft was well under way by January 1981. The Carter administration offered to take on the initial burden of presenting it to Congress; Reagan's men refused. They then let the Defense Department pin down the details before any comprehensive political review was conducted, foreign or domestic.

Reagan and his aides accepted the Weinberger recommendation to proceed with the sale, together with his laughable estimate that at most thirty-five senators would vote no. In deciding to go ahead, they rebuffed Haig, who had a far more realistic and pessimistic assessment, and who had been working out Israeli agreement to a different sales package. When Senator Howard Baker warned of serious political problems, the White House wisely deferred formal notification on the sale. But in its determination to keep the spotlight on the economic program, the White House ordered State Department officials not to argue the substantive case on Capitol Hill, thus ceding the policy battlefield to the Israelis and their well-organized U.S. allies for several crucial months. By June 24, fifty-four senators were on public record against the sale; by August, preliminary vote counts suggested sixty-five opposed and twelve in favor.

No one the president trusted seemed to understand either the policy issue or its domestic politics. Weinberger never caught on to the latter; Haig, whose October 1 Senate testimony suggested he had a clear grasp of both, remained on shaky probation in the White House and was, by personality, a mixed asset on the Hill. Allen, assigned lobbying leadership at one point, did little apparent to advance the cause. Instead, he got into a public wrangle with Haig over whether to seek Saudi concessions to Senate sentiment, and who should do the seeking. The fact that Reagan personally was able to avert an unprecedented and humiliating defeat could not conceal the fact that he had been forced into making an arms sale his most visible foreign policy involvement of the year. In complete contrast to his economic and budget program, Reagan seemed to have lost all control of his foreign policy agenda. The administration seemed to have created the worst of possible worlds for itself: enough hawkish rhetoric to send waves of alarm around the world and nourish growing domestic opposition; not enough coherence, priority, or persistence in its focus to bring any policy initiative to fruition.

In 1982 things changed for the better—at least in management of process. Reagan seized opportunities to replace first his national security assistant, then his secretary of state. Each replacement in turn moved effectively to dampen internal infighting and to engage the president more usefully and productively in the policy process. By September the Reagan administration could claim a rare combination—a secretary of state leading the formulation process for the president and generous in sharing the credit, and a national security assistant giving priority to interagency management and credible with all of the key policy players. Not entirely by coincidence, it had produced its most notable foreign policy product, a timely peace initiative for the Middle East.

The first key personnel switch, of course, was the replacement of Allen by William P. Clark. It is unnecessary to recount in detail the bizarre events that preceded this switch: how a draft Jack Anderson article caused Reagan to summon Haig and Allen to the White House woodshed a year and a day after his landslide election victory; how the man who had promised a "disappearing act" upon his appointment in December 1980 ended up with a major media controversy a year later over his acceptance of an envelope containing $1000 from a Japanese journalist; how the White House, which had planned to replace Allen before these furors broke, let the dispute fester, with the national security assistant on leave, through the December of martial law in Poland. Most important is that, on January 4, Reagan did seek and accept Allen's resignation and designate Clark as his successor. And in a reversal of the organizational downgrading of 1981, spokesman Larry Speakes declared that Clark would have a "direct reporting relationship to the president."

Clark was the same man who, as nominee for deputy secretary of state, had embarrassed himself and the administration by the foreign policy ignorance he exhibited to the Senate Foreign Relations Committee. This performance won him more negative votes on the Senate floor than all of Jesse Helms's targets combined. While he did not alter this substantive reputation in his year at State, he did prove indispensable in connecting Haig to Reagan and his trio. Beginning with the time he preceded Meese as Reagan's gubernatorial chief of staff, Clark had worked with and for all of the chief foreign policy players—Haig, Weinberger, and most important, Reagan himself. In fact, his claim on presidential confidence seemed more solid and secure than that of any of his NSC predecessors.

With Clark at the White House, things changed. To signal the new strength at the NSC, the White House released within eight days National Security Decision Directive No. 2, formally establishing Reagan's "National Security Council Structure," which had been sitting around in near-final draft since Meese pulled it together in early 1981. Visible infighting was curbed and punished, as were careless public statements: When an "official on Weinberger's plane" between Jordan and West Germany talked of the need to balance or "redirect" American policy away from Israel in February 1982, the secretary of defense was rebuked and his next proposed trip deferred. Formal National Security study directives were issued, something Allen had not accomplished. Clark led in setting the terms of reference of the studies, and while State took the lead in conducting most of them, other departments participated. NSC staff monitored the process and the conclusions went before the full National Security Council. (As in most other administrations, however, the actual policy impact of these studies seems to have been limited.)

The NSC staff was strengthened also. Clark brought from State a strong deputy, Robert C. McFarlane, and engaged an effective senior consultant in former air force secretary Thomas C. Reed. But the rest of the staff remained a notch or two below in reputation and effectiveness. Thus the strongest criticism of Clark—that he lacked substantive understanding and had not compensated for this by the quality of his senior subordinates—carried continuing weight. Over time, intertwined with gradual replacements of individuals, Clark did carry out a significant, and little-noticed, expansion in the number of staff. As of September 1982 the NSC staff had grown to forty-nine substantive professionals, more than at any time since Henry Kissinger.

Clark continued the Reagan reliance on use of the formal National Security Council, with a frequency not seen since Eisenhower. Meetings were held once or twice a week when the President was in town—more than eighty by August 1982.

Most significant, Clark's presence made Ronald Reagan a regular player in the foreign policy game. He briefed the president, usually with staff assistance, sometimes bringing Haig or Weinberger along as well. He read Reagan's sentiments and signals and tried to make policy reflect them. For the first time, there was a man in the White House who could link policy and politics, the formal and the informal, the president and his senior cabinet advisers. There remained the inevitable gap between senior advisers and their subordinates in the agencies, but Meese's black hole was no more.

Initially, the new Clark role served to strengthen Haig. The secretary had, at last, a senior ally and conduit in the White House, a man who had grown to respect him at State. And Haig seemed to be winning an increasing number of bureaucratic battles. His proposals to promote Walter Stoessel and Eagleburger were dislodged from the White House and sent formally as nominations to Capitol Hill, where they won quick approval. Haig was winning also on constraining Taiwan arms sales, on supporting Britain in the war for the Falklands, and on the U.S. negotiating position on strategic arms. The U.S. reaction to martial law in Poland was also limited and responsive to European concerns—another tilt in Haig's direction.

By all accounts, Haig's personal relationship with Reagan remained shaky. But he seemed, through Clark, to be achieving a sort of second-best solution—a presidential connection once removed. Most analysts in the spring of 1982 concluded that the secretary of state had, in spite of everything, emerged as the dominant foreign policy figure, and that his pragmatism—so infuriating to conservatives old and neo—was prevailing on issue after issue, in region after region. But Haig's base was fragile, to say the least. In June, the month of the president's trip to Europe, it suddenly collapsed.

For the White House, the trip was to be Ronald Reagan's international coming-out party: He would emerge as a respected world figure, the leader of the Free World on American (and European) television screens, with popularity and stature enhanced. For Haig and his State associates, the trip was to climax a sustained effort (described in detail subsequently) to rebuild alliance confidence, beginning with the zero-option speech on theater nuclear weapons in November, continuing through the dialogue on Poland (and avoidance of polarizing responses) in the winter and spring, and through the Eureka speech outlining the president's START program in May.

It turned out to be neither. Reagan had barely landed when the State Department provided one major embarrassment—a declaration that the United States had intended to vote differently (and less in Britain's favor) on a Falkland Islands UN Security Council resolution, but the instruction from Europe had reached the U.S. delegation too late. Haig compounded the political damage by explaining he had personally made the decision while Reagan slept, and that the reason he had not called Ambassador Jeane Kirkpatrick directly was that "you don't talk to a company commander when you have a corps in between." (This could not have pleased Reagan, who liked Kirkpatrick and listened frequently to her counsel.) The over-scheduled president went through the summit meeting, by all reports, without seriously pressing the critical (to him) issue of European participation in construction of the Soviet natural gas pipeline. Nor, to Clark's (and presumably Reagan's) increasing frustration, was the State Department successful in selling its approach—reluctant acquiescence on the pipeline issue in exchange for alliance agreement on common, much tighter credit policies for Soviet and East European trade.

If this were not enough, the Israeli thrust into Lebanon embarrassed the president, preempted his media coverage, and further exposed tensions within his senior team. Haig, the senior adviser most sympathetic toward Israel, won a relatively restrained U.S. response, but lost when he proposed to fly directly to the region and mediate. The fact that the nation he favored was believed to be deceiving the

United States about its plans and objectives further weakened Haig's position.

Meanwhile, at home, administration foreign policy was under broad conservative attack. *Commentary* editor Norman Podhoretz proclaimed his disillusionment, while the cover of *Conservative Digest* featured a fading image of Reagan and the caption, "Where's the Best of Me?"

Eleven days after the Versailles summit, Reagan delivered a rather strident anti-Soviet speech to the U.N. General Assembly, a shift from his more conciliatory rhetoric in Eureka and Bonn. One day later, following a National Security Council review conducted while Haig was meeing Andrei Gromyko in New York, the president rejected State Department counsel and decided to impose sanctions on Europe-based firms (including American subsidiaries) that were using U.S.-licensed technology in their participation in the pipeline project. European outrage was vocal and immediate.

A week later, Reagan made the surprise announcement that he had accepted Haig's resignation and named George P. Shultz as his successor. Washington immediately debated whether Haig had jumped or was pushed. The emerging evidence supported the second interpretation. Was the cause policy or personality? Haig insisted it was the former—he was leaving because the administration "was shifting from that careful course" he and Reagan "had laid out" when they began. But he did not elaborate, and though the sudden switch on the pipeline gave substance to Haig's case, the personality explanation was more convincing. A man whose personal base was always shaky finally lost the support of Clark, his last ally, and this proved decisive.

Shultz was a natural Reagan secretary of state, as suited to the low-key, collegial style as Haig was unsuited. It remains a mystery why he was not named in 1980, right-wing opposition notwithstanding. One plausible story is that Reagan wrongly believed he wasn't interested, so the offer was never made. In any case, Shultz lost no time in displaying a cool strength. In his Senate confirmation hearings he was solid though deferential, highlighting the president's role as primary foreign policy-maker, avoiding personal confrontations without substantive retreat. After his unanimous Senate confirmation he proved, as he had under Nixon, to be the quintessential inside operator, a man who listened, sought consensus, shared credit, but nonetheless moved things forward. He touched congressional and interest group bases. He reinforced special envoy Philip Habib during the complex talks over PLO withdrawal from Lebanon. He developed a dramatic *Reagan* initiative to be unveiled after that withdrawal was carried out.

The Haig style was to seize the limelight, fend off rivals, decide personally what should be done and persuade the president, one-on-one if possible, to go along. Shultz saw himself, by contrast, as the leader in constructing, with and for the president, administration-wide approaches to policy problems, and then leading in their implementation.

With Shultz and Clark, Reagan foreign policy-making was transformed. One would have preferred, of course, a Shultz with more prior exposure to political-military issues, and a Clark better versed in *all* issues. But for the first time the administration had a plausible, workable combination of foreign policy personalities and roles. To future presidents, Reagan offered an example of the gains from changing a team that clearly was not working out. Kennedy reportedly worried that replacing Dean Rusk would be an admission of initial error; Carter never faced up to the incompatibility of Brzezinski and Vance. Reagan, by contrast, showed that a timely switch could bring benefits many times the short-run costs. There was even the possibility that the Reagan administration, after a uniquely shaky start, might achieve that combination oft-prescribed but seldom attained—a strong and effective secretary of state working in tandem with a low-profile, managerial national security assistant to develop and execute presidential foreign policy.

But this change simply raised anew the question of who, in his foreign policy, Ronald Reagan was turning out to be: the mobilizer/polarizer summoning the nation and the world to pursue his noble causes, or the pragmatic political adjuster, the personal peacemaker. Clark, Shultz, and the pressure of world events had brought Reagan into the foreign policy action in 1982. Which ways would he seek to move events? In which directions had he already done so?

The Promise of "Conservative" Change

"Vote Republican, for a Change." The catchy campaign slogan understated the goals of the candidate and his committed followers, for they were running not only against the Democrats, but against "failed" establishment policies dating back at least twenty years. On foreign policy, this meant not just Jimmy Carter but Henry Kissinger, a *bête noire* of the Republican Right and a rewarding Reagan target in his 1976 challenge to Gerald Ford.

Did the 1980 election then constitute a "mandate" for Reagan to change foreign policy in his followers' preferred directions? The answer must be mixed. Reagan certainly did not carry forty-four states because of his international stands. Polls in fact gave President Carter a thin overall margin on foreign policy, and highlighted the distinction "between peace issues, which benefited Carter, and defense issues, where Reagan held the advantage."[6] In his fall campaign Reagan played defensive on foreign policy, successfully blunting the Carter effort to portray him as a reckless man likely to start a war. It was on economic issues that he took the offensive, and his overwhelming victory margin seems attributable mainly to public dismay about the economy, and rejection of Jimmy Carter.

Still, the trend of American opinion on international issues was definitely running in Reagan's direction. Support for increased defense spending grew steadily, from an average of 14 percent in 1974 polls to 60 percent in 1980, though Americans continued to be most reluctant actually to employ those forces they favored strengthening.[7] Anti-Soviet sentiment increased, as did opposition to SALT II and the belief that the United States was falling behind the Soviet Union in military strength. Among foreign policy activists, the shift of the initiative to the conservative side was even more dramatic from 1975 to 1980.

Perhaps most important, Americans who elected Reagan had no reason to doubt where he stood. He had fought the "giveaway" of the Panama Canal. The Carter foreign policy of "vacillation, appeasement and aimlessness" was bringing dishonor and humiliation "all over the world." The Vietnam War was a "noble cause," which our government had been "afraid to win." SALT II was "fatally flawed," and one reason was that "we have been unilaterally disarming at the same time we're negotiating." Détente was an "illusion"; the United States had to mobilize its allies in the worldwide struggle against "godless communism."

So if Reagan did not have a foreign policy mandate, he did have a clear opening, an opportunity to press his tough line and see how far he could get.

What, more specifically, did this line consist of? There was, needless to say, no uniform policy stance, even among devoted "Reaganites." Nonetheless, one can glean from the wealth of recent "conservative" foreign policy writing and rhetoric five central, overlapping convictions.

The first and most important was strident anti-Sovietism. The relationship with Russia was overwhelmingly one of confrontation. And while the Soviets had been engaging in the "greatest arms buildup in history" and a world political-military offensive in Angola, Ethiopia, Yemen, and Afghanistan, the United States had been abstaining, naively hooked on a discredited détente. We were losing the competition; we should be pushing as hard as the Russians to win it. And if we did push, we could win. For the Soviet Union, formidable on its military surface, was rotten in its economic and social core.

The second was ideological anticommunism. Successive administrations had been selling out our longtime friends on Taiwan in favor of ties with the mainland, something that could only undermine other small allies' faith in the United States. More generally, we should take a tough line with regimes on the ideological left—Cuba, Angola, Nicaragua—rather than try to accommodate or buy them as Carter had.

Third was a priority to military and paramilitary policy instruments—our own arms buildup, military aid and arms sales, covert action—over economic instruments or negotiated international regimes like the Law of the Sea Treaty.

Fourth was a tendency toward polarizing approaches to regional situations—supporting the antirevolutionaries in Central America or the "rightist" rebel Jonas Savimbi in Angola; forging an anti-Soviet consensus in the Middle East; favoring right-minded conservatives over suspect Socialists in Europe.

Finally there was the overriding conviction that American world preeminence should and could be restored. Our decline had been self-inflicted; it was not the product of immutable trends like the diffusion of economic strength and strategic technology. Therefore it could be reversed, and America could lead again as she had in the first two postwar decades. And this built into the Reaganites a strong unilateralist tendency, to act alone if allies could not move, even though the president's own commitment to our allies remained strong.

These then were the basic Reagan tendencies. But the practical problem was, as Clark later put it, "the conversion of that philosophy to policy."[8] There would be strong foreign and domestic pressures to compromise. And while there was little doubt about the sincerity of Reagan's commitment to foreign policy change, there was every reason to doubt his seriousness—whether he would, personally and persistently, follow through or back others who did so on his behalf. He seemed to expect that it would be simple, if not easy—a matter of persisting in principled actions and stands that heartened our friends and disheartened our foes. And the Republican platform on which he had run suggested a certain reluctance to pay costs: "The United States faces the most serious challenge to its survival in the two centuries of its existence"; yet we should cut taxes, lift the grain embargo against the Soviet Union, and abolish draft registration.

How then would the president balance philosophical conviction against situational circumstances and pressures? Would Clark's stated goal be realized? Or would Reagan vindicate instead Jimmy Carter's observation of his early 1982 foreign policy: "He's comin' toward me all the time"?[9] Assuming some pragmatic adjustment, on what issues was it most likely? One plausible prediction (henceforth Hypothesis I) was that on the big issues—NATO, U.S.-Soviet relations, arms control, China, the Middle East—the stakes would be so visibly high, and the domestic and international pressures so great, that the Reagan administration would be pulled, in Tom Hughes's phrase, "up from Reaganism."[10] In peripheral regions dear to Jesse Helms—southern Africa, or Central America, or the U.S. declaratory posture toward the Third World—the administration would have greater leeway. On these issues, "Reagan could be Reagan." Or he might strike a pragmatic political balance, ostentatiously espousing ideological goals in the peripheral areas so that he could more easily go centrist in the center.

An alternate prediction—Hypothesis II—was the opposite. The big issues would get greatest presidential, NSC, and congressional attention. They would be the most visible politically, and thus most influenced by Reagan himself. Reagan believed in a tough line on Russia; so did virtually everybody in his camp. The NSC attracts "in and out" aides politically identified with a new administration's "mandate." On the central issues, therefore, above all Soviet relations, Reaganite ideology was most likely to dominate. The established agencies, by contrast, would control the day-to-day action on peripheral issues, so greater continuity with Carter would manifest itself there.

Both hypotheses could not prove true. In all likelihood, the Reagan experience would prove more complicated than either. In early 1981, the author of this essay thought Hypothesis I would prove closer to the mark. But to form a basis for judgment of Reagan policy at midterm, we turn now to an assessment of administration experience in three issue areas: China, Central America, and (most extensive) the "central front" of dealings with NATO and the Soviet Union.

China, Taiwan, and Arms Sales[11]

Ronald Reagan's first foreign policy crisis came in August 1980, a month after his nomination. His repeated call for restoring "official" U.S.-Taiwan relations had generated alarm in Beijing. Now, while sending off vice-presidential candidate George Bush (and Richard Allen) on a mission of reassurance, Reagan sought to clarify matters. He was not advocating full diplomatic relations with Taiwan, but simply a liaison office like the one we had had on the mainland before 1979 (which Bush had headed). Beijing reacted with outrage: It was "brazen and absurd" for Reagan to propose something that the normalization accord of December 1978 had ruled out, at Chinese insistence. He had "insulted one billion Chinese people."

The Chinese gave Bush an icy reception. On his return to the United States he found Reagan repeating the "official relations" line once again, and felt it necessary to contradict his senior running mate. With the press playing up the story, and all its negative implications about the candidate's policy competence, Reagan backed down. He had made misstatements, and would be satisfied with the status quo: nongovernmental dealings under the Taiwan Relations Act of 1979. Covering his retreat, he promised not to "pretend, as Carter does, that the relationship we now have, enacted by our Congress, is not official." But he withdrew his pledge to change it, foreshadowing his March 1981 decision that the formally nongovernmental American Institute in Taiwan would not be upgraded. A major campaign "flap" then receded.

Forced to choose between his personal and ideological sympathy toward Taiwan, and the need to preserve tolerable relations with the mainland, Reagan opted—reluctantly—for the latter. So he would also two years later on Taiwan arms sales, notwithstanding cries of betrayal from the Right. But it was not an easy choice. At times during the internal U.S. policy struggle, officials at the State Department seemed to consider the president almost as volatile and sensitive on the issue as the Chinese: If the issue was not treated with extraordinary care Reagan might decide against them, obliterating twelve years of painstakingly negotiated progress with the mainland.

The central question of Taiwan sales was, of course, inherited from Carter. In their December 1978 normalization arrangement the two countries had finessed it: The United States was going to continue sales, to which Beijing "absolutely would not agree." In the Taiwan Relations Act Congress had—to Beijing's acute unhappiness—strengthened and formalized the U.S. pledge to meet Taiwan's needs for defensive weapons. Asian anticommunism was a venerable conservative cause dating from the days of William Knowland and the "loss" of China, and right-wing senators like Barry Goldwater and Jesse Helms were anti-Communist at least as much as they were anti-Soviet. They pressed for sales of more and better weapons as one way that the new administration might tilt the balance of policy in Taipei's direction. So hoped Taiwanese, who had danced in the streets upon Reagan's election, and whose officials were initially offered tickets to his inaugural celebration. So feared the mainlanders, for whom Reagan had raised the political visibility of the issue and generated doubts about the steadfastness of American commitments.

The prime issue for 1981 was the FX, an advanced fighter aircraft being produced especially for export. This represented an improvement over the F5E currently being provided to (in fact, coproduced with) Taiwan. Those sympathetic to offering it included White House aides like Allen with long-standing ties with Taipei, and perhaps Ronald Reagan himself. Secretary Haig, who consistently opposed the sale, announced during his June mainland visit that the United States would now be receptive to arms orders from Beijing. His hope, apparently, was that this might soften its resistance on Taiwan sales in general, if not on the FX. The Chinese rejected the bait, deferring concrete discussion of arms purchases, and making it clear that they would downgrade bilateral relations if an FX offer to Taiwan went forward. Congressman Stephen Solarz's House Foreign Affairs Subcommittee on Asian and Pacific Affairs tried to give weight to the mainstream consensus, sending Reagan a unanimous bipartisan letter declaring it would be militarily unnecessary, and politically "a mistake to sell the FX, or any other advanced combat aircraft to Taiwan, at this time." Indeed, no one thought Taipei needed the plane to defend itself against any near-term PRC threat. In December Haig pressed the issue, taking advantage of Allen's terminal leave and the congressional recess. Finally, in January 1982 the president opted for the State position—no FX. He did decide simultaneously on substantial further coproduction of the F5E. Assistant Secretary John Holdridge flew to China to explain and defend the decision.

For Reagan it was a substantial and painful concession, but by the time he made it China had already upped the ante. "It is conceivable," wrote A. Doak Barnett in retrospect, "that if this decision had been announced months earlier it might have forestalled the Chinese decision to broaden the issue and increase pressure on Washington."[12] But this was impossible, for administration divisions, Reagan's sentiments, and the fear of damage on the Right made such timeliness impossible—Reagan would decide against Taiwan only if the choice could not be postponed. In any case, Premier Zhao Ziyang and Foreign Minister Huang Hua had already pressed Reagan and Haig in October to set a termination date for *all* U.S. arms sales to Taiwan. This initiative was paralleled by dramatic new mainland overtures to

Chinese on that island. Beijing proposed "talks" on a "reciprocal basis" pointing toward reunification, which could allow Taiwan "a high degree of autonomy," including the right to "retain its armed forces." And it was accompanied as well by numerous signals that China might be reversing the movement of the late seventies toward a closer alignment with the United States, even moving toward rapprochement with the Soviet Union.

Reagan could not, of course, agree to a cut-off date—law, policy, and politics all stood in the way. Indeed, he was already taking considerable heat from the Right for his denial of the FX. Jesse Helms charged that aides were driving Reagan to "imitate" the "disastrous foreign policies of Carter and Kissinger." Goldwater declared that he was "bending to Peking's demands. I must call attention to the fact that the President of the United States has not kept his campaign promises regarding Taiwan." But Reagan nonetheless agreed to discussions with Beijing aiming at some general resolution of the Taiwan arms sales question. And to facilitate their rapid conclusion, he deferred formal congressional notification concerning the F5E.

The talks dragged on through spring and early summer, notwithstanding a friendly February exchange of letters to mark the tenth anniversary of the Shanghai Communiqué, and notwithstanding U.S. willingness, expressed early in the negotiations, to keep the level of sales below that of 1980 and link their reduction and elimination to a reconciliation between Taiwan and the mainland. But Beijing remained extraordinarily stubborn, and threatened a downgrading of relations unless the matter were resolved to Chinese satisfaction. So as Michel Oksenberg puts it, "The future course of Sino-American relations literally hung in the balance"[13] as Reagan sent successive letters, and Bush and Senator Howard Baker made important visits. The Defense Department worried about the military costs of a break with the PRC, whose border tied down so many Soviet forces. Haig felt it vital to come to terms, even if this meant something very close to a "date certain" for terminating the sales. Reagan resisted going this far. Taiwan attacked Reagan for ignoring "our national interests" in May, but took heart in June from the designation of Shultz, who told the Senate Foreign Relations Committee in July that he would recommend that Reagan go ahead with notifying Congress on the F5Es.

But Haig kept pressing for a resolution, sending a strong options memo to Reagan several days after his resignation. Conservatives were outraged by reports he was winning what Evans and Novak labeled "a victory from the political grave."[14] A coalition of twenty-eight New Right leaders warned of an "extremely acrimonious" political backlash from "millions of conservative supporters" if the president agreed to any Taiwan cutoff. "There is a sense of anger over this that I haven't seen on any other issue," said Paul Weyrich, president of Coalition for America.

Finally, on August 17, a joint U.S.-Chinese communiqué was issued, one that fell somewhat short of Chinese demands. The United States government denied any "long-term policy of arms sales to Taiwan," stating that such sales "*will* not exceed, either in qualitative or in quantitative terms, the level of those supplied in recent years," and that "it *intends* to reduce gradually its sales of arms to Taiwan, leading over a period of time to a final resolution" (emphasis added). This statement was loosely linked to a Chinese declaration that its "peaceful reunification" initiative toward Taiwan represented a "fundamental policy." This made it possible for the administration to claim that its reduction pledge was conditional on continuation of that policy. And the commitment was balanced by several specific assurances conveyed to Taiwan a month earlier (e.g., no terminal date, no revision of the Taiwan Relations Act) and by the August 19 transmission to Congress of the notification on F5Es. Conservative reaction was critical, but not as harsh as might have been expected. Reagan insisted, "There has been no retreat by me. We will continue to arm Taiwan." Senator S. I. Hayakawa, the semanticist, commented that any agreement with such "ambiguities" (e.g., the meaning of "final resolution") could not be all bad. But to Barry Goldwater it was a "bad agreement"; Taiwan was "one more little country we have double-crossed."

The Reagan administration had been driven, painfully, to a policy very much in the Nixon-Ford-Kissinger-Carter mainstream. Indeed, it had gone further in pledging arms sales limits than any of its predecessors. But pressure from the Right, connecting to Reagan's own philosophy, deprived the administration of the political leeway that Richard Nixon's boldness had created (and that Nixon and Jimmy Carter had exploited). How much Reagan's ideology and immobility contributed to increased Chinese pressure is impossible to determine. We may also never know whether earlier decisive action would have lessened the chances of a development that no Reaganite wanted—a Chinese shift away from Washington and toward a thaw with Moscow. But whatever the cause, the summer and fall of 1982 brought increasing evidence of just such a movement.

El Salvador and Central America

If Taiwan was Ronald Reagan's own ideological albatross, Central America was Alexander Haig's. From the outset of his tenure, he defined the problem as "a very clearly delineated Soviet-Cuban strategy to create Marxist-Leninist regimes in Central America." Here the United States had to "draw the line," perhaps even "go to the source." On matters concerning China or Europe, Haig might have been the Reagan administration's "sheep in wolf's clothing." But on Central America he moved quickly to the hardest of lines.

It was not a region with which he had much previous identification. Nor did Haig's confirmation hearings give El Salvador or Nicaragua particular attention. It was, however, the part of the world where the Reaganite, Left-Right view of the world came closest to reality. Key countries really were polarized along pro- and anti-Marxist lines, and the political center was fragile or nonexistent. And it was a region where U.S. conservatives had been very much on the offensive. In the congressional trenches, Congressman Robert Bauman had pressed a relentless substantive and procedural attack in 1979 and 1980, complicating implementation of the Panama treaties and hamstringing aid to Nicaragua. Jeane Kirkpatrick, then a professor of political science at Georgetown University, had put forward a broader indictment in her November 1979 *Commentary* article, "Dictatorships and Double Standards," accusing the Carter administration of insensitivity to the threat of Castroism and Marxism, and of having "actively collaborated" in the replacement of "moderate autocrat" Anastasio Somoza with the anti-American, leftist Sandinistas. The Central American Right, bitterly anti-Carter, had cheered Reagan's victory. And as Republicans took control of the Senate, Jesse Helms, whose seniority on the Foreign Relations Committee gave him first choice of subcommittees, opted to chair Western Hemisphere affairs.

Haig doubtless, therefore, saw toughness in Central America as a way to protect his right flank: Allen and Kirkpatrick, after all, were pressing Reagan during the transition on the crucial importance of El Salvador. He may also have seen the prospect for a relatively easy, visible, early success. The January 1981 rebel offensive in El Salvador had failed. Might not this be just the time when an intensive, menacing, public campaign could move events further in the right direction, allowing credit to be claimed and giving momentum to the new administration's foreign policy worldwide, and to Haig's drive for dominance in Washington?

In its final months, the Carter administration had increased aid to the reformist military junta in El Salvador, and challenged Nicaragua about its apparent support of Salvadoran rebels. In substance, Haig's line continued this hardening trend. But the public packaging was very different.

Haig took several dramatic steps in his first month in office. Carter administration ambassador Robert E. White, who had publicly denounced activities in San Salvador by Reagan transition aides, was promptly and visibly removed. Lawrence Eagleburger, assistant secretary–designate for European affairs, was dispatched across the Atlantic to line up NATO support to halt the arms flow to the El Salvador guerrillas. Haig himself briefed congressional committees and diplomatic representatives in Washington. And a State Department White Paper was hastily produced purporting to document Soviet-Cuban-Nicaraguan participation in arming and directing the El Salvador insurgents.

The spotlight worked: El Salvador became front-page—and prime-time—news. And the reaction was immediate. But it was not what Haig had in mind. Europeans, while granting the special U.S. concern with events in our "backyard," felt he was misdiagnosing the sources of unrest and, more important, acting disproportionately to the threat. Congressmen worried about plunging into a Vietnam-like quagmire, and an administration proposal to "reprogram" a mere $5 million in military aid survived a House Appropriations subcommittee by a cliff-hanging 8–7 vote. Most important to Haig, however, must have been the sudden chill wind from the White House. Reflecting an outpouring of mail running 10–1 against the administration, and concern that El Salvador was eroding Reagan's popularity and diverting attention from the economic program that was his overriding priority, the word went out to cool it. A "senior State official" soon identified as the acting assistant secretary for inter-American affairs told the press on March 12 that *they* were exaggerating El Salvador's significance: "The story has been running five times as big as it is."

The story continued to run through 1981 and 1982, though less often on page one. And Haig continued to take the hardest line within the administration. The White House, Weinberger, and the military services all urged greater caution, fearing costs to Reagan's popularity and to support for their cherished arms buildup. But the tough posture produced neither dramatic battlefield victories nor productive negotiations. It did, however, provide an irresistible target for congressional critics of moderate-to-liberal persuasion, as the State Department wrestled with four separate strands of the problem.

One involved the strongest strain of the "Vietnam syndrome": the overwhelming public distaste for military intervention in a morally messy internal war in an obscure country. Haig's strategy required that the United States be prepared to take direct military action—for example, to interdict the flow of arms from Cuba. But reports that he was advancing such "options" fueled public opposition and military resistance to such a costly—and presumably unpopular—"sideshow." This undermined the credibility of Haig's stance in the region.

Second was the problem of proving that the Soviet-Cuban "source" was, if not the sole cause of Central American revolution, at least a prime contributor. The February 1981 State White Paper declared that the El Salvador insurgency had been "transformed into a textbook case of indirect armed aggression by communist powers through Cuba." In support of this conclusion it sought to document what Haig had already declared to be "the large flow of arms through Nicaragua into El Salvador," and the larger "effort to impose a Communist regime in Central America," involving "close coordination by Moscow, satellite capitals, and Havana, with the cooperation of Hanoi and Managua . . . a repetition of the pattern we have already seen in Angola and Ethiopia." But the White Paper was subject to scathing dissection by the *Wall Street Journal* and the *Washington Post*. Haig continued to claim "overwhelming and irrefutable" evidence that the guerrillas were under "external command and control." But the administration never succeeded in documenting its case. Its frustration was nicely illustrated in March 1982, when the State Department produced a live guerrilla who promptly denied all the international Communist connections he had been expected to confirm. The controversy continued when a September House Intelligence Subcommittee report accused the intelligence agencies—under administration pressure— of displaying "greater certainty than is warranted by the evidence."[15]

Third was the problem of legitimizing U.S. support in a country where much of the worst political violence had long come from the Right, and specifically from the military forces we were supporting. The new administration had moved immediately to expand military and economic assistance, and to relax the Carter policy of linking this aid to the curbing of political murders by government security forces. But with the support of Foreign Relations Chairman Charles Percy, the Republican Senate joined the Democratic House in conditioning further military aid on a presidential certification, to be repeated every six months, that the El Salvador government was "achieving substantial control" of its armed forces in order to end "indiscriminate torture and murder," and that it be "implementing essential economic and political reforms," holding free elections, and demonstrating a willingness to negotiate a political settlement.

By the time this proviso became law in December, the administration had long since adjusted its policy rationales to respond to these concerns. The administration insisted, in making the necessary certification in January and July 1982, that the requisite progress was

—⟶

being made despite "severe civil strife" and challenges to the land reform program. It highlighted the need for economic support in its Caribbean Basin initiative. But it was stuck with the fragility of the "democratic center" throughout Central America. This weakness was underscored dramatically in March 1982, when the Salvadoran electorate, with no left-wing candidates on the ballot, gave fewer votes to President Napoleón Duarte's Christian Democrats than to a coalition of right-wing parties led by extremist Roberto d'Aubisson.

Fourth was the dilemma of what position to take on negotiations, both within El Salvador and among regional players more broadly. The concept was popular domestically—in March 1982 the House handed the unenthusiastic administration a 396–3 vote on a "sense of Congress" resolution calling for "unconditional discussions between the major political factions in El Salvador." It was also pressed by foreign governments—Mexican, Venezuelan, European—who wanted to deescalate the conflict and demilitarize the American approach to it. There was sporadic diplomatic activity involving Haig and the Mexicans, Assistant Secretary Thomas Enders and the Sandinistas, even General Vernon Walters and Fidel Castro. But nothing durable resulted.

In the administration's defense, one had to be skeptical about how much negotiations could accomplish, given the deep and bitter divisions within and between Central American countries. At most they might help contain particular conflicts, and perhaps provide a cover for passing on to others some of the political burdens that the United States had unilaterally assumed. But the prospects were further reduced by the administration's ambivalence about the role of regional neighbors—Mexico, Venezuela—and its tendency to interpret conciliatory behavior by Cuba and Nicaragua as a sign of weakness, to which a further twist of the screw was judged the appropriate response. Such an interpretation meshed also with political convenience. What would inflame the American Right more than visible concessions to Cuba, or lifting the ban on aid to Nicaragua even if the arms flow were stanched? But if there was little administration enthusiasm for a conciliatory policy, congressional resistance made the tough line hard to sustain, especially with the president unwilling to invest his own political capital.

One effect of these conflicting pressures was to drive policy underground, into covert investments in paramilitary forces that might, for example, weaken the Sandinistas in Nicaragua if not overthrow them. Secret operations were tempting because freedom from public debate meant greater operational flexibility. Moreover, these operations were a means of acting "tough" notwithstanding Pentagon reluctance. But large operations are hard to keep confidential, and when a November *Newsweek* cover story described their scope and evolution—from an initial decision to exclude the extreme Right, pro-Somoza forces to de facto collaboration with these forces—there was a quick political reaction. By unanimous vote, Congress added an amendment to the omnibus money bill passed in December, prohibiting provision of "military equipment, military training or advice, or other support for military activities, for the purpose of overthrowing the government of Nicaragua or provoking a military exchange between Nicaragua and Honduras."

The Reagan administration had begun highlighting El Salvador as a place to prove the effectiveness of a tough, anti-Communist approach. But Haig's self-serving ideological priorities ran head-on into the economic ones that prevailed in the White House. By late 1982 the administration had moved to treating Central America as a messy, politically entangled place where one coped as best one could given severe international and domestic constraints. It moved toward the center in terms of its stance on internal Salvadoran matters. But it remained hostile-to-skeptical about negotiations with the left, and attracted to covert collaboration with the hard Right. Shultz's strategy for Washington influence, however, did not feature ostentatious toughness on Central America. Responding perhaps to this change, Assistant Secretary Enders delivered a relatively moderate speech on August 20, 1982, linking the modest progress he claimed in Central America to "the fact that we have kept our basic course under two quite different U.S. administrations," and advocating a "process of reconciliation" within and among the key Central American countries, Nicaragua included. And two months later, in a speech whose tone was criticized by the White House, U.S. Ambassador Deane Hinton denounced, in San Salvador, what he called a right-wing "mafia," "elements of the security forces" whose acts, he said, are "destroying El Salvador."

In summary, then, Reagan's Central American policy is mixed—the polarizing tendencies of the administration were moderated (and driven underground) by the domestic and international reaction, and the unwillingness of the White House to pay the political costs of perseverance. Yet unlike on China, the balance of Reagan policy remained to Carter's Right.

The Soviet Union, NATO, and Arms Control

"Our European allies, looking nervously at the growing menace from the East, turn to us for leadership and fail to find it." So Reagan characterized the interconnection of allied and adversary relations to the Republican nominating convention. The implication was that the converse also held: as he explained in his moderate October 19 television address, strong U.S. policies would bring "unity of purpose and mutual respect" among the allies, which were a prerequisite, in turn, for "a realistic and balanced policy toward the Soviet Union." A certain American trumpet would rally our friends and impress our foes.

The naiveté of this expectation did not long go unexposed, and the precipitating factor was administration reluctance to move on arms control. Reagan had promised, in that same October speech, to "immediately open negotiations on a SALT III treaty"; he would "sit down with the Soviet Union for as long as it takes to negotiate a balanced and equitable arms limitation agreement." But a more accurate indicator of early administration attitudes was what Reagan had told the Chicago Council on Foreign Relations the previous March: "We cannot negotiate arms control agreements that will slow down the Soviet military buildup as we let the Soviets move ahead of us in every category of armaments. . . . Once we clearly demonstrate to the Soviet leadership that we are determined to compete, arms control negotiations will again have a chance."

The administration wanted to establish its arms buildup first, in order to gain the leverage necessary for effective bargaining. It was, in Weinberger's words, "a necessary prerequisite." Or, as Reagan put it more colloquially in a campaign interview, "The one card that's been missing in these negotiations has been the possibility of an arms race." Given the Russians' current "superiority," they had to be faced with a choice: "our matching what we know them to have" or "a Soviet reduction to our level."

There were other reasons to wait as well. There was a fear that excessive early emphasis on arms control could undercut support for the defense program, as most conservatives believed it had in the seventies. There was a determination to make it, at most, a subordinate element in U.S. foreign and strategic policies. There was also the Reagan commitment to "linking" arms talks to Soviet world behavior, which made it logical to wait and watch for signs of moderation, especially over Poland.

Finally there was the fact that the administration had neither a strategic arms control position nor the prospect of early agreement on one. The common Reaganite view that SALT II was "fatally flawed" masked deep differences about what sort of alternative agreement— if any—the United States should seek, and about the priority and timing of such an effort. ACDA Director Eugene Rostow, one of several semicoordinated senior officials who shared responsibility in this sphere, conceded in his June 1981 confirmation hearings that March 1982 was the earliest plausible target date. "It may be that a brilliant light will strike our officials. But I don't know anyone who knows what it is yet that we want to negotiate about."

Domestically, the administration felt it could wait. Senator Percy was pushing the matter, but he was not viewed as a major force. SALT II had been discredited, the Russians were observing its terms anyway, and the nuclear freeze movement was a year away. There were militant aides within the administration who wanted to use a forthcoming SALT I consultative meeting to confront the Soviets with their long-cherished litany of alleged treaty violations. But Haig and Weinberger squelched that by the simple expedient of postponing the meeting.

But Western Europe could not wait, and it was pressure from NATO that dragged the administration, kicking and screaming at times, toward negotiations.

In the United States the political debate sometimes seemed reduced to arms controllers versus defense advocates, with only a small group of centrist heretics suggesting that both were important, even interdependent. But the Carter administration had learned, painfully, of the political and policy need to be credible in both spheres. On the Continent, responding in particular to the concerns and political needs of West German Chancellor Helmut Schmidt, the Carter administration had negotiated in December 1979 a NATO "two-track decision" on intermediate-range nuclear forces (INF). The United States would move to deploy, by 1983, 572 intermediate nuclear missiles in Germany and other allied countries, and over the same period would seek to reach an INF deal with the Soviet Union whereby this deployment might be reduced or eliminated in exchange for cutbacks in Soviet intermediate forces, especially the modern, mobile SS-20s capable of hitting Western European targets.

European leaders, facing active challenge from a growing anti-nuclear "peace" movement, needed the arms control side of this decision in order to maintain support for INF deployment within their ruling coalitions. Public attitudes were ambivalent toward nuclear defense and dependence on the United States. So were they also ambivalent, to a lesser degree, toward conventional defense, notwithstanding a considerable rise in defense spending by European NATO countries in the seventies. Schmidt had signaled his political need for a U.S. arms control commitment rather egregiously in November 1980, when he extracted a brief courtesy appointment from Reagan's transition schedulers, and used it to assure the German Bundestag that on the SALT process, Reagan's "thoughts point in the same direction" as his own. More generally most Europeans saw a need for balanced relations with the Soviet Union, for a strong military alliance but trade and arms control agreements as well. Détente was not a dirty word to them but rather a description of a complex reality, which included major two-way trade with the Warsaw Pact countries and extensive human contact, especially among Germans. But their stake in détente made even conservative Europeans very reluctant to risk current transactions in order to exert leverage on the Soviet Union, even on matters like Poland.

All of this meant that the Reagan trumpet was likely to have effects contrary to those the president predicted. Unless the new policy line was developed, explained, and executed with extraordinary care, it was likely to undercut America's European friends and energize her increasingly vocal European critics. Schmidt and other European leaders had long since lost patience with Jimmy Carter and his administration. They hoped Reagan would be easier personally, and that his administration would follow a clearer policy line. But the truculent, careless, confrontational words they heard from Washington in early 1981 were enormously unsettling.

In his first news conference, the president led off by reiterating his belief that the Soviets were seeking world domination, and that they "reserve unto themselves the right to commit any crime, to lie, to cheat" in order to achieve it. His professional reputation was hardly enhanced when he later defended this by saying he had not volunteered these remarks; he was just answering a question. The secretary of state, in his first news conference, accused the Russians of promoting international terrorism, and stressed that any arms control negotiations would be linked to Soviet world behavior. Two subsequent settling-in flaps sent hard but confusing signals—the secretary of defense stated in February his support of production and deployment (in Europe) of the controversial neutron bomb; the secretary of the navy told a group of reporters over breakfast in March that SALT II limits were not binding for U.S. defense planning. In both cases, Secretary Haig quickly offered a public rebuttal—these statements were not official policy and Europeans should therefore disregard them. Nor was there presumably an official U.S. view that war with Russia was inevitable if the Soviets did not change their system (as NSC aide Richard Pipes told Reuters in March) or any calculated White House decision to express alarm about "outright pacifist sentiments" in Europe (as did Pipes's boss, Richard Allen). But such comments, combined with El Salvador and the Haig–White House flaps, suggested a chaotic hawkishness that created serious problems for America's European friends.

These friends pressed for moderation, and for concrete steps they could use politically. By the end of March, their friends in the State Department made a tentative commitment to move ahead on INF talks while deferring SALT, and in early May Reagan authorized a pledge to the NATO ministerial meeting—INF talks by the "end of the year." But more visible in Europe were Reagan's lifting of the embargo on Soviet grain sales in April, which seemed to expose his toughness as hypocrisy, and a series of actions and statements in the summer and early fall: Weinberger's announcement that Reagan had decided to produce and stockpile the neutron bomb, overriding Haig's recommendation for a more gradual, less visible strategy; Haig's suggestion to the Senate Foreign Relations Committee that the United States had plans for a "demonstration" detonation of a nuclear weapon in time of crisis (immediately denied by Weinberger); and above all the president's October musings to a group of out-of-town editors, "I could see where you could have the exchange of tactical weapons against troops in the field without it bringing either of the major powers to pushing the button." This translated, in the minds of hypersensitive European critics, into a readiness to consider waging a nuclear war limited to Europe.

This sort of talk did more to buttress antinuclear sentiment in Europe than anything the Soviet Union could accomplish. But the Russians were doing their part, too, with a surprisingly sophisticated propaganda campaign tailored to European sensitivities—e.g., a Brezhnev offer to freeze Euromissiles at their current levels. A quarter-million anti-INF demonstrators gathered in Bonn on October 10, increasing the squeeze on European governments. They also set the stage for Reagan's most effective foreign policy declaration of 1981—the "zero-option" speech of November 18.

Haig and Soviet Foreign Minister Andrei Gromyko had announced, following their September meetings in New York, that INF talks would begin on November 30. The question now was what the United States would offer. The decision was to put forward a dramatic, appealing, and almost certainly nonnegotiable proposal. NATO would eschew deployment of all its planned 572 missiles if the Soviets would "dismantle" all their SS-20s and other intermediate-range missiles, including those deployed against China. Hardliners in Defense saw it as a masterful propaganda stroke, a brilliantly packaged, one-sided proposal, trading what Moscow already had for what we hoped European politics would allow us to deploy in response. State officials, though worried that it might complicate future negotiations, saw the immediate tactical advantages in the European political market: Reagan was one-upping the Russians in proposing to remove nuclear weapons from European soil.

The speech itself, beamed live to prime-time European television audiences, was conciliatory and appealing, calling for continuation of the NATO policies of "restraint and balance" that had "preserved the peace in Europe for more than a third of a century," and could do so "for generations to come." Reagan stressed the urgent need to control arms, citing the Soviet buildup but dropping linkage, undercutting the stereotype of the gun-slinging actor cowboy that had spread so widely on the Continent. And though Brezhnev did counter by offering to remove "hundreds" of his weapons, Reagan's stroke was clearly effective. Not only had he bought some political time, he had also planted the seeds of a counterimage, of Ronald Reagan as a good man of peace. Throughout that fractious Washington summer and fall, he had wisely resisted proposals that he deal with confusions within and about his administration by giving a general foreign policy speech. Not for him the trap of Jimmy Carter at Annapolis. He had saved his international speaking debut for the right subject and occasion, which could give his remarks both structure and impact. He had deployed his greatest asset—his platform style.

He had not eliminated differences within his administration. Indeed, two weeks after he declared us "willing to listen to and consider the proposals of our Soviet counterparts," Assistant Secretary of Defense Richard Perle was on Capitol Hill likening an INF compromise to the appeasement of Nazi Germany. But Reagan had set a constructive tone. He had also inaugurated a seven-month period when his administration, under Haig's leadership, with Clark's White House engagement, seemed to be moving toward a conservative-centrist, alliance-based approach to dealings with Europe and the Soviet Union.

One sphere where relative moderation seemed apparent was on the contentious issue of East-West economic relations. From the start there had been bitter internal debate. Weinberger and his allies took what amounted to an economic warfare position—restrict trade as much as possible, particularly on items of strategic consequence; seek by all means to block, delay, or render more costly the Soviet national gas pipeline despite commitments by European firms and governments to help construct it. Haig, seeing the pipeline as undesirable but not worth a bitter NATO wrangle, favored emphasis on controlling military-related trade and limiting European credits to Russia and Eastern bloc countries.

At the July 1981 Ottawa economic summit the administration followed the Haig approach. The United States raised East-West trade to the level of a primary summit concern, and won a very general communiqué commitment: to consultations and coordination so "our economic policies continue to be compatible with our political and security objectives," and "to improve the present system of controls on trade in strategic goods and related technology with the U.S.S.R." Haig parried reporters' questions about the United States having sought a stronger declaration; Reagan, in his brief concluding statement, did not mention East-West trade issues at all. Thereafter, Undersecretary of State Myer Rashish led an interagency mission to Europe urging energy alternatives to the pipeline project, without apparent result.

The Soviet-supported suppression of Solidarity in Poland forced renewed attention to the issue in December, this time in the context of sanctions. The administration, with the State Department in the lead, balanced rather carefully the need to consult with reluctant allies with the U.S. determination to take some concrete punitive steps, unilaterally if necessary. Included was a ban, announced December 29, on major pipeline-related sales by General Electric and Caterpillar Tractor. But the INF talks were continued, and proposals to force a Polish default on its debts were rejected. There was a Reagan commitment to take further (unspecified) punitive steps at some (unspecified) future time if martial law continued unabated. But on balance the immediate reaction to Poland was such as to win the plaudits of Anthony Lewis and the condemnation not just of neoconservative Norman Podhoretz but of Henry Kissinger as well.

Early 1982 brought intensive governmental preparation for Reagan's June trip to Europe for the Versailles and NATO summits. The rejuvenated White House national security staff took the lead in brokering sharp interagency differences on strategic arms to formulate the START (strategic arms reduction talks) proposal Reagan had promised in November. Adding to the antinuclear pressure in Europe was the explosion of popular—and then congressional—pressure for a nuclear freeze, a movement fueled by fears the administration had exacerbated. The resulting formula, announced in May in Reagan's Eureka College commencement speech, was judged a modest victory for the State Department, in alliance with the Joint Chiefs of Staff. The first phase of START talks would concentrate on reducing the total number of launchers and warheads, deferring to a second phase the goal cherished by Defense Department civilians: equalizing overall missile throwweight.

Nonetheless, START very much resembled the "zero-option" INF proposal: politically attractive to doves as well as hawks because it stressed reductions; diplomatically unpromising because the cuts would be made, as the proposal was drawn, overwhelmingly on the Soviet side. This was fully consistent with the Reagan campaign goal of giving the Russians a choice between our building up and their cutting back. Indeed, its adoption would force such a drastic reshaping of Soviet forces as to leave the United States with a substantial strategic advantage. It was supplemented, however, by Reagan's carefully worded Memorial Day promise: "As for existing strategic arms agreements, we will refrain from actions which undercut them as long as the Soviet Union shows equal restraint."

On East-West trade, administration divisions were equally deep. For some, like NSC Soviet specialist Richard Pipes, the goal went beyond linkage to Poland and beyond blocking the pipeline. Their aim was squeezing the Soviet Union economically across the board, "compelling the Soviet regime to bear the consequence of its own priorities." Weinberger and his aides tended toward this view, and so, evidence suggests, did Ronald Reagan and William Clark. No one took the opposite view (still widely held in Europe) that East-West trade was intrinsically good because it might promote constructive interdependence, with beneficial impact on Soviet society and policy. Rather, State officials argued the practicalities: A restrictive policy could work only if pursued by Western nations collectively; we should not, above all, pursue a unilateralist approach that would transform a crisis of the Warsaw Pact into one for the Atlantic Alliance. The best way to proceed, therefore, was to seek allied agreement on tightening trade credits to Eastern bloc countries.

Throughout the spring, this view maintained a shaky primacy in Washington. State, represented by Undersecretary James Buckley, sought to negotiate what *seemed* clearly in the common interest—an allied agreement not to subsidize the Eastern bloc through competitive, below-market-rate credit financing. But the going was hard, with the French showing greatest resistance. There was wide European disagreement with the United States concerning the desirability of détente and East-West trade. There was the immediate employment cost of trade restrictions during a recession that threatened to become a depression. There was the embarrassment of huge U.S. grain sales, suggesting that America too was giving priority to commercial interests. There was the complexity of the issue of export subsidies in general, which complicated negotiations over trade within the West. But the U.S. position was further weakened by its unwillingness to give on the economic matters that most concerned Europeans—high interest rates and the overstrong dollar. An American readiness to negotiate on what Europeans perceived as most burdening them— our macroeconomic or exchange rate policies—would presumably have increased our leverage on East-West trade as the Versailles summit approached. But no such readiness existed. In any case, the "domestic" issues were well outside of Haig's (and State's) bureaucratic domain.

So this issue remained unresolved when the president arrived in Paris on Thursday, June 3. Before his departure eight days later, he would, in sequence, be embarrassed by Israel's invasion of Lebanon and by the flap over the Falkland Islands vote, discuss economics with his advanced industrial counterparts at Versailles, pay a brief visit to Rome and the Vatican, deliver impressive speeches celebrating freedom in London and peace in Bonn, and participate in a NATO summit. He would then return home with the U.S. print media declaring his trip a modest success. "After some early stumbles," wrote Lou Cannon in the June 13 *Washington Post,* "President Reagan recovered in the final half of his European odyssey and largely accomplished his major political goal of reassuring the nations he visited that he is not the sort of man who would lead the Western alliance into war." Or as Hedrick Smith put it in that same Sunday's *New York Times,* Reagan "apparently succeeded in softening the damaging, negative, warlike image of him in Europe."

The success would last all of one week. The reason, apparently, was acute White House dissatisfaction with what Versailles had accomplished on Eastern bloc credits. Reagan had refrained from pressing the pipeline issue there, but the only reward he got for his restraint was communiqué language pledging the seven "to handle cautiously financial relations with the U.S.S.R. and other Eastern European countries," recognizing "the need for commercial prudence in limiting export credits." Negotiations remanded to the OECD did complete, later that June, an agreement to raise the nonbinding guideline interest rate for loans to the Soviet Union to about 12 percent. But in terms of clear, visible policy changes, the accomplishment was small— and made visibly smaller when the host, French President François Mitterrand, suggested right after the summit that the credit language was meaningless. Each nation remained "sovereignly responsible for deciding what is prudent."

Meanwhile, repression continued in Poland. And Reagan had yet to determine the substance of the follow-up sanctions he had promised to impose. One possibility—not raised by the President at Versailles— was that he might decide to tighten the screws on the natural gas pipeline. Europeans generally read his acceptance of the communiqué language as a commitment not to do so; they had hoped, in fact, he would ease his pipeline sanctions as part of the summit agreement. But the idea of broadening them instead was very much alive in Washington. Clark—presumably reflecting Reagan's personal senti-ments—felt that Haig had painted the president into a corner by not pressing the credit question forcefully enough with the Europeans. So he scheduled a meeting of the National Security Council on June 18 to review this issue—a date for which Haig had a previous com-mitment to meet with Soviet foreign minister Andrei Gromyko in New York. On that day Reagan listened to competing arguments and quickly decided to extend sanctions against participation in the pipe-line project to the subsidiaries of U.S. firms operating abroad and to European firms using technology under American licenses. Pressing the winning case were Weinberger, Meese, and Clark. In Haig's ab-sence, Undersecretary Eagleburger made the main argument against this action, supported by Commerce Secretary Malcolm Baldrige. The decision was almost immediately announced to the press.

The allies were dumbfounded, and the European response was fierce and unanimous. From Thatcher's Tory England to Mitterrand's Socialist France, all major West European countries denounced the "unilateral and retroactive" steps and took legal action to protect their firms. Haig, having been done in both substantively and procedurally, launched the protest that led promptly to his departure. This loss of their champion upset the Europeans more. To allies like Helmut Schmidt, it looked as if the administration had blown it, wasted half a year's alliance repair work. After a patient, frequently sophisticated effort to show that the United States could be sensitive to European concerns and that Reagan was a reasonable man, he had now taken just the sort of action that recalled all the worst stereotypes—simplistic, ideological, unilateral, ineffective, and probably illegal. French For-eign Minister Claude Cheysson, his government no longer Reagan's special friend, said a "progressive divorce" was under way in trans-Atlantic relations.

Why did Reagan do it? He was under broad right-wing attack for compromising his convictions on a range of issues. He had little to show for the moderate sanctions policy he had pursued up to that time and little reason to feel that the Europeans were even taking him seriously. So it seems that his visceral hardline instincts prevailed, reinforced by the senior aides he trusted the most. Clark, in his desire to implement Reagan's philosophy, failed the president in a more profound way by not giving adequate weight to the European political costs of this course of action. This, and the administration's subsequent surprise at the ferocity of the European reaction, laid bare the thinness of its expertise and understanding regarding Europe. There seems to have been nobody of cabinet rank at the NSC table June 18 who knew what a mess they were making for themselves. Nor was there adequate preparatory staff work, presented to the president, on questions like the legality and economic effects of such an "extraterritorial" assertion of U.S. power.

Reagan reinforced the impression of a president not grasping what he was doing at his televised press conference of June 30, 1982. Asked to respond to "those who say there is confusion in your foreign policy," Reagan volunteered the information that when he came to office "there was disarray with our European allies. I think that has been largely eliminated and they have confidence in us once again." Closer to the mark was James Reston's critique three months later: "He came to office promising to unify the Atlantic alliance but has divided it over trade with the Soviet Union more seriously than at any time since World War II." On August 12, the European Community declared the sanctions "contrary to international law, and apparently at variance with . . . U.S. law," and "unlikely" to "delay materially the construction of the pipeline or the delivery of the gas." Instead, the harm would be mainly to European firms and U.S.-European economic relations: "to call in question the usefulness of technological links between European and American firms, if contracts could be nullified at any time by decision of the U.S. administration."

Well before this statement, however, work had begun to limit the damage. Prodded in part by U.S. Trade Representative William Brock (who was in Europe when the decision was taken and felt the full brunt of the reaction), Clark convened meetings in the White House exploring ways of climbing off this limb with pride intact. Shultz employed in his July confirmation hearings the most transitory of the administration's several antipipeline rationales: it was not to prevent European energy dependence or to deprive Russia of foreign exchange, but to show our displeasure over Poland. Then, in a small peace offering to Europe, the scope of their firms' punishment was reduced. Following the widely quoted Cheysson statement about an Atlantic "divorce," rhetoric from Europe grew cooler also.

In the fall, Shultz took on the issue personally. He sought to provide Reagan a basis for yielding on pipeline sanctions by negotiating a broad allied agreement on East-West trade restraint, like that sought at Versailles. What Shultz accomplished on the latter remains unclear, and partly by design, given the loud French insistence that since the U.S. sanctions were "unilateral and unjustified," Paris would give nothing directly to secure their removal. In fact, when Reagan announced on November 13 the removal of all U.S. pipeline sanctions because "we've achieved an agreement with our allies which provides for stronger and more effective measures," the French government felt compelled to insist it was "not a party" to any such agreement. The truth, apparently, is that France was in substance a party, but also that the agreement was very general—to study means of coordinating and tightening policies and to refrain from additional Soviet natural gas contracts (which no country was contemplating) in the meantime. For Reagan it was, in essence, a retreat packaged as an advance. In any case, in December Shultz and Cheysson met in Paris and visibly, at least temporarily, buried the hatchet.

There was no comparable adjustment of the U.S. position on arms control. The November death of Leonid Brezhnev and his rapid replacement by Yuri Andropov brought general expressions, in both Washington and Moscow, of readiness for constructive dialogue. But when Andropov increased the pressure in December by making public a Soviet proposal to reduce its Europe-based intermediate missiles to the numbers deployed by Britain and France—a significant softening of Moscow's earlier position—the immediate Washington response was to reject it. The U.S. positions for both START and INF remained fully consistent with the Reagan campaign stance: the choice was between Soviet cutback and American buildup. It seemed unlikely that this position would be politically sustainable through 1983, the time of reckoning for INF deployment. For added to the antinuclear pressure in Europe was the freeze movement in the United States, which won general endorsement at the polls in November. Growing concern over Reagan's arms control credibility surfaced in early 1983, as the Senate reacted negatively to the firing of ACDA Director Eugene Rostow and the nomination of a young ideologue as his successor. There was also erosion of support for military buildup, reflected in the unprecedented (if not necessarily permanent) congressional rejection, in December 1982, of funds to deploy a major new strategic weapon, the MX missile.

Whether Reagan would adjust in 1983 only events would reveal. The best judgment at midterm was that on alliance-adversary relations, Ronald Reagan had kept the faith more than his right-wing critics realized. He was sticking with his military budget and his arms control positions. And in pressing so hard on Soviet matters, he had compounded the already-difficult problems of alliance management.

Summing Up:
Faith versus Works

Three issue areas are less than the sum of Reagan administration foreign policy. More would have been added had space and time permitted. If one looked for cases where the administration adhered strongly to its philosophical convictions, there was the failure to sign the Law of the Sea Treaty, or international monetary policy, or energy, where only the oil glut saved the Reagan free market policies from sustained domestic and international attack. If one looked for cases of pragmatism, there was trade policy, Falkland Islands diplomacy, and, surprisingly, southern Africa, where Assistant Secretary Chester Crocker was pressing an ambitious diplomatic effort to broker a regional political settlement, with Angola rebel Jonas Savimbi held at arm's length and Jesse Helms and his allies remarkably quiet. There was, finally, the Middle East journey from Haig's pursuit of that elusive anti-Soviet, Israel-based "strategic consensus" to the brilliantly timed, effectively presented Reagan-Shultz peace initiative of September 1, 1982, whose content was what any recent U.S. administration might have proposed.

Still, enough experience has been recounted in these pages to suggest some broad, if necessarily tentative conclusions.

We can begin with the alternatives set forth on page 131. Hypothesis I suggested that the Reagan administration would be ideological in the peripheral regions, pragmatic about the Soviet-NATO center. Hypothesis II argued the opposite, and as of summer 1982 it seemed closer to the mark. It is true that on the strategic issue posing the starkest choice, arms sales to Taiwan, the President proved unwilling to risk provoking a new "loss" of China, so he swallowed hard and took the pragmatic course. But on Central America, where policy seemed to take an initial sharp rightward lurch, the reaction forced it back somewhat in the Carter direction. And on the European front, where policy seemed to be moving in a moderate direction from November 1981 to June 1982, this evolution was abruptly reversed by the afternoon decision of June 18.

Hypothesis I may have reflected Alexander Haig's political strategy. He may well have been seeking to buy, through a hard hemispheric line, the leeway he needed on alliance relations. Cede Central America to Jesse Helms and his cohorts so as to fend them off in Europe. But as of summer 1982, if one asked in which region the administration has most clearly risked conflict in pursuit of ideologically grounded principles, the answer was in Europe, with hardline policies on East-West trade and arms control. And this reflected the clear inclinations of the president and his close aides in the White House.

This was accomplished through a decision-making process that was a marked improvement over the chaos that preceded it. In appointing a management-oriented California associate as national security assistant, Ronald Reagan made central foreign policy-making possible in 1982, as it was not in 1981. And he found means to connect himself to the process—as he was not connected, for the most part, in 1981—without shutting other senior players out.

Yet it was Clark who orchestrated the disastrous pipeline decision, seeing his job as "the conversion of philosophy to policy," and responding, one must assume, to Reagan's strong personal impulses. And the way that that decision was handled—hastily scheduling an NSC meeting on a date that Haig, the prime cabinet negotiator and advocate of caution, was known to be out of town—raises serious questions about Clark's commitment to fair process, even if one aim was to precipitate Haig's departure.

Hence a certain irony: a policy process undeniably more orderly, with a strong presidential coordinator adhering, in the main, to the appropriate "inside" role of policy management, tended to produce, in the Reagan presidency, more extreme policies. One reason was that this was what the president, in the end, seemed to want. Another is Clark's limited expertise, making him less sensitive to likely decision results, and thus more likely to respond to Reagan's ideology—and perhaps his own. Still another reason was that the cast around the National Security Council table—Weinberger, Meese, Casey, and others—would provide ample, semi-informed support for many hardline options that are advanced. A strong NSC staff role meant less free-wheeling by Defense, but less also by State. And after listening to the range of argument, Reagan (or Clark) was likely to come down in a tougher place than the fractious Haig did, or the cooperative Shultz would.

Alexander Haig dealt with this problem by fending the White House off. This style doubtless won him some short-run victories, but it led also to his political demise. And the policy results were brittle, because Ronald Reagan himself was not really committed to them. Once the president, using Clark, began to have a central foreign policy process, it was bound to put him in repeated touch with U.S.-Soviet issues above all others. Policy tended to be hardline here, because countering the Soviets directly was what Reagan cared most about. If this Reagan system did not also connect him with enough of their complexity, this reflected the limited background of Clark and most other senior advisers, but more fundamentally the limits in what the Reagan presidential market would bear.

⌠ As of summer 1982, then, the Reagan system tended to produce positions and proposals that reflected and reaffirmed conservative goals but did not yield productive results. It kept the faith, but at the cost of works.

At that very time, however, a conservative pragmatist, a man of works, was taking over as Ronald Reagan's secretary of state. And quietly but quickly he made his mark. On July 1, as war raged in Lebanon and George Shultz began to prepare for his succession, there was no American peace program for the Middle East beyond the battered Camp David framework. Shultz insisted on the centrality of the Palestinian problem during his confirmation testimony, consulted experts inside and outside government, and engaged the president carefully and continuously. So on September 1 there was such a program, and Reagan could announce it, in what was generally judged his most impressive international initiative to date.

That fall, as already noted, Shultz tackled the impasse in U.S.-European relations, recognizing that the pipeline sanctions were a no-win proposition, but recognizing equally that Reagan could not yield without something to claim in their place. And as 1982 drew to a close, the secretary was turning his attention increasingly to other critical issues, such as the deepening global depression.

With Shultz and Clark, the administration had a smooth complementary foreign policy team—working with Ronald Reagan, restraining Caspar Weinberger, beginning to link international politics and international economics. Shultz had not yet gotten seriously into U.S.-Soviet relations and arms control; this allowed Defense to exploit White House anti-Sovietism to reject a promising INF compromise, even to harden the START negotiation position. But where he was effectively engaged, Shultz's impact in his first six months was to pull policy toward the center. And that was all to the good.

For most foreign policy accomplishment requires, inconveniently, the cooperation of people outside the United States. It is easy to strike a resonant tone on trading with the adversary. But concrete accomplishments to implement this kind of goal require ability to work with, and adapt our policies to, people and movements outside our borders, as Philip Habib could testify. The less dominant our power position, the more cultivation and adjustment will generally be required. A tough stance may be productive in a particular situation, even if the State Department—usually biased toward short-term accommodation—argues against it. Had Haig "gone to the brink" on Eastern bloc credits before Versailles, he might have gotten more of what Reagan wanted. But this turned on a judgment of the players and interests within each country: how much leeway they had on the issue, what would move them and what would not.

Making such calculations and trade-offs is a hard business, and one attraction of ideological approaches is that they render them irrelevant, perhaps even immoral. In fact, he who persists in raising practical problems with the faith can be labeled a heretic. But keeping the faith in a world where most others do not share it draws lines separating us from them and makes it unlikely that works can be accomplished. In other words, ideology isolates, as the Soviet experience should have shown us by now.

It also can create for us brand new foreign policy problems, as if we do not already have enough. Whether it be over "official" ties to Taiwan, "going to the source" in Central America, or pipeline sanctions in Europe, the Reagan regime generated reactions abroad, to which U.S. officials then had to devote enormous time and energy in order to contain the damage. They had to search for ways to back off, at least a bit, at least for now, without seeming to repudiate the concept that caused the trouble in the first place.

Yet another problem is the impact efforts to implement ideology have upon support for the president's policy at home. Ideology polarizes by nourishing its adversaries. Ernest Lefever gave a shot in the arm to human rights advocates; Reagan and Weinberger were the best recruiters the peace and freeze movements could hope for. In 1982 the United States Congress was much more a force for democratic reforms in Central America, or strategic arms limitations, than it was in 1980, because of the reaction the administration had produced.

In the short run, such a reaction is manageable. Congress is unlikely to seize control: El Salvador can be certified as making human rights progress, and bills to support the freeze or reverse the pipeline sanctions can be beaten back by one expedient or another, in one house or another. But when the president needs constructive support, positive congressional action, the result is less impressive. In 1981, for example, Reagan compromised on aid with development liberals and won endorsement of the first foreign assistance appropriations bill in three years. In 1982, he pressed for increments heavily weighted to the military side, and lost.

If foreign policy were inherently popular, if our overseas entanglements had broad popular support, then an ideological approach that mobilized half of the elite that cares about foreign policy might be viable, even if the other half were arrayed against it. In fact, the mass public is skeptical-to-hostile about most foreign policy actions that have visible dollar or human costs. Unless an administration can mobilize support from activists across a broad spectrum, its foreign policy fast becomes politically fragile, as Carter's became in his last two years, as Reagan's threatened to become as 1983 began.

Part of the administration recognized this problem and was moving to address it. This part included, one must assume, some portion of Ronald Reagan. He was certainly as aware as George Shultz that one cannot build a political majority, or a policy base, by subtraction. The question was how successful the secretary would be in nurturing the president's pragmatic side—as he had on the Middle East and the pipeline. The goal of Shultz's careful, consultative, inclusive style of consensus-building was, presumably, to envelop everyone in policies that were visibly Reagan's, and linked to certain Reaganite goals, but somehow articulated and pursued in ways that took the edge off conflict externally as well as internally. And as long as Clark adhered, in the main, to the "inside" role of process manager, he could play a key connecting role in policy development and policy enforcement.

One key test in 1983, certainly, will be alliance-adversary relations, with arms control the central issue. As the year began, there were many signs that the hard Reagan line could not be sustained.

At home, the number of Americans who favored more defense spending had been falling ever since Inauguration Day 1981. Reagan could claim some credit for this, in the sense that most Americans now believe they have a president who gives the armed forces at least their due. But he had also undercut his defense cause by generating anxiety about nuclear war, and by the deep gouge his economic program has taken out of the tax base. This, combined with domestic program cuts and anxiety about social security, increasingly forced moderates and liberals to take on the Pentagon. Thus, Reaganomics had done its part to repolarize the national security debate, at the very time when many Democrats were moving out of the "antidefense" posture of the Vietnam era.

In Europe, there was the still-potent antinuclear movement, with the INF deployment scheduled for the end of 1983 offering a ripe target for political mobilization. Notwithstanding generally supportive governments in London, Bonn, and (on nuclear issues) Paris, the administration would find the Germans, in particular, squeezed by this movement unless it showed readiness to entertain an arms control compromise. And European resistance to INF deployment would, in turn, fuel unilateralist sentiment in the United States, further eroding an alliance that has contributed far more to American security than anything new the Reagan Pentagon will produce.

In Moscow, the emerging post-Brezhnev regime was proving—by initial appearances—more aggressive and imaginative diplomatically, though whether its prime goal was disruption of NATO or a serious deal on arms control was not yet clear.

Did the administration's immediate (and diplomatically defensible) rejection of Andropov's December INF proposal reflect a determination to "stay the course" on Reagan's zero option, come what might? Or would the president repeat in 1983 his successful political performance of November 1981, but with the major substantive adjustments that would be required to assuage concerns in Europe, and move toward agreement with Moscow? Could such a retreat be skillfully managed, even packaged (persuasively) as an advance, so as to gain more backing on the center-left than was lost on the right, which was insisting that Reagan arms control diplomacy had been too accommodating? Could an administration where Paul Nitze was suspected of softness manage such a pragmatic adjustment without enormous internal strife? Was Ronald Reagan, the man, up to this demanding leadership challenge?

It is too soon, at midterm, to offer confident answers. But the first two Reagan years posed the questions and established the alternatives. Over the next two, Americans will learn whether, in the main, it will be faith or works that prevail.

Notes

I am grateful to Jonathan Sack for research assistance, and to William P. Bundy, Fred I. Greenstein, Robert H. Johnson, Leon V. Sigal, and Michael O. Wheeler for their comments on earlier drafts.

This essay draws mainly on public sources, supplemented by a few interviews and off-the-record conversations. Footnoting is limited to important analytic references, and unfamiliar quotations not reported in the major, contemporary print media.

1. See I. M. Destler, "National Security Management: What Presidents Have Wrought," *Political Science Quarterly* 95 (Winter 1980–81): 573–88; and "The National

Security Adviser: Role and Accountability," Hearing before the Committee on Foreign Relations, U. S. Senate, April 17, 1980.

2. Lou Cannon, *Reagan* (New York: G. P. Putnam's Sons, 1982).

3. McGeorge Bundy, "Mr. Reagan's Security Aide," *New York Times,* November 16, 1980.

4. Zbigniew Brzezinski, "The Best National Security System," interview in *Washington Quarterly* 5 (Winter 1982): 77.

5. For a more extended treatment of the AWACS affair, see I. M. Destler, "Reagan, Congress, and Foreign Policy in 1981," in Norman Ornstein, ed., *President and Congress: Assessing Reagan's First Year* (Washington, D.C.: American Enterprise Institute, 1982), pp. 71–77.

6. William Schneider, "The November 4 Vote for President: What Did It Mean?" in Austin Ranney, ed., *The American Elections of 1980* (Washington, D.C.: American Enterprise Institute, 1981), p. 233.

7. Bruce Russett and Donald R. DeLuca, " 'Don't Tread on Me': Public Opinion and Foreign Policy in the Eighties," *Political Science Quarterly* 96 (Fall 1981): 383.

8. William P. Clark, "National Security Strategy," Address, Center for Strategic and International Studies, Georgetown University, May 21, 1982.

9. Jimmy Carter, quoted in Hedley Donovan, "A Vacuum in Leadership," *Fortune,* March 22, 1982, p. 86.

10. Thomas L. Hughes, "Up from Reaganism," *Foreign Policy,* no. 44 (Fall 1981), pp. 3–22.

11. This section draws substantially on A. Doak Barnett, *U. S. Arms Sales: The China-Taiwan Tangle* (Washington, D.C.: Brookings Institution, 1982), and Michel Oksenberg, "A Decade of Sino-American Relations," *Foreign Affairs* 61 (Fall 1982): 175–95.

12. Barnett, *U. S. Arms Sales,* p. 30.

13. Oksenberg, "Sino-American Relations," p. 193.

14. Rowland Evans and Robert Novak, *Washington Post,* July 30, 1982.

15. "U.S. Intelligence Performance in Central America: Achievements and Selected Instances of Concern," Staff Report, Subcommittee on Oversight and Evaluation, House Permanent Select Committee on Intelligence, September 22, 1982, p. 4.

6 Reagan and the Lore of the Modern Presidency: What Have We Learned?

Fred I. Greenstein

In the post-1932 universe of nine presidencies, each case is exemplary, if not necessarily admirable. Variations in incumbents, administrations, operating procedures, policies, and political circumstances are so great and the number of presidencies so small (even though presidencies do change as they proceed) that each incumbent and administration corrects or modifies the lore about the possible modes of filling and executing the job of chief executive.

Laws versus Lore of the Presidency

The problem of small numbers makes it more appropriate to speak of lore than of laws in discussing the conduct of the presidency. By 1970 scholars began to see law-like patterns in the operations and properties of the presidency that expanded so massively in the post-Hoover years. Interpretive categories for identifying the properties of presidential leadership were provisionally set forth. As of the early 1980s, however, further study of the Roosevelt through Nixon presidencies had cast doubt on many of the seeming empirical regularities from which the interpretive categories were derived. And aspects of the presidencies since Nixon's—those of Ford, Carter, and now Reagan—further undermined the categories. In short, by the 1980s patterns of presidential leadership seemed less clearly distinguishable than they had appeared to be a decade earlier.

Nevertheless, the effort to identify patterns and construct typologies has led to an increasing awareness of questions that need to be asked and criteria that are likely to be useful in analyzing presidencies. For example, Reagan and his presidency cannot adequately be analyzed by two widely discussed classifications, one of presidential advising patterns and the other of presidential personality. Yet the issues about the conduct of the presidency that led these classifications to be developed provide insight into, and are illuminated by, Reagan's leadership. Moreover, viewing Reagan's leadership through the prisms of the two typologies leads to examination of his presidency from a broader perspective that includes not only personality but also other aspects of his political psychology and his advising arrangements and other elements of his political context.

Reagan and Types of Presidential Advising

One typology that seemed promising a decade ago distinguishes different ways presidents organize the many aides necessary to run the modern presidency and predicts the consequences of how they do so. The distinction seemed evident as long ago as the late 1950s, when Richard Neustadt was completing the research for the first exercise in realistic appraisal of the strategies open to American presidents in advancing their purposes.[1]

In a chapter of his *Presidential Power* entitled "Men in Office," Neustadt compared the Roosevelt, Truman, and Eisenhower modes of employing advisers, seeking information, and canvassing tactical and substantive options. On the basis of the evidence then available to him as a close reader of the press who had also interviewed a number of White House aides, Neustadt accepted the contemporary portrayal of Eisenhower's approach to taking advice as hierarchical. The former supreme commander had, after all, introduced a chief of staff to the White House. He relied extensively on delegation. And he used formal channels of advising, such as frequent cabinet and National Security Council meetings, with elaborately prepared agenda papers. Eisenhower conveyed the sense that he was part of a team— that he was on tap in, but not consistently on top of, his administration.

Roosevelt, by contrast, exhibited virtually the opposite of Eisenhower's style, with Truman falling somewhere in the middle. Roosevelt employed an extraordinary diversity of advisers, took counsel in endless informal meetings rather than making serious use of his formal meetings with his cabinet, and communicated to Washington insiders and the public alike that he personally was the moving force in his presidency, if not the entire government. Instead of employing a staff chief and working through channels, Roosevelt made himself the nerve center of his advising system.

Neustadt was persuaded that the way presidents used advisers made a difference. Roosevelt's leadership was consummately professional. Eisenhower's seemed amateurish. A significant component of the Roosevelt professionalism, Neustadt suggested, was his steady intake of advice and information. This alerted him to possible ways of exercising influence that would not occur to Eisenhower, who absorbed a narrower range of communications through formal channels.

In the decade after Neustadt's book appeared, Kennedy and Johnson followed the Roosevelt practice of running presidencies in which numerous aides reported independently to the president. There emerged a textbook symbol of this leadership style: the president was the hub of a wheel, his aides the spokes. Then Nixon used with a vengeance the leadership mode that until recently was thought to have been Eisenhower's practice—hierarchical ordering of aides with single gatekeepers funneling advice and information to the president on domestic policy (H. R. Haldeman seemed analogous to Eisenhower's Sherman Adams) and foreign policy (Henry Kissinger appeared parallel to John Foster Dulles).

A pattern seemed to have emerged. Presidents had the option, in the phrase of Stanford Business School Professor Richard Tanner Johnson, to array their advisers "formalistically," as Nixon and Eisenhower evidently did. In doing so, Johnson argued, they gained orderly policy assessment and implementation but lost the diversity of information and advocacy necessary to make effective policy. On the other hand, presidents could adopt a "collegial" mode of organization, running their staffs by fostering numerous personal links with each of their principal aides and encouraging give-and-take among them, an approach with virtues and vices reciprocal to those of formalism. The president was availed of richly varied information and advice that added to his knowledge and protected his ability to consider policy alternatives, but under such an arrangement policy formulation might be unsystematic and implementation might fail to take place.[2]

Even before Reagan took office, it became clear that the formalistic versus collegial dichotomy inadequately captured the variations in how modern presidents take advice. Nor did the dichotomy explain whether presidents became exposed to a diversity of information and advice. Moreover, in the mid-1970s presidential library archives yielded evidence that Eisenhower's advising system was neither formalistic nor collegial but rather made systematic, coordinated use of both modes.[3] And Johnson library records were released documenting many claims made during his incumbency that LBJ manipulated his collegial advisers, eliciting from them support for his preestablished policy aims.[4]

Richard Tanner Johnson's classification also proved to be incomplete because it did not leave room for different advisory modes in different policy areas. In the Ford presidency foreign policy advising was hierarchical, with Kissinger reporting directly to Ford. Domestic policy-making, however, especially in the area of economics, was marked by what might be called formalized colleagueship, an approach in which the major administration economic actors engaged in regular give-and-take with each other, often in the president's presence, by means of their participation in an official entity, the Economic Policy Board.[5]

Although the formalistic versus collegial advising dichotomy no longer seems adequate for classifying presidential advising patterns and predicting their consequences, the lore summarized in Professor Johnson's distinctions does provide criteria for assessing and learning from Reagan's use of advisers. It is evident, for example, that in Reagan's first year in office, foreign affairs advising was totally unhierarchical and lacking in formal organization. The substitution of George Shultz for Alexander Haig as secretary of state and of William P. Clark for Richard Allen as White House assistant for national security has produced greater orderliness, teamwork, and advising cooperation but does not appear to have left Reagan dependent upon a single foreign policy advice conduit. The shift in foreign affairs advising appears to have been from acrimony to harmony among colleagues, but not to formalism.

In certain respects Reagan's domestic advising appears, on the other hand, to be the paradigm of hierarchical formalism. Reagan, for example, has an officially labeled chief of staff. But his chief of staff,

James Baker III, is actually the White House political operations specialist. Edwin Meese, who holds the title of counselor, comes closest to being in charge of staff work. And Baker and Meese share with Michael Deaver the authority to report directly to Reagan. With his propensity to be (in Lou Cannon's phrase) the Great Delegator, even though he employs three rather than one principal White House aide, Reagan seems formalistic. But since the formalism is distinctly non-pyramidal, and his top aides have had disagreements, he also has institutionalized elements of collegial advising. He additionally relies on kitchen cabinet advisers such as Senator Paul Laxalt, and the Baker and Meese groups operate as exceptionally flexible and informal, if not always wholly amicable, colleagues. Indeed in some policy areas, especially ones like the economy, which have many actors in both the presidential office and the cabinet, advising arrangements appear to be downright disorderly.

Although Reagan's domestic operations add to the evidence that the formalist-collegial distinction is inadequate for identifying the available ways of organizing a president's counselors, the lore derived from observation of modern presidential advisers and summarized in Johnson's and other typologies[6] clarifies the kinds of questions we can ask about Reagan presidency advising and presidency advising in general. These include questions about its cognitive functions: How well does the system inform the president? How does he receive counsel and information? Is he exposed to sharply joined presentations of the choices before him? If so, how do he and his advisers use the information and recommendations that reach him? They also include questions about the noncognitive personal "chemistry" of advising. For example, to what degree are presidents capable of choosing advisers with whom they can effectively work, and who can work together, supplementing each other's strengths and weaknesses and, above all, the president's? Questions about the psychology of selecting and working with advisers lead us to consider the second typology—that of presidential personality.

Reagan and Types of Presidential Personality

James David Barber's account of presidential character and his general formulation of the array of elements (character, world view, style, and political context) that affect presidential performance are more often discussed than turned to analytic use.[7] When set with some care against the most reliable reports of the qualities Reagan brings to his leadership, however, Barber's psychological contribution to the lore of the modern presidency illuminates and is illuminated by the Reagan experience. Moreover, his overall conceptualization of the elements of presidential performance provides a useful framework for iden- tifying lessons of Reagan's presidency.

Barber, in research on state politicians done in the 1950s, provi- sionally identified four types of political actors with distinctive political styles, and by implication personality patterns, that could be detected by using two criteria.[8] One criterion is whether the emotional energy leaders invest in political activity is positive or negative—whether they derive pleasure or pain from politics. The other is whether these energies are turned to active or passive role-performance.

Reagan manifestly participates in politics with relish.[9] In the title phrase of his 1965 memoir, politics enabled him to find "the rest of me." He seems cut out to fit Barber's positive type, in contrast to the relentlessly hard-working Carter and the periodically tormented Johnson and Nixon. But are his nine-to-five work habits, punctuated by vacations and midweek horseback rides, active or passive? Asking the question reveals the ambiguity of the terms "active" and "passive." When called upon to be active, largely in his additional roles as chief administration communicator and persuader, Reagan has been un- stinting. Certainly he also has been an activist in the traditional policy sense of that ambiguous term. He knows what he wants and does everything he can to attain his goals. (Franklin Roosevelt, it may be added, is viewed as a classical activist, but he was no workaholic.) Thus, Reagan is not readily placed in a passive-active continuum.

Suppose, however, we use Barber's analysis as a sensitizer rather than as a predictor. Consider, for example, the political psychological insights Barber sought to condense in his use of the passive-positive category, which he once tentatively applied to Reagan.[10]

In *The Lawmakers*, Barber identifies through the use of the passive- positive category the traits that he found united in a political type he called the "spectator." This is the politician who, like the people iden- tified in David Riesman's account of the other-directed character, seems more interested in the status derived from leadership than in policy accomplishment and who is highly compliant to advisers.[11] As an issue-oriented ideologue, Reagan has *not* been an "easy sell"— indeed, according to some accounts he has been overly disposed to steer his advisers, signaling in advance the recommendations he wants. Furthermore, if presidential leadership has been fundamentally an occasion for Reagan to bask in a sense of exalted status, he has kept this need well concealed.

Nevertheless, the Barber category does fit certain other-directed qualities Reagan seems to manifest. For example, his beliefs clearly are not so deeply rooted in characterological needs that he refuses to bend them when compromises are necessary. Overall, his career and practices display other-directed, context-dependent qualities of the sort that cognitive psychologist Herman Witkin calls "field dependence."[12] Reagan's beliefs have followed a parabola from keen Roosevelt liberalism to enthusiastically strong conservatism in close synchronization with the changes in his own life circumstances from Depression child to big business spokesman. And while he is capable of overruling his advisers, he is widely said to be reluctant to discipline them or even to tolerate heated disagreement (in contrast to civil, measured debate) among them in his presence. Thus, although the "passive" Barber category does not work for Reagan, themes in Barber's account of passive-positive presidential personality alert us to compliant elements in Reagan's political psychology.

In his analyses of modern era presidents, Barber's overwhelming preoccupation is with the active types. (The only modern president Barber treats in *The Presidential Character* as passive is Eisenhower, who, he notes, does not easily fit his classification scheme.[13]) Underlying the distinction between the active-positive and -negative types in Barber's analysis is a set of issues that derive from Harold D. Lasswell's work on political personality.[14] Lasswell was profoundly impressed by the danger that psychologically wounded leaders will use politics not only for seeking to influence the real world dilemmas of national and international politics, but also for giving vent to their inner distresses by means of "symptoms" such as irrational anger, rigidity, or grandiosity. At a minimum, the bulk of observers of the presidency have felt that neurotic needs of one type or another have influenced—indeed distorted in ways that undermined their own policies—the performance in office of at least two modern presidents, Nixon and Johnson, and (here there is the most agreement) one of the major precursively modern presidents, Woodrow Wilson.[15]

Reagan would never have rigidified in the face of a League of Nations conflict. On one often-quoted occasion as California governor, he announced that his feet were set in concrete. Later he accepted a compromise with a characteristically disarming one-liner: "You are hearing the sound of concrete cracking." Reagan also is no insomnia-haunted Johnson, waking to nightmares, and he cannot be imagined as a cornered Nixon denying that he is "a crook" and allowing himself to become immersed in self-destructive acts that culminate in a forced resignation from office. Yet the tension between ideological faith and pragmatic works has—as the preceding chapters make clear—been a continuing element in Reagan's leadership. Evidently Reagan's leadership is significantly influenced by his psychological "wiring," but by other aspects of it than are illuminated by Lasswell's and Barber's studies of presidents who "rigidify" because of neurotic motivations, such as compulsive power needs.

Reagan and the Modern Presidency: Parallels and Departures

Although the typologies just discussed provide a partial perspective on Reagan and his presidency, it is now necessary to go beyond them, first examining additional aspects of his personality, then considering his beliefs and political style. This leads to consideration of the context of the Reagan presidency, part of which includes the constellation of advisers around him, but much of which is not as open to his control as his advising—for example, the leaders he faces on Capitol Hill and the state of the economy.

Personality

The official campaign photograph of Ronald Reagan portrays a rugged-faced westerner in modified cowboy attire. This public relations image, however, is clearly *not* the outward manifestation of a president with the impulses of a gunslinger. Reagan's anti-Soviet rhetoric and his commitment to increased military expenditures have understandably aroused antinuclear and more generally dovish concerns about dangers that may ensue from his leadership. Even his adversaries, however, recognize that he exhibits none of the personal insecurities that characterize the power-preoccupied leaders about whom Lasswell and Barber write.

In responding to being shot by a would-be assassin, Reagan revealed neither bravado nor panic. Instead, he displayed his almost reflexive proclivity to be ingratiating, including the familiar humor. ("I hope you fellows are Republicans," he said to the emergency room surgeons.) Reagan may be "militaristic," but he illustrates the fallacy in political psychology writings that treat all commitments to enhance military strength as "neurotic," rather than recognizing that a pro-armaments position may stem from beliefs about the nature of world politics. The psychological roots of a leader's political beliefs are of profound significance. Neurotically rooted beliefs are less open to change when they lead to unproductive consequences than are beliefs that mainly serve to provide a map of the political universe. And it is instructive that throughout his political career this emotionally secure leader has been willing to adapt the positions he derives from doctrine if circumstances force him to recognize that they cannot be achieved or will not work.]

Reagan's ability to be ingratiating, like many outward manifestations of his conduct of the presidency, stands in particularly distinct relief against the personal attributes that, according to many press, memoir, and research reports, flawed his predecessor's leadership. University of Maryland scholar Allen Schick, for example, interviewed a congressman who found the experience of meeting with Reagan strikingly more persuasive than that of consulting with Carter. In a meeting with Carter on proposed legislation, the congressman recalled that "we had barely got seated and Carter started lecturing us about the problems he had with one of the sections of the bill. He knew the details better than most of us, but somehow that caused more resentment than if he had left the specifics to us."[16] In his meeting with Reagan, the congressman reported admiringly that he was only in the president's office for "a couple of minutes, but I didn't feel rushed and I'm not quite sure how I was shown the door. A photographer shot the usual roll of pictures; the president gave me a firm, friendly handshake. He patted me on the back and told me how much he needed and appreciated my vote. He said that I should call if I needed anything."]

All of the modern presidents, including Carter, have had successes in patting—and scratching—backs. All also have learned that charm is a marginal rather than a decisive political influence, especially in the long haul. After all, other political leaders are more responsive to their own convictions, their constituency interests, and such elements of external reality as the state of the economy than to personal niceties. Reagan, described in chapter one as a "generic politician," does, however, illustrate the capacity of a chief executive, especially early in a presidency, to derive substantial benefits from being gifted at small-group persuasion. By extension, this side of Reagan's performance contributed to a general impression that post-Watergate assertions stressing the limits on presidents' capacities to achieve their goals have underplayed the potential of the Oval Office as a base for skillful politicking.

⌐Reagan's adeptness at using the politics of persuasiveness in face-to-face settings is paralleled by his professionalism in projecting public messages through the broadcast media.⌐ Of the nine modern presidents, Reagan's capacity for what Hamilton in *Federalist* 68 cuttingly called "the little arts of flattery" most resembles that of the president he admired so greatly during his young adulthood—Franklin Roosevelt. Both are examples of political dramatists and charmers. Both spent more time than most modern presidents have in writing their speeches, not wholly delegating this task to speechwriters. Both also typify politicians who publicly exude confidence and optimism, qua. ities that can be extraordinarily important when inspirational lead ership and morale building are needed.⌐

In Roosevelt's case, however, optimism was not enough to end the Great Depression that had led to his election in 1932. The Depression ended when preparations for war stimulated the economy. Critics of the "fit" between Roosevelt's personality and the national needs of the time focus on the flaw in the cognitive side of his personality, echoing the oft-quoted description of him as a man whose temperament was first-rate, but whose mind was second-rate.[17] What they refer to is the tatterdemalion nature of the policies that Roosevelt supported. The Hundred-Days legislation included both public assistance programs and a federal pay cut—policies likely to cancel each other in their macro-economic consequences.[18]

Lou Cannon believes that Reagan's attraction to the painless remedy implicit in supply-side economics resonates with Reagan's own high-spirited optimism, a trait that has been reinforced continually throughout his career by lucky breaks—finding lucrative employment in the Depression, becoming a well-paid political spokesman just as his film career was about to end, unexpectedly achieving national political prominence through a single television broadcast, and the like. Cannon also portrays Reagan's approach to analyzing policy much as the media reports based on first- and second-hand personal contact with him do. He is said not to apply rigorous thought to policy issues; not to have a "hypothesis-testing" cast of mind. Rather, he defends his positions with anecdotes or highly selective statistics that support his initial predilections.⌐Unlike Roosevelt, Reagan has long had difficulty using his sound political temperament to conceal any cognitive limitations he may have. Aides keep his press conferences to a minimum and at first did not schedule them at prime time. In general, his spontaneous discourse with the press has shown conspicuous gaps of information and flaws in reasoning when compared with the comportment of his predecessors in comparable unrehearsed circumstances.[19]

Reagan is like Roosevelt in being personally and politically flexible, even though he is unlike him in his ardent commitment to abstract beliefs. Discussing Reagan's conversion to conservatism in the 1950s, Cannon writes, "his views changed, as his views would change on other things, but he rarely became obsessive about his new opinions. . . . Reagan had changed his mind . . . not his personality."[20]

But the two obviously are not psychological clones. Roosevelt evinced extraordinary curiosity about people and programs and delighted in being personally at the center of an inordinately complex network of political intelligence. Reagan, for all of his outward bonhomie, is a private man. What and whom he knows are unclear. He seems to be an instinctive political strategist but is said to be bored with political tactics, just as he seems not to be interested in close analysis of his policies.

As usual, however, the qualifier "seems" is vital at this stage in assessment of Reagan's leadership. It is, after all, as Heclo and Penner point out, strategically advantageous for the president to keep public distance from the details of the policies his aides are advancing, thus retaining maneuverability for retreat, bargaining, and compromise. And Reagan manifestly does not seal himself off from criticisms of his policies and leadership. He follows the *Washington Post, New York Times*, selected regional newspapers, the White House press summary, and television news—a diet of communication scarcely calculated to induce the illusion that he and his policies only receive accolades. Again, he is like Roosevelt in ardently following the news media. The difference seems to be that Reagan's reading serves especially to inform his rhetoric. Roosevelt's reading also guided his leadership tactics and was more likely than Reagan's to lead him to make independent judgments about what policies to pursue, when, and how.

This speculative exercise in comparative Reagan-Roosevelt character analysis points to a type of politician better able to sell policies than to analyze them. In this respect, although Reagan's White House is seething with organizational entities (whereas Roosevelt's was still an extension in many respects of the presidential household), neither man has left a record of having addressed his aides to the task of systematically analyzing and anticipating the workability of alternative policies. In certain respects Reagan has more extended contacts with his official associates than Roosevelt did, meeting regularly with the cabinet and encouraging cabinet discussion (as long as it takes place in the spirit of discourse rather than combat) and also meeting regularly with a body that was not formed until the Truman years, the National Security Council. But both presidents and their practices may prove to be particularly instructive to students of the modern presidency because they illustrate the difficulties that arise when a president is so constituted that his political skills far exceed his skills at or impulses toward policy analysis.

Jimmy Carter gave policy analysis a bad name by immersing himself in policy content and failing to assess adequately the political feasibility of his programs. But the flaw was in Carter's analytic mode. Feasibility and substance both need analysis. Carter made the mistake of seeking to break complex issues into a multitude of technical components and attempting to evaluate them by politically neutral criteria. Effective policy analysis should be neither apolitical nor atomized. Rather, it should identify the grand contours of policies and project their consequences in order to weigh their substantive and political costs and benefits.

In Reagan's case, the most conspicuous time in which political skill was wedded to defective policy analysis was during the months leading up to the 1981 spending and tax cuts. Within the year, these enactments were haunting the administration by contributing to massive budgetary deficits. As budget politics proceeded in the course of 1983, the dilemma of massive projected deficits led to unusually intense disagreement among Reagan's advisers and between groups of them and Reagan himself.

Perhaps the most extreme modern display of short-run exercise of presidential skill in getting a result that had long-run catastrophic results for a president and his presidency was Lyndon Johnson's 1965 success in rallying his aides and other political leaders behind an open-ended commitment of American combat troops to Vietnam. Johnson himself sensed the danger in the decision. When a military adviser observed that "the Gallup Poll shows people are basically behind our commitment," Johnson presciently posed this parallel: "If you make a commitment to jump off a building and you find out how high it is, you may want to withdraw that commitment."[21]

Johnson's skepticism about the viability of a policy he was undertaking did not lead him to back off or even to apply analytically neutral staff resources to examining the consequences that were likely to ensue from escalation and exploring alternatives to such action. Reports of Reagan's style of thinking about policy consequences and employing advisers to extend his personal cognitive capacities suggest he does not find it natural even to worry about possible negative consequences of actions like the 1981 tax decrease.[22] And reports of the White House debates on the tax cut and about the views of others in Reagan's coalition, such as key congressional actors, suggest that in 1980 Reagan's personal political effectiveness (much augmented by presidential and other administration lobbying and successful efforts to manufacture a mandate out of the ambiguous 1980 Republican election victory) discouraged even skeptical advisers from bringing their views to his attention.[23] Here, in a fashion similar to the account Destler gives of the administration's difficulties in tempering its ideological stances when practical necessity seemed to make doing so desirable, Reagan has been especially resistant to reconsidering policies in the areas closest to his most central beliefs.

Belief System

In charting Ronald Reagan's political rise, I stressed that he is unique among the modern presidents in his depth—and one might add, duration—of ideological commitment. Some of the slogans he wove together in his 1950s public addresses, through which he perfected "The Speech" that won him acclaim in 1964 (see p. 5), appeared again in his 1980 campaign pronouncements. Yet Reagan is less than the compleat ideologue in two senses. In an Eric Hoffer world of "true believers"—individuals who rely on detailed elaborations of doctrine to guide their day-to-day actions and even to lend meaning to their lives—Reagan is a tame specimen.[24] His beliefs are important to him, but so are his wife, his family, his friends, his avocations, and much else that keeps him from being a Savonarola descended upon Washington to purge it of evil. His beliefs did not stop him from making immediate, amiable contact with the old New Dealer and urban-machine politician, House Speaker Thomas O'Neill. Indeed, to the distress of his conservative supporters, one of Reagan's first postelection social gatherings in Washington was with a Nixon enemies-list liberal—*Washington Post* publisher Katherine Graham.

If Reagan's beliefs are not branded on his skin, neither are they highly specific in terms of their policy implications. One of the dilemmas of Reagan aides such as Budget Director David Stockman has been to translate Reagan's broad conservative aphorisms—some of them in conflict with one another (for example, cutting spending is not always the best way to "eliminate waste and fraud")—into policy. Turning the coin over, the generalized nature of his beliefs contributes to his public (and allegedly private) ability to rationalize the compromises he makes in terms of his overarching political philosophy. That Reagan does state broad precepts, albeit in general form, serves his political purposes in another fashion. His enunciation of a broadly conceived but unequivocal conservative commitment has enabled his administration to recruit a roughly like-minded core of committed supporters to staff White House and administrative branch positions, as well as to shape a bloc of local allies in Congress.

Basic agreement on broadly stated principles has helped promote overall cohesion in his forces and maintain solid relations with his main allies in the face of extremely sharp disagreements among his associates and allies as the hard budgeting and economic policy choices had to be made after 1982. When options are debated, the possibilities for reaching compromises are enhanced because all parties concerned have a good general idea of what kind of policy will or will not be acceptable to Reagan. Their task then is to convert his principles into legislation and executive orders, establishing what is politically feasible, but still plausibly susceptible to interpretation as Reagan orthodoxy.

Again comparisons with Carter are inescapable. Carter, his speechwriter James Fallows complained, knew an enormous amount about innumerable matters but had no general conceptions of the direction that public policy should take.[25] In Reagan's case the general direction is always identifiable, no small advantage for influencing the policy agenda.

Advisers have complained that it is difficult to bring Reagan's attention to bear on the specifics of converting the principle to the policy. Some of them have also told journalists that Reagan's ease at enunciating generalities, his broad commitment to them, and his resistance to the hard work of policy analysis foster a kind of duplicity among them that is the opposite of the "yea saying" George Reedy describes in *The Twilight of the Presidency*.[26] Rather than blindly adhering to Reagan's views, his advisers seem sometimes to develop new positions for him and privately apply to him the same kind of casuistry that is used publicly to keep him from being (in the cruel Reagan administration locution for vacillation) "Carterized." They seek to persuade him by providing him with the rationale that what in fact are policy changes really are reflections of his principles. Thus, for example, a tax increase may become a closed loophole in the tax code or a user's fee in his thinking as well as in his public rhetoric. The shortcomings of such advising are obvious. Relabeling programs in order to change them may blunt an already flawed presidential ability to assess policies, depending on whether the president is unaware of what he is doing or is merely participating in a face-saving political charade.

Political Style

If we provisionally draw on Lasswell and Barber to identify those presidents who in their leadership emphasize rhetoric, those who put self-conscious effort into their direct personal relations with aides and others, and those who devote substantial time to perusing documents and other sources of substantive information, we find that Reagan scores highest in his use of the first two elements of leadership. Compared with his predecessors, he is lowest in the third category.

On the matter of rhetorical facility, Anthony King[27] appropriately remarks on Reagan's career as an actor and on the other prepresidential activities that made oral communication second nature to him. Americans—politicians and scholars, as well as members of the general public—place a high premium on the chief executive's oratorical powers. The emphasis stems in part from the nation's egalitarian traditions that contribute to the widespread American distrust of parties and the other institutions that mediate between citizens and leaders in democracies.

It is taken for granted that the citizen should directly observe candidates and leaders and judge them by their words and actions. The premium on rhetoric has been much augmented in the era of the modern presidency. One of the characteristics of the expanded presidency that took shape during Franklin Roosevelt's incumbency was that citizens increasingly came to view the workings of the government in terms of the actions of the president. And his most conspicuous actions are his utterances. Not coincidentally, the evolution of the modern presidency roughly parallels the explosion of opportunity for direct presidential appeal to the public via radio, newsreels, television, and other forms of communication.[28]

Curiously, despite the weight scholars' and politicians' assessments of presidential effectiveness give to rhetorical skill, Reagan is only the third modern president (the others being Roosevelt and Kennedy) who could be said to have exhibited a professionally adept podium manner. Given the belief that rhetorical gifts are a major political resource, it is less surprising that a professional mass communicator made his way to the White House in 1981 than that such a figure did not become a serious presidential contender sooner. In 1982, immediately after Edward Kennedy announced he would not seek the 1984 Democratic nomination, one of the two foremost "obvious" Democratic candidates was Senator John Glenn. The crucial point made against Glenn by politicians and press commentators was not that his understanding of issues, political skills, or policy positions are deficient, but rather that he is an uninspiring public speaker.

Reagan, of course, has used his public speaking skill to the hilt. There have been accounts of the self-conscious attention he has given to perfecting his speaking technique—his fund of anecdotes and catchphrases, his insistence on rehearsing important presentations, his facility in using the teleprompter (quite unconvincingly turning blank pages on the podium as he makes eye contact through the television camera lens with his audience), and, above all, of his ability to convey a humble but eloquent image of sturdy middle-Americana. Although his mass media presentations are pitched to the public, their impact on other leaders is highly significant. As Neustadt suggests in *Presidential Power*, the Washington politicians who must be influenced if the chief executive is to achieve results are less impressed by their own response to the president than by their perception of their constituents' view of him. In the case of a rhetorically gifted president, however, they are likely to be persuaded that he has public support not only from standard sources such as polls and constituent mail, but also from observing how he makes his appeals to the public and intuiting that a presentation they feel *should* have been effective *must* have been.

But *is* Reagan as effective a communicator as has generally been assumed? As we saw in chapter one, close analysis of the 1980 election results does not support Reagan's use of the inevitable claim of just-elected politicians—that their victory carries with it a mandate for their policy proposals. Although experienced politicians discount such presidential claims, members of Congress, bolstered by near uniformity in mass media accounts and by partially engineered constituency pressure, clearly were persuaded at the time of the 1981 Reagan tax and expenditure cuts that the president was riding high. One reason they were persuaded was that it was difficult to believe that such an effective communicator had not won the public over. It must be added that they also correctly perceived the general if short-lived national enthusiasm he aroused in the dramatic appearance before Congress that marked the end of his convalescence from the assassination attempt. He was confident and buoyant, radiating unpretentious self-assurance. From the good will he engendered, it was not hard to conclude that the legislators' constituents backed the specifics of his proposals and would be prepared to accept their consequences.

In retrospect, it is illuminating to look at Gallup support for Reagan from inauguration through the midterm elections. Table 1 shows public response to the question Gallup has regularly asked since the 1940s: "Generally speaking, how do you think President [name of incumbent] is doing his job?" During the key period in June and July 1981, when Reagan was the most visible performer in the brilliantly orchestrated legislative campaign that produced the tax and expenditure cuts, he had begun already to slip. His top Gallup rating of 68 percent approval in early May had followed his recovery from the

Table 1.   Approval/Disapproval of How President Reagan Is Doing His Job

Gallup poll findings from Inauguration Day through 1972 midterm election			
		Approve	Disapprove	No opinion
1981	Jan. 30–Feb. 2	51	13	36
	Feb. 13–16	55	18	27
	Mar. 13–16	60	24	16
	Apr. 3–6	67	18	15
	Apr. 10–13	67	19	14
	May 8–11	68	21	11
	June 5–8	59	28	13
	June 19–22	59	29	12
	June 26–29	58	30	12
	July 17–20	60	29	11
	July 24–27	56	30	14
	July 31–Aug. 3	60	28	12
	Aug. 14–17	60	29	11
	Sept. 18–21	52	37	11
	Oct. 2–5	56	35	9
	Oct. 30–Nov. 2	53	35	12
	Nov. 13–16	49	40	11
	Nov. 20–23	54	37	9
	Dec. 11–14	49	41	10
1982	Jan. 8–11	49	40	11
	Jan. 22–25	47	42	11
	Feb. 5–8	47	43	10
	Mar. 12–15	46	45	9
	Apr. 2–5	45	46	9
	Apr. 23–26	43	47	10
	Apr. 30–May 3	44	46	10
	May 14–17	45	44	11
	June 11–14	45	45	10
	June 25–28	44	46	10
	July 23–26	42	46	12
	July 30–Aug. 2	41	47	12
	Aug. 13–16	41	49	10
	Aug. 27–30	42	46	12
	Sept. 17–20	42	48	10
	Nov. 5–8	43	47	10

Source: Gallup Report No. 203 *(August 1982) with later figures supplied to me by the Gallup organization.*

attempted assassination and triumphant April 28 appearance before Congress. But by late spring his approval rate dropped to the upper 50 percent range. And just after he signed the tax and expenditure cuts in August, a steady erosion of support began. By the spring of 1982 more Gallup respondents disapproved than approved of his job performance. This continued through to the midterm election. As of early 1983 Reagan was running behind both John Glenn and Walter Mondale in "trial heat" polls of whom citizens would support in 1984. Reagan's approval rating at the end of his second year in office was lower than the second-year ratings of any of the presidents who initially reached the White House by election for the period during which Gallup has surveyed—lower, that is, than the ratings of Eisenhower, Kennedy, Nixon, and even Carter.

Reagan and his lieutenants found it far more necessary to bargain and form coalitions in 1982 policy-making than in 1981, just as the results of the midterm election pushed them even further toward the traditional mode of White House–congressional negotiation rather than White House dominance. Nevertheless, even in the midterm election, the Democrats took great pains to avoid personal attacks on the "popular" Reagan. The political wisdom was that attacks on such a well-meaning, personally liked president would backfire.

Midterm election Democratic political commercials stressed the links between Republican leadership in the 1980s and the Depression leadership of Herbert Hoover, barely recognizing Reagan's existence, in fear of encouraging a sympathy vote for him. In retrospect, we can see from the Gallup data on perceptions of Reagan (table 2), that citizens were less impressed with Reagan than politicians thought they were.

He did score favorably (as Carter before him had, even in defeat) in such personal traits as likeability, loftiness of moral principles, and intelligence. But the single most common perception was that he "cares about the needs of upper-income or wealthy people" and the two least common were that he is "sympathetic to problems of the poor" and "sides with the average citizen." A mere 39 percent agreed that he "has well thought out, carefully considered solutions for national problems." In short, quite early in his presidency, Reagan was in trouble with the public, though he and his allies were able to limit opposition leaders' impulses to take advantage of his vulnerabilities for longer than might have been expected. The popular judgment of Reagan as "bright" undoubtedly departed from the views many Washington professionals had begun to form precisely because they felt he lacked the initiative and capacity to do his homework. But even if

Table 2.   Reagan Personality Profile—Trend

Question: "Here is a list of terms (respondents were handed a card)—shown as pairs of opposites—that have been used to describe Ronald Reagan. From each pair of opposites, would you select the term which you feel best describes Reagan? Just read off a number and letter from each pair."

	May 14–18, 1982	Sept. 12–15, 1980	June 27–30, 1980
Cares about the needs of up-per-income or wealthy peo-ple	75	na	na
Bright, intelligent	70	73	65
A man of high moral princi-ples	69	70	60
A likeable person	65	na	61
Has strong leadership quali-ties	60	65	56
The kind of person who can get the job done	56	56	na
Would display good judgment in a crisis	54	55	58
A religious person	51	40	28
Has a clear understanding of the issues facing the coun-try	46	55	na
Takes moderate, middle-of-the-road positions	43	48	46
Cares about the needs and problems of women	42	na	na
Cares about the needs and problems of middle-income people	41	na	na
Cares about the needs and problems of the elderly	41	na	na
Adaptable, willing to compro-mise on his positions	40	na	na
Has well thought out, care-fully considered solutions for national problems	39	45	na
Cares about the needs and problems of people like yourself	39	na	na
Cares about the needs and problems of black people	37	na	na
Has modern, up-to-date solu-tions to national problems	36	51	na
Sides with the average citi-zen	28	43	40

Table 2. (*continued*)

	May 14–18, 1982	Sept. 12–15, 1980	June 27–30, 1980
Sympathetic to problems of the poor	24	41	35
A colorful, interesting personality	na	70	na
Decisive, sure of himself	na	69	60
Says what he believes even if unpopular	na	54	44
You know where he stands on issues	na	54	48
Has a well-defined program for the country ahead	na	53	41
Offers imaginative, innovative solutions to national problems	na	52	45
A man you can believe in	na	na	42
Puts country's interests ahead of politics	na	na	37
A person of exceptional abilities	na	na	35
na = not available			

Source: Gallup Report No. 203 *(August 1982).*

citizens did not cast aspersions on Reagan's brain power, their sense that he lacked "carefully considered solutions" (table 2) converged with Washington (and media) concerns about whether this president was seriously at work with his aides on devising coherent problem-solving strategies.

The emphasis on oratory in Reagan's political style adds to the lore of modern presidential leadership in several ways. One, specific to Reagan's performance, is the possibility that his oratory oversold political leaders on his popular appeal.[29] A second is that oratory without results is as dead as faith without works. But how then do we explain the success of another oratorical president—FDR—in an era when the economy was misperforming far more profoundly than now? Among the differences surely are low national expectations in the 1930s about the inevitability of expanding economic well-being; Roosevelt's efforts to provide direct assistance to victims of the Depression; and, most pertinent to Reagan's circumstances, Roosevelt's studious resistance to making precise predictions and specific promises about what results he would achieve when.

Reagan, as Heclo and Penner show, went much further than he had to in promising results. The promises were glowing. But as daily television news portrayals of soup kitchens and closed factories began to occupy public attention, the raised expectations were bound to engender disillusionment, exacerbated by the eloquence of the leader who raised them.

In general, as Ceaser, Thurow, Tulis, and Bessette suggest in "The Rise of the Rhetorical Presidency,"[30] there are costs to presidential reliance on addressing the public to get results. The greatest communicator among modern presidents, Roosevelt, was concerned in a way that Reagan evidently is not to avoid overexposing himself to the public and thus inducing indifference. He also was less disposed than Reagan has been to use his utterances as a direct means of placing pressure on Congress. Even so, the emphasis on rhetoric of both presidents early in their administrations contributed to congressional enactments that were passed without the customary degree of deliberation. Thus, on the one hand, without presidential rhetoric certain enactments would not have come to pass. But on the other, some legislation that was passed in the wake of presidential oratorical appeals later came under fire or, in the case of many New Deal measures, was repealed or invalidated on the ground that it had been ill-considered.

A final comment on rhetorical presidencies: even though an FDR may be sparing in making detailed promises, and even though the second of the three modern oratorical presidents, John F. Kennedy, addressed some of his oratory to the need for coolly rational policy-making, Henry Fairlie is persuasive in suggesting in *The Kennedy Promise*[31] that oratorical leadership fosters lack of realism in public political thinking and discourse. At a minimum, if the speech making is compelling, it encourages citizens to expect more of the same from other presidents and consequently adds to the personalization of the presidency and to preoccupation with the chief executive rather than with the full policy-making establishment. Further, even if they do not traffic in promises that cannot be kept, rhetorical presidents may be institutionally costly. In particular, they may weaken the presidency by being hard acts to follow. Truman suffered in part because he lacked FDR's histrionic gifts. Johnson had difficulties that arose from his failure to sway audiences as Kennedy had.

I have already touched on Reagan's political style in his direct personal relations with others and his use of documentary and other intelligence sources. Further observations are that he does not seek systematically staffed position papers with the contending views of his advisers carefully distinguished and defended, the practice Eisenhower used to prepare his associates for National Security Council meetings. His strength has been less in working with his aides to clarify policy than in rallying them around him and his policies. In general, with both Executive Office of the President staff and the cabinet he manages to delegate extensively but nevertheless keep administration members' actions in line with his political principles.

On the matter of the contention among foreign policy aides, if the Reagan presidency stretches to eight years, the first year—marked by feuding among the secretary of state, the secretary of defense, and (covertly) the assistant for national security—will seem no more than a ripple. After all, by 1982 the kind of harmony-without-groupthink that Reagan prizes had been achieved in foreign policy–making. William P. Clark had replaced Richard Allen as NSC assistant, providing the White House with a foreign policy aide who is a general policy broker and who reports directly to the president. And it would be difficult for any cabinet change to receive more favorable press than did the shift from Haig to Shultz in the State Department. Further, for whatever reasons, Shultz's accession was accompanied by an end to the Pentagon disagreements with the State Department. As Destler remarks, Reagan has been far more successful than a number of his predecessors in reshaping his foreign policy team when its initial members were working together inadequately.

In choosing his three top White House advisers—Meese, Deaver, and Baker—Reagan exhibited an ability unusual in presidents. Influential White House aides often get the reputation of being "yes men," or at any rate of being extensions of the president's own proclivities rather than complementary actors who compensate for the president's weaknesses and augment his strengths. H. R. Haldeman was as disposed as Richard Nixon to think the White House was surrounded by enemies. Harry Hopkins shared Roosevelt's love of manipulative leadership. However, in appointing his triumvirate, Reagan seems to have been sensitive to ways in which he, as communicator, overarching strategist, and proponent of broad doctrine, needs to be supplemented. He requires help in organizing his staff to transform political philosophy into policy and needs a tactician to establish what is or is not politically feasible. In addition, he clearly values a friend and confidant who empathizes with him and has an intuitive understanding of what demands on his time and requests for his approval will be personally congenial to him. As indicated in chapter one, Meese, Baker, and Deaver respectively have carried out these three roles.

In general, Reagan appears to have a good sense of how to judge personnel and motivate his associates. Although we have no account of his rationale in choosing this constellation of aides, it is difficult to believe that they came together without Reagan's conscious choice or stayed together without his continuing encouragement. He shows every sign of having a genuine gift for casting major supporting actors in positions that will back up the leading man.

As in his change of foreign policy teams, Reagan's White House staffing practices contribute to the lore of effective presidential leadership. In insisting neither on sycophants nor on aides who duplicate his own style, Reagan teaches future presidents that it is feasible and even desirable to shape their official family to their distinctive needs, whether or not in doing so they organize the White House in a manner that defies orthodox organization theory.

The Context of Reagan's Presidency

The political environment that impinges most directly on a president is of his own making—the staff of the Executive Office of the President (EOP), the top cabinet-level officials, and the second- and third-level officials who back up their principal associates. A common proposition states that presidents make policy by ratifying advisers' choices. Since Robert Gallucci's analysis of bureaucratic politics in United States' involvement in Vietnam is also germane to domestic policy, I have elided the adjective "foreign" in this quotation from his formulation:

> The president makes . . . policy only in the sense that a customer in a restaurant makes dinner when he orders his food; he chooses from a limited menu prepared for him by the establishment and usually must accept the interpretation of his choice as it is reflected in the execution of his order. That is to say, he "makes" it hardly at all, although those dining with him are likely to hold him responsible for the choice if they are made to consume it also.[32]

If only as a corrective to the tendency of many former presidential aides to treat the EOP as a mere extension of the president, this passage provides a valuable reminder that because a presidency is collective, it must be analyzed with close attention to the major members of the president's support staff, to how they are organized, and to how they operate. Enough has been said earlier in this chapter and in chapter one about Reagan's advisers to make it clear that he uses aides who are skilled professionals. In press accounts and in my informal conversation with White House staff, the distinction is usually made between whether middle- and lower-level members of the staff are on the "Meese side" or the "Baker side" of the White House. Journalists in contact with the aides who take part in the many animated White House staff policy and strategy planning meetings portray a fragmented White House, full of rivalries extending from the triumvirate down. A sociologist of groups posing the abstract question of what to expect of a relationship with an advisory group in which three individuals of equal responsibility report to a single chief might readily predict conflict, especially two-against-one coalitions that form in triads.

What seems most remarkable about the Reagan White House, however, is not its conflicts, but rather the substantial collegiality at the level immediately below the president and extending to the key middle-level aides. Accounts of what Heclo and Penner dub the "working committee of the presidency"—the endless strategy meetings—suggest a flexible operating style much like the Kennedy White House, but without a Kennedy regularly immersing himself in policy and tactics. Perhaps even more remarkable was the ability of White House aides to join informally in a policy-framing, support-building working group with leading congressmen of both parties ("the gang of seventeen") as early as 1982.

The available evidence also suggests that, apart from the initial conflicts among his foreign policy-makers, Reagan's cabinet, subcabinet, and White House staff have worked together generally smoothly. Although much journalism reporting intra-administration policy debate has appeared, in the final analysis Reagan's associates have presented a remarkably consistent common front. Inevitably, of course, as the decisions faced by the administration became more difficult—for example, in the post-midterm election deliberations to frame the next budget presentation late in 1982 and early in 1983—differences among Reagan's advisers found their way into print.

Overall, however, personal and general philosophical commitment to Reagan has contributed to cohesion in the White House staff and cabinet. In addition, to a degree that is still undocumented by research, the cabinet council system devised by Meese has, most notably in economic policy, been an institution designed to foster *esprit*, air diverse options, but then weld consensus among aides.

The narrow policy agenda of the Reagan administration (see chapter 2) has led most investigative journalists to focus on White House performance at the higher staff levels. A widespread impression in Washington is that middle- and lower-level staff functions, while often carried off with skill, are not well coordinated and do not funnel effectively into White House decision-making. There is, for example, no evidence that the Office of Policy Development, successor to the influential domestic staffs in the Johnson through Carter presidencies, has much impact on the performance of the Reagan presidency. In addition, as we have seen, Reagan's personal style encourages effective short-run political performance more than well-considered analyses of whether policies will have their desired effects in the longer run. When the administration memoirs are written and, eventually, when its archives are opened, it will be possible to see whether Reagan allowed himself to accede to policies that were made by subordinates who, to spare the president, compromised their differences and produced "least-common-denominator" recommendations that made more sense as bureaucratic politics than as good policy.

What is not in doubt, however, is that a great effort has been made to keep the staff operating effectively, especially at its upper level. It is, for example, taken as a matter of course that Meese's leadership and Baker's are coordinated by seeing that each man has an able, well-informed and energetic deputy (Craig Fuller and Richard Darman respectively) and that these deputies are in communication with each other, usually many times each day. One Reagan advantage is that in staffing the White House he has at his disposal members of the impressively large cadre of younger Republicans who developed skills in Washington operation during the Nixon and Ford years and whose tactical expertise undoubtedly will provide continuing lessons for the presidential teams that follow Reagan's.

More generally, whatever the political and policy fates of Reagan's administration, his early successes in domestic legislative and administrative politics demonstrate that in the post-Watergate period both scholars and political operators have underestimated the ability of gifted EOP aides to help the president influence the federal political agenda and have a significant impact on policy.

The president can dismiss his aides. But he has far less control over the extended political environment in which he works—Congress, other Washington groups, the performance of the economy, and the state of international affairs. He can seek to influence congressional elections, but he cannot dissolve Congress and does not have a decisive impact on who heads his party in the Senate and House. Forces in the larger society are obdurately resistant to White House influence. Cutting across all of the aspects of presidential foreign policy performance that Destler analyzes is the special intractability of the international political environment.

Since the external environment that impinges on a presidency is virtually unbounded, I simply note two areas in which what the Reagan presidency can and cannot do has depended on factors largely out of its control. Both can hamstring any president no matter how skillful: the Congress and the economy.

More Democratic than Republican votes were cast for the Senate in 1980 (see p. 16). Nevertheless, electoral arithmetic put the Republicans in control of the Senate. The extraordinary exercise of presidential influence in the 1981 tax and budget cuts could not have occurred without Republican control of the Senate and the able cooperation of Senate Majority Leader Howard Baker and Finance Committee Chairman Robert Dole. Without the thirty-three-vote Republican surge in the House in 1981, a conservative coalition could not have been put together to bring the Senate initiative to fruition.

By 1982, however, it was apparent that the 1980 victory had not abolished the separation of powers and produced presidential government pure and simple. Much of the legislation Reagan signed in the second year of his presidency had been intricately worked out by his White House strategists and was powerfully influenced by legislators' responding to constituency pressures stemming from the poor performance of the economy.

The August 1982 tax increase represented a significant rite of passage from what might be called quasi-presidential government to government-as-usual, but with persistent, often effective, exercise of presidential influence. Both congressional leaders and key Reagan aides had become convinced that economic recovery would be profoundly impeded without a serious effort to reduce the federal deficit. The subsequent legislation departed sufficiently from supply-side theory to add significantly to Reagan's right-wing backers' already existing disillusionment with his failure to promote such social issues as antiabortion legislation.[33]

The 1982 midterm election brought the decline in presidential party seats that regularly follows a seat gain in the presidential year. But, given a 10 percent unemployment level and languishing indicators of economic growth, the loss was widely accepted as a "message"—perhaps with not much more accuracy than Reagan's 1980 victory, which had been treated as a mandate. Even in the Senate, which suffered no Republican seat loss, leaders clearly would be putting their moderate imprint on legislation and carefully examining presidential initiatives.

Throughout the Reagan presidency economics has been the prime issue. One source of the early legislative victories was the president's willingness to subordinate other programs to a single-minded effort on this front. The Reagan administration predicted favorable results from its economic program. An economic upturn would be a political boon. However, continuing unemployment and other failings in the economy throughout 1983 would inevitably undermine the survival of the Reagan presidency. These matters are too well developed by Heclo and Penner to be profitably expanded on here. But it takes no specialized scholarly knowledge to realize that the fate of this administration—no matter how remarkable its political gifts—will be overwhelmingly influenced by the performance of the economy, whether or not that performance can be "scientifically" traced to Ronald Reagan's political stewardship.

Despite early successes, should the Reagan presidency become politically ineffective, this would not prove definitively that ideologically based policy-leadership provokes presidential catastrophe. However, such an outcome would promote a major ex post facto analysis of what went wrong—and why—in formulating and pressing for the decisive Reagan-sponsored domestic policies of 1981.[34] The ensuing research would be a boon for scholarship, just as the Reagan presidency already has added substantially to the lore at the disposal of future American chief executives. But the demise of still another presidency could not fail to weaken further the capacity of the nation's political institutions to meet the demands of the century's final decades.

Notes

1. Richard E. Neustadt, *Presidential Power: The Politics of Leadership* (New York: John Wiley & Sons, 1960).

2. Richard Tanner Johnson, *Managing the White House* (New York: Harper & Row, 1974). Johnson also used a third category, "competitive advising," to capture the practice of one of the modern presidents, namely Roosevelt, of encouraging advisers to vie with one another for the president's attention. He did not, however, have in mind advisory competition that was not congenial to the president, and did not serve his purposes, as in that of Reagan's first year in foreign affairs and the beginning of his third year in domestic affairs.

3. Fred I. Greenstein, "Eisenhower as an Activist President," *Political Science Quar-*

terly 94 (Winter 1979–80):575–99, and *The Hidden-Hand Presidency: Eisenhower as Leader* (New York: Basic Books, 1982).

4. Larry Berman, *Planning a Tragedy: The Americanization of the War in Vietnam* (New York: W. W. Norton, 1982).

5. Roger B. Porter, *Presidential Decision Making: The Economic Policy Board* (New York: Cambridge University Press, 1980).

6. The most thorough and intelligently qualified analysis of these matters—addressed to foreign policy but relevant to presidential use of information and advice in general—is Alexander L. George, *Presidential Decisionmaking in Foreign Policy: The Use of Information and Advice* (Boulder, Colo.: Westview Press, 1980).

7. James David Barber, *The Presidential Character: Predicting Performance in the White House* (Englewood Cliffs, N.J.: Prentice-Hall, 1972).

8. James David Barber, *The Lawmakers* (New Haven: Yale University Press, 1965).

9. My remarks on Reagan are inevitably speculative. They rely heavily on Lou Cannon's excellent *Reagan* (New York: G.P. Putnam's Sons, 1982), but also draw on extensive "Reaganology" in the mass media.

10. James David Barber, "Worrying about Reagan," *New York Times*, September 8, 1980, p. 19.

11. David Riesman, *The Lonely Crowd: A Study of the Changing American Character* (New Haven: Yale University Press, 1950).

12. Herman A. Witkin and Donald R. Goodenough, *Cognitive Styles: Essence and Origins* (New York: Inter-Universities Press, 1981).

13. Moreover, the data on Eisenhower and his leadership that became available after Barber wrote clearly make it inappropriate to treat him as passive. Greenstein, *The Hidden-Hand Presidency*, ch. 2.

14. The seminal Lasswell book on personality and politics is Harold D. Lasswell, *Psychopathology and Politics* (Chicago: University of Chicago Press, 1930; reprinted with "afterthoughts" and a new preface by the same publisher in 1979). The following work reprints later key Lasswell writings on the topic and has a valuable introduction and a bibliography of Lasswell's writings: Dwaine Marvick, *Harold D. Lasswell on Political Sociology* (Chicago: University of Chicago Press, 1977).

15. Dorothy Ross, "Review Essay: Woodrow Wilson and the Case for Psychohistory," *Journal of American History* 64 (December 1982):659–68.

16. Allen Schick, "How the Budget Was Won and Lost," in Norman J. Ornstein, ed., *President and Congress: Assessing Reagan's First Year* (Washington, D.C.: American Enterprise Institute, 1982), pp. 14–43.

17. See, for example, James MacGregor Burns, *Roosevelt: The Lion and the Fox* (New York: Harcourt, Brace & Co., 1956).

18. Pendleton Herring, *Presidential Leadership: The Political Relations of Congress and the Chief Executive* (New York: Rinehart, 1940; reprint ed., Westport, Conn.: Greenwood Press, 1972).

19. Again, the qualification is necessary that I am writing from presently available information and echoing themes in current journalism. Eisenhower, who often seemed innocent of fundamental current information in his press conferences, can now be seen (on the basis of transcripts of pre–press conference briefings) to have deliberately feigned ignorance on controversial matters. His professions of ignorance, however, were not "bloopers," like Reagan's confusion about the circumstances that led to the creation of North and South Vietnam and, in general, his press conference texts, although full of fractured syntax, reveal a better informed, more clear-headed president than do Reagan's. See Greenstein, *The Hidden-Hand Presidency*.

20. Cannon, *Reagan*, p. 87.

21. Berman, *Planning a Tragedy*, p. 119.

22. For a typical example of such a report, see "How Reagan Decides: Intense Beliefs, Eternal Optimism and Precious Little Adaptability," *Time*, December 13, 1982, pp. 12–17.

23. Steve Weisman, "Reaganomics and the President's Men," *New York Times Magazine*, October 24, 1982, p. 26.

24. Eric Hoffer, *The True Believer: Thoughts on the Nature of Mass Movements* (New York: Harper, 1951), first ed.

25. James Fallows, "The Passionless Presidency: Part I," and "The Passionless Presidency: Part II," *Atlantic Monthly*, May and June 1979.

26. George Reedy, *The Twilight of the Presidency* (New York: World Publishing Co., 1970).

27. Anthony King, "How Not to Select Presidential Candidates: A View from Europe," in Austin Ranney, ed., *The American Elections of 1980* (Washington, D.C.: American Enterprise Institute, 1981), pp. 303–28.

28. See, for example, the essays and sources cited in Doris A. Graber, *The President and the Public* (Philadelphia: Institute for the Study of Human Issues, 1982).

29. Since an oratorical president may get results less by "going over the heads" of other leaders than by conveying the impression that he is succeeding in doing so, it would be instructive to have evidence about citizens' responses to Reagan the communicator that were more subtle than those allowed by standard public opinion polls. I have in mind such procedures as the market research discussion group technique of arranging "focus group" conversations between people who have just seen by live television or videotape a presidential communication. The essence of the procedure is to encourage "natural" discussion of *both* the president's specific television presentation and his leadership in general. My hypothesis is that in spite of Reagan's extensive reliance on polls to gauge the effects of his leadership, group interviews would show rather little public attention to Reagan's skill and persuasiveness as a communicator. Rather, the packaging of the message, especially in a controversial area such as economic policy, probably would be beside the point. Discussion would quickly move to his stewardship, especially of the economy, not the skill with which he justifies his policies or his attractive human qualities.

30. James Ceaser, Glen E. Thurow, Jeffrey Tulis, and Joseph M. Bessette, "The Rise of the Rhetorical Presidency," *Presidential Studies Quarterly*, Spring 1981, pp. 158–71.

31. Henry Fairlie, *The Kennedy Promise: The Politics of Expectation* (Garden City, N.Y.: Doubleday, 1973).

32. Robert L. Gallucci, *Neither Peace nor Honor: The Politics of American Military Policy in Viet-Nam* (Baltimore: Johns Hopkins University Press, 1975), p. 7.

33. See, for example, "Ronald Reagan Won the Election; Now He's Lost the White House," *Conservative Digest* 8 (February 1982):2–32.

34. On administration recriminations after two years see, for example, Kenneth H. Bacon, "Fiscal Frustration: Many Reaganites Call the Economy's Course Major Disappointment; Big Deficits, Inflation Fears, High Interest Rates Kill Hopes for Fast Recovery; Were Tax Cuts Oversold?" *Wall Street Journal*, December 21, 1981.

About the Contributors

I. M. DESTLER is senior associate and director, Project on Executive–Congressional Relations in Foreign Policy, Carnegie Endowment for International Peace, in Washington, D.C. He was awarded a Ph.D. degree from Princeton University in 1971. His previous positions include assistant to Senator Walter F. Mondale, staff aide or consultant to various government agencies, lecturer at the Woodrow Wilson School at Princeton University, and senior fellow at the Brookings Institution. He has authored or coauthored five books: *Presidents, Bureaucrats, and Foreign Policy; Managing an Alliance; The Textile Wrangle; Making Foreign Economic Policy;* and *Coping with U.S.–Japanese Economic Conflicts.* He has written extensively on Congress and foreign policy, the policy-making and organization of the executive branch, and U.S.–Japan relations.

FRED I. GREENSTEIN is professor of politics at Princeton University. He received his Ph.D. degree from Yale University in 1960 and has taught at Wesleyan University, Yale University, the University of Essex, University of Melbourne, and University of Virginia. His early work in political psychology led to such books as *Children and Politics* and *Personality and Politics.* He has also written general books on politics, including *The American Party System and the American People* and (with Martin Shapiro and Raymond Wolfinger) *The Dynamics of American Politics.* His work on the development of the modern American presidency includes *The Hidden-Hand Presidency: Eisenhower as Leader* and numerous articles and chapters in compendia.

HUGH HECLO is a professor of government, Harvard University. He received his Ph.D. degree from Yale University in 1970 and has taught at Yale, the University of Essex, and Massachusetts Institute of Technology. He has served as an assistant to the vice president on domestic policy and has been at the Brookings Institution as a senior fellow and research associate. His books include *Modern Social Politics in Britain and Sweden, The Private Government of Public Money, Comparative Public Policy*, and *A Government of Strangers*. He has written many articles on the presidency and public policy.

SAMUEL P. HUNTINGTON is Clarence Dillon Professor of International Affairs and director of the Center for International Affairs at Harvard University. He has served as coordinator of security planning for the National Security Council, 1977–78, and he was a founder of the quarterly journal *Foreign Policy* in 1970. His books include: *American Politics: The Promise of Disharmony; No Easy Choice; The Crisis of Democracy; Political Order in Changing Societies; Political Power: USA/USSR; The Common Defense;* and *The Soldier and the State*. He is the author of more than sixty articles in scholarly journals and journals of opinion.

RICHARD P. NATHAN is professor of public and international affairs and director of the Princeton Urban and Regional Research Center at Princeton University. He received his doctoral degree from Harvard University in 1966. He has served as legislative assistant to Senator Kenneth Keating, director of domestic policy research for Nelson A. Rockefeller, associate director of the U.S. National Advisory Commission on Civil Disorders, assistant director of the U.S. Office of Management and Budget, deputy undersecretary in the U.S. Department of Health, Education, and Welfare, and as senior fellow at the Brookings Institution. His books include *Public Service Employment, Monitoring Revenue Sharing*, and *The Administrative Presidency*.

RUDOLPH G. PENNER is director of tax policy studies at the American Enterprise Institute. With a Ph.D. from The Johns Hopkins University, he has taught at McCoy College, University of Rochester, and Princeton University. He has also consulted for the United Nations, the U.S. Federal Aviation Agency, the Canadian government, the government of Tanzania, the U.S. Treasury, and the Philadelphia Federal Reserve Bank, among others. Before joining AEI, he was deputy assistant secretary for economic affairs in the U.S. Department of Housing and Urban Development and assistant director for economic policy in the Office of Management and Budget, Executive Office of the President. His books include *Nixon, McGovern, and the Federal Budget, Public Claims on U.S. Output, The 1978 Budget in Transition*, and *Social Security Financing Proposals*. He has published numerous articles.

Index